MLA
Handbook
for Writers
of Research
Papers

MLA Handbook for Writers of Research Papers

Seventh Edition

THE MODERN LANGUAGE ASSOCIATION OF AMERICA

New York   2009

The Modern Language Association publishes two books on its documentation style: the *MLA Handbook for Writers of Research Papers* (for high school and undergraduate students) and the *MLA Style Manual and Guide to Scholarly Publishing* (for graduate students, scholars, and professional writers). These volumes provide the most accurate and complete instructions on MLA style.

If updates of the information in this handbook become necessary, they will be posted at the MLA's World Wide Web site.

Library of Congress Cataloging-in-Publication Data

MLA handbook for writers of research papers. — 7th ed.
    p. cm.
  Prev. ed. entered under: Gibaldi, Joseph, 1942–
  Includes index.
  ISBN 978-1-60329-024-1 (pbk. : alk. paper) — ISBN 978-1-60329-025-8 (large print : pbk. : alk. paper)
  1. Report writing—Handbooks, manuals, etc. 2. Research—Handbooks, manuals, etc. I. Gibaldi, Joseph, 1942– MLA handbook for writers of research papers. II. Modern Language Association of America. III. Title: Handbook for writers of research papers.
  LB2369.G53 2009
  808'.027—dc22   2008047484

Third printing 2011

Book design by Charlotte Staub. Set in Melior and Lucida Sans. Printed on recycled, acid-free paper

Published by The Modern Language Association of America
26 Broadway, New York, New York 10004-1789
www.mla.org

Contents

Foreword

"Why do I need to learn MLA style?" It is a question we sometimes hear at the Modern Language Association, and the answer is simple. Every time you write a research paper, you enter into a community of writers and scholars. The disciplines in this community all use conventions—think of the ways chemists, mathematicians, and philosophers use symbols and special terms to transmit information. MLA style represents a consensus among teachers, scholars, and librarians in the fields of language and literature on the conventions for documenting research, and those conventions will help you organize your research paper coherently. By using MLA style, you will direct your readers to the sources you consulted in arriving at your findings, and you will enable them to build on your work.

MLA style is especially useful in today's research environment, and humanities scholars and classroom teachers generally prefer it over other documentation systems. One advantage of MLA style is its simplicity. When you write a paper in MLA style, you place in parentheses brief references to the sources you are using to make your argument, and at the end of your paper you place an alphabetical list of the works you cite. By requiring in citations only the information readers need to locate a source in your list of works cited, MLA style makes reading a research paper easier on the eyes—and the brain—than other styles do. Further, MLA style is known for its flexibility: you have options when it comes to including elements in your list of works cited. When you need to improvise, the modular format outlined in this book gives you the knowledge and confidence to make consistent choices so that you can produce an authoritative and persuasive research paper.

The *MLA Handbook for Writers of Research Papers* will not only teach you MLA style, it will also help you at all stages of your project. It will guide you through virtually any question you may have about writing a research paper, from formulating a topic to using abbreviations in the list of the works that you cite in the paper. If you are like most users of the *MLA Handbook*, you will return to it many times as you work on your research papers. In the course of your research, you may encounter unfamiliar sources that you want to cite, or you may have doubts about proper punctuation or abbreviations. Perhaps you will want to learn how to cite texts in a language other than English, to document material you found on a Web site, or to quote from an e-mail message you received. The *MLA Handbook* is an easy-to-use reference tool for solving these problems.

Going beyond documenting sources, the *MLA Handbook* helps you understand how to work with them in your writing. A chapter on plagiarism covers summarizing, paraphrasing, and quoting from sources. The chapter explains the different forms of plagiarism, how to avoid them in your work, and what to do if you discover you have unknowingly plagiarized. The *MLA Handbook* also teaches you how to evaluate the authority of the sources you consult, guiding you especially through the sometimes difficult process of determining the reliability of material on the Web.

How long has MLA style been in circulation among students and scholars? In 1951 the Modern Language Association published "The MLA Style Sheet," compiled by Executive Director William Riley Parker, and ever since then the association has been refining the elements of MLA style and adding information that helps researchers perform their work. Founded in 1883 and based in New York City, the MLA is an organization of over thirty thousand scholars and teachers in English and other modern languages. The MLA publishes a range of journals and books designed to promote teaching and scholarship in languages and literatures. While most of our publications are intended for teachers and advanced researchers, the *MLA Handbook* was created with the student in mind. Sometimes students ask us how we devise the style that we recommend in the *MLA Handbook*. The process is collaborative: our editorial and publications staff members, in consultation with expert MLA members, discuss the relevance of MLA style and attempt to seek a balance between concision and informativeness. Librarians, students, classroom teachers, editors, scholarly authors, and many others contribute to the formulation of MLA style.

The seventh edition of the *MLA Handbook* is accompanied for the first time by a Web-based component that helps users learn MLA style and understand better the activities of researching and writing a paper. Students, instructors, and librarians have shown great interest in gaining access to the *MLA Handbook* on the Web, and we responded by developing a site that contains the full text of the book with complementary materials. The site includes sample papers with step-by-step narratives showing how the papers were prepared, and each narrative can be explored from a number of perspectives. For example, if you are having trouble defining a topic, you can look at the ways the authors of the sample papers did it. If you are unsure how to evaluate sources for inclusion in your project, you can follow the steps outlined in the narratives. We hope that the new electronic component will help students in every stage of their work. Scholarly research is increasingly conducted in a digital environment, and we are pleased to usher the *MLA Handbook* into that world.

Much has changed since I used the 1977 edition of the *MLA Handbook* to write my two undergraduate theses. Its instructions for preparing the paper noted that a "fresh black ribbon and clean type are essential" and advised against using "thin paper except for a carbon copy" (44). I imagine most readers of the current edition have never handled a black ribbon and have little concept of how carbon copies work. In just thirty years, there has been a dramatic shift in the way we conduct research, find primary and secondary materials, process information, and prepare a paper for submission. I was grateful that I had the *MLA Handbook* when I was a student, and I cannot imagine tackling a research project in today's world without the careful, concise, and authoritative edition you hold in your hands.

Many people contributed to the seventh edition of the *MLA Handbook*. A full list of acknowledgments appears in the preface, but I wish to single out four MLA staff members for special thanks. David G. Nicholls, director of book publications, revised the *MLA Handbook* and oversaw the development of the Web content for the project. Judy Goulding, director of publishing operations, guided the editing and production of this edition with the capable assistance of Eric Wirth, associate editor of MLA publications, and Judith Altreuter, director of print and electronic production. Finally, I want to pay tribute to my predecessor, Phyllis Franklin, who always made sure the *MLA Handbook* was at the center of the association's work and who used to ask me regularly how the new edition was coming along.

Rosemary G. Feal
Executive Director
Modern Language Association

Preface

For over thirty years, millions of college and high school students have turned to the *MLA Handbook for Writers of Research Papers* for guidance. The *MLA Handbook* explains how to identify a topic and develop it through research. It also shows you how to work with sources in your writing, gives advice on the mechanics of academic prose, and authoritatively presents MLA documentation style. Reorganized and revised, the new, seventh edition evaluates the kinds of research resources available today and demonstrates techniques for finding reliable information online. The seventh edition is the first to include a Web component; by logging in, you can access the full text of the print volume along with additional examples, research project narratives with sample papers, and answers to frequently asked questions (see "Note on the Web Component").

This edition introduces student writers to a significant revision of MLA documentation style. In the past, listing the medium of publication in the works-cited list was required only for works in media other than print (e.g., publications on CD-ROM, articles in online databases); print was considered the default medium and was therefore not listed. The MLA no longer recognizes a default medium and instead calls for listing the medium of publication in every entry in the list of works cited. This change helped us standardize and simplify our recommendations throughout chapter 5. Following the advice of instructors, librarians, and scholars, we further simplified the guidelines for citing works on the Web. For example, the MLA no longer recommends including URLs in the works-cited-list entries for Web publications. Because issue as well as volume numbers of journals are useful for finding articles in electronic databases, the MLA now requires inclusion of both for every journal article in the list of works cited. The *MLA Handbook* also presents new guidelines for citing forms that are gaining more scholarly attention, such as graphic narratives and digital files. Graduate students, scholars, and professional writers will already be familiar with the MLA's revised documentation style, for it was presented to them in the third edition of the *MLA Style Manual and Guide to Scholarly Publishing*, released in 2008. Since then, we have refined the guidelines for citing works in newspapers and articles in reference works; the refinements appear for the first time in this edition of the *MLA Handbook* (in 5.4.5 and 5.5.7, respectively). Similarly, we have clarified our guidance on the punctuation of titles of works (presented in 3.6.1 of the *MLA Handbook*).

Additional updates and revisions appear throughout this edition of the *MLA Handbook*. Chapter 2, for example, gives an expanded discussion of when documentation is not needed, and it also offers guidance on what to do if your research involves human subjects. Several changes affect the guidelines for preparing a printed paper. The volume now assumes the use of italics, not underlining, for text that would be italicized in a publication (see 3.3). Chapter 4, which discusses the format of the research paper, is completely reorganized and revised under the assumption that all students write papers using word-processing software. It presents new instructions for preparing figures, tables, and captions. The appendixes now lead readers to writing guides and specialized style manuals.

Each edition of the *MLA Handbook* is developed by many collaborators, as previous lists of acknowledgments make clear. The first three editions were written by Joseph Gibaldi and Walter S. Achtert, and the fourth, fifth, and sixth editions were prepared by Gibaldi. In taking on the task of preparing the seventh edition, I knew that I would be carrying over much material from the previous one; I also knew that I would work with colleagues in writing the new material for the Web component. I decided that the new edition should be considered the product of corporate authorship. I was responsible for writing or revising the entire print volume and for preparing the additional examples that appear in the Web version of it, and I was supported in my work by members of the book-publications department. James C. Hatch, Sonia Kane, Margit A. Longbrake, and Joshua Shanholtzer helped develop the research project narratives and the sample papers. Lucy D. Anderson and Will Kenton provided research assistance. I consulted the MLA's Publications Committee at several stages in the development of the research project narratives and sample papers, so thanks are due to Dudley Andrew, Bradin Cormack, Rena Fraden, Sara Friedrichsmeyer, Irene Kacandes, Amy Katz Kaminsky, E. Ann Kaplan, Steven Mailloux, Saree Makdisi, Cristanne Miller, Karen Newman, Gerald Joseph Prince, C. P. Haun Saussy, Elaine Savory, Shu-mei Shih, Diana Sorensen, Richard Terdiman, and Susan Wells. The research project narratives and accompanying sample papers were reviewed by consultant readers, whose expert advice helped us make improvements.

The preparation of this new edition involved many members of the MLA staff. The editorial department, under the direction of Judy Goulding, played an important role in planning and producing the publication. Eric Wirth served as principal copyeditor. Judith H. Altreuter coordinated print and electronic production. Others in the department who assisted in editing and producing this edition include Paul J. Banks, Anna S. A. Chang, Lisa George, Angela L. Gibson, Kathleen M. Hansen, David W. Hodges, Elizabeth Holland, Vivian S. Kirklin, Kerry Marino, Sara Pastel, Pamela Roller, Laurie Russell, and Christopher Zarate. Terrence Callaghan, director of operations, and Leonard J. Moreton, manager of Member and Customer Services, assisted in developing the technical and commercial infrastructure supporting the Web component. Barbara A. Chen, director of Bibliographic Information Services and editor, *MLA International Bibliography*, offered comments and suggestions, as did Nelly Furman, director of programs and ADFL. In planning the new edition, the MLA benefited from the advice of focus groups representing graduate students, librarians, high school teachers, and college teachers. A letter from Vernon Nargang led us to update our advice on citing works in newspapers. Soelve I. Curdts assisted in the evaluation of features in the Web component that describe figures for users with visual impairment. Finally, the new Web component featured in this edition would not exist without the leadership of Rosemary G. Feal, executive director, and the MLA's Executive Council. I thank everyone who contributed to the development of the seventh edition.

David G. Nicholls
Director of Book Publications
Modern Language Association

Note on the Web Component

Every copy of this edition of the *MLA Handbook for Writers of Research Papers* comes with an activation code for an accompanying Web site. The code and instructions for using it are located on the inside back cover of each book. Once you establish a personal account, you will have continuous access throughout the life of the seventh edition of the *MLA Handbook*.

New to this edition, the Web site provides enhanced ways of consulting, learning, and searching the contents of the *MLA Handbook*. You will find the full text of the print volume on the site, as well as over two hundred examples that do not appear in print. The site also presents several research project narratives, with sample papers, illustrating the steps successful students take in researching and writing papers. Each research project narrative shows about thirty steps in the preparation of a paper for an instructor. The steps are linked to sections in the *MLA Handbook*, so you can move easily between the specific situation encountered by the student and the general topic discussed in the *MLA Handbook*. Similarly, if you are reading a section in the *MLA Handbook*, you can go directly to any steps in the research project narratives that illustrate the topic of that section. You might, for example, want to look at how several students approach the problem of defining a topic as you read section 1.3, "Selecting a Topic." The sample papers demonstrate how the various steps in researching and writing culminate in a complete document. Examine the sample papers to identify strategies for organizing an argument and working with sources. The papers also serve as models for formatting the margins, line spacing, and other physical attributes of a printed paper. Each narrative shows the instructor's comments, which should help you understand the kinds of concerns instructors have and what you can learn from their reading of your work.

The Web site allows keyword searching of the entire site, including the full text of the *MLA Handbook*. There is also a section where frequently asked questions are answered.

1 Research and Writing

1.1. THE RESEARCH PAPER AS A FORM OF EXPLORATION

Personal Essays and Research Papers

During your school career you have probably written many personal essays that presented your thoughts, feelings, and opinions and that did not refer to any other source of information or ideas. Some assignments, however, require us to go beyond our personal knowledge. We undertake research when we wish to explore an idea, probe an issue, solve a problem, or make an argument in relation to what others have written. We then seek out and use materials beyond our personal resources. The outcome of such an inquiry appears in the research paper. The term *research paper* describes a presentation of student research that may be in a printed, an electronic, or a multimedia format.

Types of Research

The research paper is generally based on a combination of primary research and secondary research. *Primary research* is the study of a subject through firsthand investigation, such as analyzing a literary or historical text, a film, or a performance; conducting a survey or an interview; or carrying out a laboratory experiment. Primary sources include statistical data, historical documents, and works of literature or art. *Secondary research* is the examination of studies that other researchers have made of a subject. Examples of secondary sources are articles and books about political issues, historical events, scientific debates, or literary works.

Using Secondary Research

Most academic papers depend at least partly on secondary research. No matter what your subject of study, learning to identify and analyze the work of other researchers will play a major role in your development as a student. The sorts of activities that constitute a research paper—discovering, assessing, and assimilating others' research and then articulating your own ideas clearly and persuasively—are at the center of the educational experience.

Combining Research and Original Ideas

Research increases your knowledge and understanding of a subject. Sometimes research will confirm your ideas and opinions; sometimes it will challenge and modify them. But almost always it will help to shape your thinking. Unless your instructor specifically directs you otherwise, your research paper should not merely review publications and extract a series of quotations from them. Rather, you should look for sources that provide new information, that helpfully survey the various positions already taken on a specific subject, that lend authority to your viewpoint, that expand or nuance your ideas, that offer methods or modes of thought you can apply to new data or subjects, or that furnish negative examples against which you wish to argue. As you use and scrupulously acknowledge sources, however, always remember that the main purpose of doing research is not to summarize the work of others but to assimilate and to build on it and to arrive at your own understanding of the subject.

Different Approaches to Research and Writing

A book like this cannot present all the profitable ways of doing research. Because this handbook emphasizes the mechanics of preparing effective papers, it may give you the mistaken impression that the process of researching and writing a research paper follows a fixed pattern. The truth is that different paths can and do lead to successful research papers. Some researchers may pursue a more or less standard sequence of steps, but others may find themselves working less sequentially. In addition, certain projects lend themselves to a standard approach, whereas others may call for different strategies. Keeping in mind that researchers and projects differ, this book discusses activities that nearly all writers of research papers perform, such as selecting a suitable topic, conducting research, compiling a working bibliography, taking notes, outlining, and preparing the paper.

Exploration and Discovery

If you are writing your first research paper, you may feel overwhelmed by the many tasks discussed here. This handbook is designed to help you learn to manage a complex process efficiently. As you follow the book's advice on how to locate and document sources, how to format your paper, and so forth, you may be tempted to see doing a paper as a mechanical exercise. But, ideally, writing a research paper is intellectually rewarding: it is a form of exploration that leads to discoveries that are new—at least to you if not to others. The mechanics of the research paper, important though they are, should never override the intellectual challenge of pursuing a question that interests *you* (and ultimately your reader). This pursuit should guide your research and your writing. Even though you are just learning how to prepare a research paper, you may still experience some of the excitement of developing and testing ideas that is one of the great satisfactions of research and scholarship.

Research Papers and Professional Writing

Skills derived from preparing research papers are by no means just academic. Many reports and proposals required in business, government, and other professions similarly rely on secondary research. Learning how to write a research paper, then, can help prepare you for assignments in your professional career. It is difficult to think of any profession that would not require you to consult sources of information about a specific subject, to combine this information with your ideas, and to present your thoughts, findings, and conclusions effectively.

1.2. THE RESEARCH PAPER AS A FORM OF COMMUNICATION

A research paper is a form of written communication. Like other kinds of nonfiction writing—letters, memos, reports, essays, articles, books—it should present information and ideas clearly and effectively. You should not let the mechanics of gathering source materials, taking notes, and documenting sources make you forget to apply the knowledge and skills you have acquired through previous writing experiences.

This handbook is a guide for the preparation of research papers. It is not a book about expository writing. (See Λ.2–4 for a selected list of useful books on usage, language, and style.) Nonetheless, no set of conventions for preparing a manuscript can replace lively and intelligent writing, and no amount of research and documentation can compensate for a poor presentation of ideas. Although you must fully document the facts and opinions you draw from your research, the documentation should only support your statements and provide concise information about the sources cited; it should not overshadow your own ideas or distract the reader from them.

1.3. SELECTING A TOPIC

1.3.1. Freedom of Choice

Different courses and different instructors offer widely varying degrees of freedom to students selecting topics for research papers. The instructor of a course in a specific discipline (e.g., art, history, literature, science) may supply a list of topics from which to choose or may, more generally, require that the paper relate to an important aspect of the course. If you are given the latter option, review course readings and class notes to find topics that particularly interest you. Discuss possibilities with other students and with your instructor. If your choice is limited to a set list of topics, you will probably still need to decide which aspect of a topic to explore or which approach to use.

In a writing class, you may have more freedom to select a topic. The instructor may assign a general problem that can generate many kinds of responses—for example, you might be asked to choose a modern invention and show what benefits and problems it has brought about. If you have complete freedom to choose a topic, consider using a personal interest that lends itself to research (e.g., education, the environment, movies, new technologies, nutrition, politics, the business of sports) or an issue that has recently generated public interest or controversy (e.g., immigration policy, global warming, stem cell research, terrorism).

Teachers understand the importance of choosing an appropriate topic for a research paper. When freedom of choice is permitted, students are commonly required to submit topics to the instructor for approval early in the research project. If your campus has a writing center, find out how to make use of the resources there. It is preferable to contact the writing center in the early stages of your project.

1.3.2. Finding an Appropriate Focus

As you choose a topic, remember the time allotted to you and the expected length of the research paper. "International politics in the modern age" would obviously be too broad a subject for a ten-page term paper. You may prefer to begin with a fairly general topic and then to refine it, by thought and research, into a more specific one that can be fully explored. Try to narrow your topic by focusing on an aspect of the subject or an approach to it. A student initially interested in the general subject of "violence in the media" might decide, after careful thought and reading, to write on "the effects of cartoon violence on preschool children." Likewise, an interest in architecture could lead to a focus on the design and construction of domes, which could in turn be narrowed to a comparison between the ancient Roman dome and the modern geodesic dome.

Preliminary reading is essential as you evaluate and refine topics. Consult, in print and electronic form, general reference works, such as encyclopedias, as well as articles and books in the areas you are considering (see 1.4 on conducting research). You can also refine your topic by doing subject searches in reference databases (see 1.4.4c) and in online catalogs (see 1.4.5a) and through Internet search tools (see 1.4.8d). Such preliminary reading and searches will also let you know if enough work has been done on the subject to permit adequate research and whether the pertinent source materials are readily accessible.

Selecting an appropriate topic is seldom a simple matter. Even after you discover a subject that attracts your interest, you may well find yourself revising your choice, modifying your approach, or changing topics altogether after you have begun research.

1.3.3. SUMMING UP

- Give yourself plenty of time to think through and rethink your choice of a topic.
- Look for a subject or an issue that will continue to engage you throughout research and writing.
- Consult library materials and other print and electronic information resources to refine the topic and to see if sufficient work has been done on the subject to make it a viable topic for the research paper.
- Before settling on a final topic, make sure you understand the amount and depth of research required and the type and length of paper expected.
- If you encounter problems at any point in the project, do not hesitate to consult your instructor, whether to clarify the assignment or to get help in choosing, developing, or researching a topic or in preparing the paper. A campus writing center can be a useful resource.

1.4. CONDUCTING RESEARCH

1.4.1. The Modern Academic Library

The library will generally be your most reliable guide as you conduct research for papers that draw on the published work of experts. Librarians evaluate resources for authority and quality before acquiring them for use in research. You should therefore become thoroughly acquainted with the libraries available to you and take full advantage of the resources and services they provide on-site and over the Internet.

Resources and Services

The modern academic library typically offers resources in print and electronic forms and in other nonprint media (e.g., films, sound recordings), as well as computer services, such as word processing, high-quality printers, and access to the Internet. Whereas some important resources are available only in the library building (e.g., most books and other publications solely in print form, microfilm materials, special collections), your library probably provides a number of electronic resources, such as bibliographic and full-text databases, that are accessible not only through computer terminals in the library but also from outside through the library's Web site.

Orientation and Instruction

Most academic libraries have programs of orientation and instruction to meet the needs of all students, from beginning researchers to graduate students. Ask about introductory pamphlets or handbooks and guided tours as well as lectures and classes on using the library and on related subjects like developing research strategies and searching the World Wide Web. The library's Web site likely contains scheduling information on such classes as well as descriptions of available resources and services. The site may also offer online tutorials.

Professional Reference Librarians

Nearly all public and academic libraries have desks staffed by professional reference librarians who can tell you about available instructional programs and help you locate sources. Specialist librarians often prepare and distribute, in print and electronic forms, research guides to specific fields of study. Consulting a librarian at key points in your research may save you considerable time and effort. Librarians may be available in person or by telephone, e-mail, or instant messaging.

1.4.2. Library Research Sources

Touring or reading about your library will reveal the many important sources of information it makes available to researchers. Information sources fall into four general categories.

Electronic Sources

Your library probably offers reference works in electronic form (see 1.4.4) and full-text databases (see 1.4.6) and may also recommend useful Web sites (see 1.4.8). Your library likely subscribes to journals available in electronic form.

Books and Similar Publications

The library typically houses a vast number of books as well as similar publications such as pamphlets and perhaps dissertations. Books are essential sources for many projects, and some instructors require that students use books—in addition to articles, Web sites, and other materials—during research. You can usually borrow most books from the library. A common exception is the library's collection of reference works in print (see 1.4.4). Although reference works usually cannot be borrowed, many important ones are likely available to you through the library's Web site.

Articles and Other Publications in Print Periodicals

The library gives access to numerous articles and similar writings (e.g., reviews, editorials) published in print periodicals such as scholarly journals, newspapers, and magazines.

Additional Sources

Most libraries provide nonprint sources such as sound recordings and video recordings and possibly also unpublished writings (e.g., manuscripts or private letters in special collections).

1.4.3. The Central Information System

Most academic libraries provide an online central information system to guide students and faculty members to research sources. The system ordinarily includes

- **the library's catalog of holdings** (books, periodicals, electronic sources, audiovisual materials, etc.; see 1.4.5)
- **bibliographic databases**, such as the *MLA International Bibliography* and *Science Direct*
- **other electronic resources**, including reference works (see 1.4.4), full-text databases to which the library subscribes (see 1.4.6), and recommended Web sites to which the library provides links (see 1.4.8)
- **other information about the library**, such as its location, hours, and policies

If your campus library does not hold a work you seek, consult *World-Cat*, on the Web. This database lists the holdings of over ten thousand libraries and can help you find a copy in a nearby library.

1.4.4. Reference Works

A useful way to begin a research project is to consult relevant reference works. Some reference works, like indexes and bibliographies, categorize research materials by subject and provide data that permit you to locate sources—author, title, date of publication, and so forth. Other reference works, like encyclopedias, dictionaries, and biographical sources, give basic information about subjects. This section provides a brief introduction to the kinds of general and specialized reference works you should know about. Your library probably has reference works in print and electronic forms.

- **Print.** Print works may be located in a reference room. General reference books, like dictionaries, encyclopedias, biographical sources, yearbooks, atlases, and gazetteers, may all be shelved together in one place, while specialized reference books may be grouped according to subject area—biology, business, literature, psychology, and so forth. The volumes of reference works published annually—indexes, bibliographies, and abstracts collections—are likely lined up in chronological order.

- **Electronic.** Reference works available as electronic databases are usually online or on CD-ROM or DVD-ROM. Searching and drawing material from the library's databases can be done in the library building and probably from outside as well, over the Internet. In some electronic environments, you can search several kinds of works in a single query. *Reference Universe*, for example, allows you to search the indexes of more than ten thousand reference works.

The electronic medium has obvious advantages for the researcher, such as currency, broad coverage, ease of downloading and printing, hypertextual links to other works, and sophisticated search capabilities. But do not ignore printed reference works, for many valuable works exist only in print. Sometimes when a work is available in both media the electronic version is partial, and so the print version provides better coverage. For example, some longstanding reference publications, such as indexes, bibliographies, and encyclopedias, have parts available in print that have not been converted for electronic publication. You will want to consider the scope of coverage in electronic versions you consult.

a. Reference Works That Provide Data about Research Materials

Indexes and bibliographies are lists of publications usually classified by subject. Depending on the scope of coverage, they may guide you to material in newspapers, magazines, and journals as well as to writings in books and on Web sites.

- *The New York Times Index* covers all articles published in the newspaper. For a research paper on the military draft in New York City during the Civil War, you can use this index to locate relevant articles in 1860–65.
- *Readers' Guide to Periodical Literature* indexes the contents of widely circulated periodicals. If you are writing about American women's fashion during the 1970s, you can identify magazine articles on the topic here.
- Most subject areas and scholarly disciplines have their own specialized bibliographies. You can use *The Philosopher's Index*, for example, to create a list of scholarly-journal articles about Immanuel Kant's ethical theory published since 1995.
- Some publishers combine several indexes in one electronic environment. Using *Wilson OmniFile Full Text*, you can search six indexes,

covering education, science, business, the humanities, social science, and journalism, with one query. For a research project in an area that crosses disciplines, such as ethnic studies, a search here will yield a useful variety of results.

- *Bibliographic Index* cites bibliographies that are published as books or pamphlets, as parts of books, or in periodicals.

Collections of abstracts present summaries of journal articles and other literature. Abstracts help you screen out works irrelevant to your research, so that you look for and read only the most promising sources.

- *Newspaper Abstracts* covers over fifty major newspapers in the United States.
- *Periodical Abstracts* treats a wide range of English-language academic journals and newsmagazines. It also indexes transcripts from about eighty television and radio programs that present news and other information.
- An entry in *Book Review Digest* provides an abstract of a book, excerpts of reviews it received in major publications, and bibliographic data for the reviews. This resource can help you understand how a book was evaluated when it was first published.
- Many collections of abstracts focus on a specific discipline or subject. *Biological Abstracts* covers over 3,700 journals in the life sciences from around the world. The index goes back to publications from 1926, illuminating the history of biology as well as contemporary research.
- Summaries of doctoral dissertations are available in *Dissertation Abstracts International*.

Guides to research seek to direct you to the most important sources of information and scholarship in the area you are researching. Unlike indexes, bibliographies, and collections of abstracts, which tend to strive for comprehensiveness and objectivity in presenting information, guides to research are usually selective and evaluative.

- Some research guides cover entire fields, such as *Literary Research Guide: An Annotated Listing of Reference Sources in English Literary Studies* and *Philosophy: A Guide to the Reference Literature*.
- Some guides to research are devoted to specific subjects within fields (e.g., *Reference Guide to Mystery and Detective Fiction*).

To learn of any guides that might be useful to your project, consult the latest edition of the American Library Association's *Guide to Reference Books*, your instructor, or a librarian.

b. Reference Works That Give Basic Information about Subjects

Dictionaries provide information, usually concise definitions, about words or topics.

* Among the most authoritative dictionaries for English words are *Webster's Third New International Dictionary of the English Language* and, especially for the history of a word's meanings and usages, *The Oxford English Dictionary*.
* More concise English-language dictionaries often recommended for student writers are *The American Heritage College Dictionary*, *Merriam-Webster's Collegiate Dictionary*, and *The New Oxford American Dictionary*.
* Dual-language dictionaries typically present words in one language followed by translations of those words into another language— for instance, *The New World Spanish-English, English-Spanish Dictionary* (also titled *El New World diccionario español-inglés, inglés-español*). Some language dictionaries in specialized fields are in a multilingual format, such as *Elsevier's Dictionary of Environment in English, French, Spanish, and Arabic*.
* A thesaurus lists groups of synonyms—words with similar meanings. It is useful for writers who wish to find the most precise word for a particular context or to vary their choice of words. Examples are *Merriam-Webster's Collegiate Thesaurus* and *Roget's International Thesaurus*.
* Major fields of study have specialized dictionaries, such as *Black's Law Dictionary*, *Dorland's Illustrated Medical Dictionary*, *The New Grove Dictionary of Music and Musicians*, and *The Penguin Dictionary of Sociology*.

Encyclopedias give introductory information about subjects.

* Popular general encyclopedias are *The Columbia Encyclopedia*, *The Encyclopedia Americana*, and *The Encyclopaedia Britannica Online*.
* Specialized encyclopedias include *The Corsini Encyclopedia of Psychology and Behavioral Science* and *Stanford Encyclopedia of Philosophy*.

Biographical sources describe the lives of prominent persons.

- Information on living persons is collected in such works as *Current Biography*, *The International Who's Who*, *Who's Who in America*, and *Who's Who in the Arab World*.
- Sources for persons no longer living are often organized by nation, as in *American National Biography* (for the United States), *Dictionary of Canadian Biography*, and *Oxford Dictionary of National Biography* (for Great Britain).

Yearbooks present facts about years in the past. Examples are *The Americana Annual*, *Britannica Book of the Year*, and *The Europa Yearbook*. Most are updates to encyclopedias, published between editions.

Almanacs are annual publications containing data, especially statistics, about many subjects. Examples are *The World Almanac and Book of Facts* and *The World Factbook*.

Atlases are collections of maps. Along with the many useful atlases published as print volumes, prominent atlases available on the Web include *The National Atlas of the United States of America*, the official atlas of the United States; *Google Earth*, which covers the entire globe; and *Perry-Castañeda Library Map Collection*, at the University of Texas, Austin, a historical collection.

Gazetteers provide geographic information. Examples are *The Columbia Gazetteer of the World* and *Merriam-Webster's Geographical Dictionary*.

Statistical resources provide numerical or quantitative facts.

- The United States government regularly publishes collections of statistics. For example, *Statistical Abstract of the United States* is issued by the Bureau of the Census. *American FactFinder*, produced by the same bureau, is a source for population, housing, economic, and geographic data. *FedStats*, an interagency publication, gives access to statistics and other information produced by more than one hundred United States government agencies. The Congressional Information Service provides statistical information from federal, state, business, professional, and international sources.
- Intergovernmental and nongovernmental organizations are also good sources of quantitative information. For instance, the United

Nations publishes the *Statistical Yearbook* and the *Demographic Yearbook.*

c. Searching a Reference Database

Every field of study has standard reference works. One such work is the *MLA International Bibliography*, which lists studies in the fields of language and literature. This work is published in electronic and print formats.

VERSIONS

- **Electronic.** The *MLA International Bibliography* is published in on-line and CD-ROM versions, which contain all citations published in annual volumes of the bibliography from 1926 to the present. Therefore, while an annual print volume of the *MLA International Bibliography* lists around 67,000 titles, the electronic versions offer information on more than 2,000,000 titles. Using these electronic editions, which are available from different vendors, involves searching techniques common to most databases. The standard ways of searching this database and similar ones are by author, title, and subject. Each vendor's system has help screens to guide you through its software interface.
- **Print.** The printed library edition of this work is published annually in two clothbound books. The first contains listings in five areas: literature in English, literature in other languages, linguistics, general literature and related topics, and folklore. The second book provides a subject index to the first.

TYPES OF SEARCHES OF THE ELECTRONIC VERSION

- **Author searches.** By entering the name of a scholar, you can obtain a list of the titles by the author that are collected in the database. For example, if you want to know what studies by Judith Butler have been published in the fields covered by this bibliography, you can enter her name and receive a list of titles.
- **Title searches.** If you know only the title of a work—like the essay "Sexual Linguistics" or the book *Talking Voices*—you can call forth complete bibliographic information about the work from the database by entering the title. If you remember only part of the title (e.g., "city"), you can request a listing of all titles containing that term (e.g., "Fun City: TV's Urban Situation Comedies of the 1990s,"

"The City in Modern Polish and Hungarian Poetry," "The London Scene: City and Court," "Japanese Adolescent Speech Styles in Hiroshima City: An Ethnographic Study").

- **Subject searches.** Since every work added to this bibliography is accompanied by at least one descriptor—a term that describes the work's subject matter—you can also search the database by subject. Thus, if you ask for studies that discuss, for instance, "detective fiction," the system will search through its files and present you with all titles that have "detective fiction" as a descriptor. If you want studies of Toni Morrison's novels, you can search for records with "Toni Morrison" as a descriptor. (Some vendors require that persons' names be inverted for searching—e.g., "Morrison Toni.")
- **Expanded searches.** Databases like the *MLA International Bibliography* also permit you to expand or narrow your searches usefully. While you are trying to decide on a topic, you may want to do expanded searches to get a broad sense of possibilities. An expanded subject search of this database can be particularly helpful when you are developing a suitable research topic. If you have a general idea that you want to write on detective fiction, you can find related subjects by entering the word "detective" in your expanded subject search. The following is a sampling of the related topics you will receive, with links to relevant bibliographic listings:

detective comics	female detective
detective drama	French detective
detective fiction	hard-boiled detective
detective film	American detective fiction
detective magazines	Egyptian detective fiction
detective novel	English detective fiction
detective story	paranormal detective fiction
detective television	Senegalese detective fiction

Also useful for expanded searches is the truncation (or wild card) feature. By using a truncated, or shortened, term—for example, a word root—followed by an asterisk (or the symbol *:* or *$*, depending on the vendor's software interface), you can retrieve all variants of it. If you wish, for instance, to do a paper on feminism but cannot decide what aspect to focus on, you can enter as a search term "femini*" and receive records on, among other subjects, "feminine discourse," "femininity," "feminist literary theory and criticism," "feminist movement," and "feminist writers."

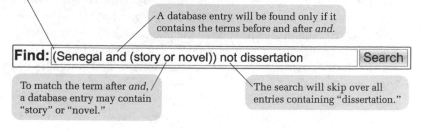

Parentheses group related parts of the query.

A database entry will be found only if it contains the terms before and after *and*.

Find: (Senegal and (story or novel)) not dissertation   Search

To match the term after *and*, a database entry may contain "story" or "novel."

The search will skip over all entries containing "dissertation."

Fig. 1. Boolean searching. When using the *MLA International Bibliography* through *EBSCOhost*, you can enter this search phrase to find scholarship about short stories or novels relating to Senegal. The search will exclude PhD dissertations.

- **Boolean searches.** The electronic *MLA International Bibliography* also permits searching according to Boolean logic—named after the nineteenth-century British mathematician and logician George Boole. In this kind of searching, you customize your search request with the operators *and*, *or*, and *not* (see fig. 1). For example, you can use the Boolean operator *or* to expand your search. The following search expression will furnish more titles than either "Arthur Conan Doyle" or "Sherlock Holmes" by itself would:

Arthur Conan Doyle or Sherlock Holmes

If you want to perform narrower searches, the Boolean operators *not* and *and* can limit the field of titles accessed. If you are interested in finding studies on, say, versions of the story of Othello other than Shakespeare's, enter the following:

Othello not Shakespeare

Or if you would like to identify studies that compare Shakespeare's play with *Otello*, Verdi's operatic adaptation of it, keying the following rather than just "Othello" will result in a shorter, more focused list of sources:

Othello and Otello

- **Other advanced searches.** The *MLA International Bibliography* in its electronic versions offers other ways to restrict your search. It allows you to retrieve titles from a single publication source—for instance, articles on *Othello* that have appeared in *Shakespeare Quarterly* over the last several decades. The database also allows you to limit your search according to language of publication (e.g., Japanese, Spanish), publication type (e.g., book, journal article), and publication year. You can obtain a list, for example, of books on Goethe's *Faust* that were written in German and published in 2000 or later.

BIBLIOGRAPHIC INFORMATION PROVIDED

The database allows you to print out and download bibliographic information. It also gives you a choice of how to view, print, or download data. The display style varies among the interfaces through which the *MLA International Bibliography* is offered. Figures 2 and 3 present two ways in which the bibliographic information may appear in the ProQuest interface. The first record you see (fig. 2) includes the author, title, and publication details. By clicking on the title, you open an expanded record (fig. 3), which lists the author, title, publication details, publication year, publication type, language of publication, international standard serial number (ISSN), an indication of whether the publication was peer-reviewed, subject descriptors, update code, accession number, and sequence number.

The expanded record allows you to click on the subject descriptors to find additional items on the same topics. In some cases, you can follow a link from a bibliographic record directly to a PDF or Web version of the work.

1.4.5. The Online Catalog of Library Holdings

An important part of a library's central information system is the online catalog of holdings (e.g., electronic publications, books, serials, audiovisual materials). There is no standard system for online catalogs. Systems differ, for example, in how users access information and in what appears on the screen. All systems, however, permit searching.

a. Searching an Online Catalog

When using an online catalog, you can locate a work in a number of ways. The most common are by author, by title, and by subject.

• **Author searches.** If you enter the author's full name—whether a personal name (e.g., Maxine Hong Kingston) or a corporate name

> Butler, Judith: "On Never Having Learned How to Live"
> Differences: A Journal of Feminist Cultural Studies, (16:3),
> 2005 Fall, 27-34. (2005)

Fig. 2. The initial record resulting from a search of a bibliographic database.

Document Author:	Butler, Judith
Title:	On Never Having Learned How to Live
Publication Details:	Differences: A Journal of Feminist Cultural Studies, (16:3), 2005 Fall, 27-34.
Publication Year:	2005
Publication Type:	journal article
Language of Publication:	English
ISSN:	10407391
Peer-reviewed:	Yes
Subjects:	
National Literature:	French literature
Subject Classification Term:	prose
Period:	1900-1999
Author as Subject:	Derrida, Jacques (1930-2004)
Literary Theme:	(treatment of) death
Update Code:	200601
Accession Number:	2006871262
Sequence Number:	2006 2 4178

Fig. 3. An expanded record in a bibliographic database.

(e.g., United States Central Intelligence Agency)—the screen displays a list of all the works the library has by that author. If you know only an author's last name (e.g., Kingston), you can obtain a list of all authors with that last name.

- **Title searches.** Entering the title produces a list of all works the library has with that title. The online catalog contains not only book titles but also titles of other works in the system, including journals (e.g., *Psychology and Marketing*), databases (e.g., *Anthropological Literature*), and book series. If you enter the name of a book series, such as "Approaches to Teaching World Literature" or "Loeb Classical Library," you will receive a list of all book titles in the series. If you know only the beginning of a title—for example, only *Advertising,*

Competition, instead of *Advertising, Competition, and Public Policy: A Simulation Study*—you can enter what you know, and the screen will display all titles that begin with those words.

- **Subject heading searches.** If you have no author or title in mind, you can enter a subject heading to produce a list of works about the subject. Most academic libraries exclusively use the subject headings that appear in the *Library of Congress Subject Headings*. Many headings have more specific subheadings. For example, you can enter "Mass media and the environment" and receive a list of all works assigned that general subject heading, or you can obtain a more specialized list by entering one of the following:

      Mass media and the environment—Great Britain
      Mass media and the environment—India
      Mass media and the environment—Latin America
      Mass media and the environment—United States

- **Call number searches.** If you know a work's call number, the designation by which the work is shelved in the library, you can enter it and receive bibliographic information about the work. For example, if you enter "PA817.B43 1992," you will learn that it applies to the book *An Introduction to New Testament Greek*, written by Frank Beetham and published in London by Bristol Classical Press in 1992.

- **Keyword searches.** An online catalog also helps you to initiate more sophisticated searches. A keyword search looks for individual words regardless of their location in a name, title, or subject heading. You can, for example, call up a list of all works that contain "competition" anywhere in their titles, such as

      Information Agreements, Competition, and Efficiency
      Conglomerate Mergers and Market Competition
      Competition and Human Behavior

  A subject heading search using the keyword "competition" will produce the titles of all works whose subject descriptions include the word, such as *Europe versus America? Contradictions of Imperialism*, one of whose subject headings is "Competition, International," or *Unequal Freedoms: The Global Market as an Ethical System*, one of whose subject headings is "Competition—Moral and ethical aspects."

- **Boolean searches.** Online catalogs also typically permit searching according to Boolean logic—that is, using the operators *and*, *or*, and *not*. For instance, suppose you are interested in studies on the relation between nutrition and cancer. A search using "nutrition" alone or "cancer" alone would yield a list of all works having anything to do with the subject of each search, and you would have to pick out the items dealing with the two subjects together. In contrast, a Boolean search using "nutrition *and* cancer" excludes all works not about both subjects. Likewise, if you want to see which authors besides Goethe wrote about the Faust theme, you can enter "Faust *not* Goethe." In addition to narrowing lists of titles, Boolean searching is useful for expanding them. For example, if you wish to research solar heating, you might enter "solar *or* sun *and* heating," which will produce more titles than would just "solar *and* heating." (On using Boolean logic in searching a reference database, see 1.4.4c.)

- **Other advanced searches.** Online catalogs allow you to limit your search in various ways. You may ask for titles published during a certain range of years (e.g., 2000 to the present) or titles located only in one specific part of your library (e.g., the main collection). You may be able, too, to limit your search to specific media (e.g., books, serials, electronic publications, archives, manuscripts, musical scores, films, video or sound recordings). This feature will permit you, say, to request a list of books that were published in Spanish between 1990 and 2000 about cave paintings in Spain, or it will let you find out if your library has any video recordings about mythology or the Civil War.

b. Bibliographic Information Provided

When you access a title, the screen shows something like the example in figure 4. The top lines of the screen image contain the author's name (Elaine Freedgood), the full title (*The Ideas in Things: Fugitive Meaning in the Victorian Novel*), and complete publication information (the book was published by the University of Chicago Press in Chicago in 2006). The following lines describe the physical characteristics of the book (it has 10 pages of front matter—material before the main text—and 196 pages of text and measures 23 centimeters in height); indicate that it contains a bibliography and an index; show the subject headings under which the book is cataloged; and give its international standard book numbers (ISBNs). Then follow hyperlinks to an electronic version of the table of contents and to records on the borrowing status of copies in the main collection and in a

Standard View	Name Tags View	MARC Tags View	
Author	Freedgood, Elaine.
Title	The ideas in things : fugitive meaning in the Victorian novel / Elaine Freedgood.
Publisher/Date	Chicago : University of Chicago Press, 2006.
Description	x, 196 p. ; 23 cm.
Note	Includes bibliographical references (p. [159]-186) and index.
Subject (LCSH)	English fiction -- 19th century -- History and criticism.
	Material culture in literature.
	Material culture -- Great Britain -- History -- 19th century.
ISBN	0226261557 (cloth : alk. paper)
	9780226261553
Library Holdings:	Unrestricted / Internet Resources / Electronic access
Library Holdings:	NYU Bobst / Main Collection PR788.M37 F74 2006
Library Holdings:	New School Fogelman Library / Main Collection PR788.M37 F74 2006

Fig. 4. An entry in an online catalog.

related collection. The call number of the book appears in the listings of the libraries' copies.

c. Information Needed for Research and Writing

For the purposes of researching and writing your paper, you normally will not use most of the information that appears in the catalog entry. You need to know the call number, of course, to locate the work in the library (see 1.4.5d); and, for your paper's works-cited list, you also need to know the author, title, and full publication information (see 1.5 on compiling a working bibliography; see ch. 5 on information needed for compiling the list of works cited). Following is the entry in the works-cited list for the title given above:

> Freedgood, Elaine. *The Ideas in Things: Fugitive Meaning in the Victorian Novel.* Chicago: U of Chicago P, 2006. Print.

Transcribe this information carefully. Online catalog systems typically give the option of printing out or downloading the bibliographic data displayed on the screen. This feature saves you the effort of copying the information and eliminates the possibility of transcription errors. You should, of course, verify the information you derive from the catalog against the source itself; errors sometimes occur during cataloging.

d. Call Numbers

The call numbers in your library probably follow one of two systems of classification: the Library of Congress system or the Dewey decimal system. Learning your library's system will not only help you to find works and know their contents from their call numbers but also guide you to sections of the library in which to browse.

The Library of Congress system divides books into twenty major groups:

A   General works
B   Philosophy, psychology, and religion
C   Auxiliary sciences of history
D   World history and history of Europe, Asia, Africa, Australia, New Zealand, etc.
E–F   History of the Americas
G   Geography, anthropology, recreation
H   Social sciences
J   Political science
K   Law
L   Education
M   Music and books on music
N   Fine arts
P   Language and literature
Q   Science
R   Medicine
S   Agriculture
T   Technology
U   Military science
V   Naval science
Z   Bibliography, library science, and information resources (general)

The Dewey decimal system classifies books under ten major headings:

000   Computers, information, and general reference
100   Philosophy and psychology
200   Religion
300   Social sciences
400   Language
500   Science
600   Technology
700   Arts and recreation

800   Literature
900   History and geography

e. Location of Library Materials

The library catalog normally indicates not only the call number for a title but also the section in which to find the work, whether in the main collection or in a different location. It may also indicate if a title is checked out, missing, at the bindery, or on order. Ask at the circulation desk to see if it is possible to recall a checked-out book or search for a missing book.

- **Open shelves and closed stacks.** Most library holdings are kept on open shelves, to which the public has direct access. To obtain a work in closed stacks, you usually have to present a call slip to a library staff member, who will locate the work for you.
- **Sections for reserved works and reference works.** If the word *Reserved* appears in a catalog entry, it indicates that the work is required in a course and stored in a special section, at the instructor's request, so that the work may not be borrowed but stays available for students in the course. A work shelved in the reference section, often designated in the catalog entry by *R* or *Ref*, is too widely used to be borrowed and thus must also remain in the library.
- **Other sections.** Libraries also commonly set aside areas for other types of materials—current periodicals, pamphlets, and nonprint materials, like CD-ROMs, films, and audio and video recordings. Some libraries have additional special collections, such as rare books or government documents, that are similarly kept separate from the main collection. Consult the library directory or a librarian for locations.

1.4.6. Full-Text Databases

Modern academic libraries subscribe to and make generally available a wide variety of databases: not only those containing bibliographic citations and abstracts (see 1.4.4a), which guide researchers to relevant sources, but also full-text databases, which offer complete texts of many sources. Some of these databases may be limited to use in the library, but many probably can also be accessed from outside, through the library's Web site. Virtually all full-text databases are searchable by author, title, and subject and through more sophisticated strategies (e.g., keyword searching, Boolean searching), as discussed in 1.4.4c and 1.4.5a. This section describes a few well-known full-text databases and explains how you might use them in your research.

- **AnthroSource.** This resource collects the contents of over thirty scholarly journals published by the American Anthropological Association. For a paper on the methods for recording folklore in the 1930s, you can perform a keyword search ("folklore") of all articles in the database published during that decade. You can then read the articles that relate most closely to your topic. If an article you read cites a source not included in the collection, you may be able to follow a link from the citation into another full-text database in your library where you can retrieve it.
- **ARTstor.** Over 700,000 images relating to art and architecture are available in this database for browsing and searching. If you are studying the architecture of Buddhist temples in Vietnam, you can use *ARTstor* to locate relevant images of temples and other works of art with a search by geographic area. You can also save images on disk for use as figures in your paper or in a class presentation.
- **Early English Books Online (EEBO).** A digital collection of over 100,000 books, tracts, and pamphlets published in England between 1473 and 1700, *EEBO* allows users to view and search rare material that is fragile in its original state. A student in a music history course can look at early English ballads here, for example, and identify patterns of imagery in the lyrics.
- **EBSCO.** Your library may subscribe to a number of EBSCO's bibliographic databases as well as to its full-text databases, such as *Academic Search Premier* (articles from over 4,500 scholarly publications in all major disciplines), *Business Source Premier* (articles from over 2,000 scholarly business periodicals), *Newspaper Source* (articles from some 200 United States and international newspapers), and *Masterfile Premier* (articles from nearly 2,000 periodicals on a variety of subjects, including general science, business, and psychology). These databases are good resources for research papers covering current events.
- **Project Muse.** You can view recent issues of nearly four hundred scholarly journals in the humanities and social sciences in this collection. A listing in an online bibliography or in your library's catalog may provide a direct link to a journal or article here. If you are interested in learning about, for instance, the propagation of

native species, you might read through several issues of *Native Plants Journal.*

By making a careful record of your research findings, you can save time and effort when you later prepare the list of works cited. Most databases allow you to print or download citation data as well as the full text of sources. Whether you print or download materials from a database or take notes on your own, be sure to check the citation data to see if you have everything you need to prepare an entry in the list of works cited (see 1.5 on compiling a working bibliography; see ch. 5 on preparing the list of works cited). Remember to record the date of access (day, month, and year).

1.4.7. Other Library Resources and Services

Besides knowing about the materials discussed above, you should become familiar with the library's other resources and services.

a. Microforms

Microform designates printed matter greatly reduced in size by microphotography; common types are microfilm, microfiche, and microcard (see fig. 5). Libraries use microforms to store such materials as back copies of periodicals (newspapers, magazines, scholarly journals) and rare books. Microforms are usually kept in a special section of the library. To use them, you need a reader that magnifies them; a special photocopier can reproduce microform pages. Library staff members are usually on hand to assist researchers in locating microform materials and operating the readers and photocopiers.

b. Media Center

Many libraries have a special section devoted to audio recordings (e.g., compact discs, audiotapes, long-playing records), video recordings (e.g., on VHS or DVD), and multimedia materials. These resources are generally kept in closed stacks and used only in the library, although there may be exceptions, such as for use in the classroom. Some materials may be available for listening or viewing on the Web, inside or outside the library.

MODERN LANGUAGE ASSOCIATION OF AMERICA.
  PUBLICATIONS OF THE MODERN LANGUAGE *
Vol 115   No 1   JAN 2000

Fig. 5. An enlargement of part of a microfiche containing pages from the journal *PMLA*.

c. Electronic and Other Resources

Photocopying machines are typically located at various sites in the library, as are computer terminals that give access to the central catalog and other databases and to the Internet. Your school may also permit students to borrow laptop computers, with Internet connections, for use in the library. Some schools have computer centers in the library and in other locations on campus as well. Such centers provide, for student use, a variety of software applications for tasks such as word processing, spreadsheet analysis, database management, drawing, image processing, and drafting. Services might include high-quality printing and image and text scanning. Some schools have facilities for photographic, audio, and video production.

d. Interlibrary Loans

Most libraries have agreements for the exchange of research materials on a regional, statewide, national, or even international basis. If your library does not have the materials you need, ask whether it can borrow them from another library. If it can, ask your librarian for help in initiating an interlibrary loan. Finding the source in a nearby library rather than a faraway one will save considerable time. To discover which libraries own your title, you may search other library catalogs over the Internet or consult *WorldCat*, which lists the holdings of over ten thousand libraries.

1.4.8. Web Sources

a. Range of Sources

Through the World Wide Web, a researcher can read and transfer material from library catalogs and millions of other useful sites, created by professional organizations (e.g., American Chemical Society, American Philosophical Association), government agencies (e.g., Library of Congress, United States Census Bureau), commercial enterprises (e.g., publishers of encyclopedias, news organizations), educational entities (e.g., universities, libraries, academic departments, research centers, scholarly projects), and individual scholars. These sites provide access to historical papers, literary works, articles in periodicals (e.g., journals, magazines, newspapers), and audiovisual materials (e.g., photographs, paintings, sound and video recordings).

b. Using Recommended Sites

Using the Web for research requires practice and training just as using a library does. Whenever possible, follow the guidance of an instructor, an academic department, or a librarian in selecting Internet sites for research. In addition to offering online databases, your library's Web site may provide links to important Internet sources, which were likely selected after careful evaluation and consultation. A librarian might also be able to advise you about sites relevant to your research. Similarly, you may find recommended sites on Web pages for your academic departments, instructors, or courses.

c. Gateway Sites

Your librarian or instructor might direct you to a "metapage" or "gateway" that provides links to other sites. Some editors of gateway sites are broadly inclusive, while others are highly selective. Examples of such sites follow:

- *Voice of the Shuttle* (Univ. of California, Santa Barbara) offers on its home page a menu of subjects in the humanities—anthropology, archaeology, architecture, history, literary theory, philosophy, and so forth. Selecting "media studies," for example, gives you a list of specific fields (e.g., journalism, film and video, popular music, comics, cyberculture). The choice of "media theory and theorists" presents links to numerous resources in this area: professional organizations, bibliographies, journals, articles and papers, and other related sites, including many created and maintained by scholars in media studies. The home page also provides general links to libraries and museums, reference works, journals, publishers and booksellers, e-mail discussions and news groups, conferences, and travel resources.

- *Crossroads* (Amer. Studies Assn.) is a comprehensive resource for research and teaching in American studies. A section of the site, "American Studies Web," provides annotated listings of Web sites by subject category. Under the topic "Nature and the Environment," for example, you will find links to over seventy sites relating to environmental issues in the United States.

- *Intute* (Intute Consortium) is published by a consortium of seven universities. The consortium says that "all material is evaluated and selected by a network of subject specialists." The site has four main areas: science and technology, arts and humanities, social sciences, and health and life sciences.

d. Searching the Web

Search tools. Whether you are developing a research topic or looking for research sources, use the tools for locating Internet materials. You have probably used Internet search engines such as *Google, Windows Live,* and *Yahoo!* to find all sorts of information, but you may not have explored all the ways of searching provided by these services. Most search engines offer help pages that explain strategies for basic and advanced searching. You may be able to define the scope of your search, limiting it, for example, to images or to books. Consider the criteria the search engine uses to sort results and how those criteria relate to your research. A search engine that weights results by commercial sponsorship, for example, may provide useful information if you are looking to purchase a product, but the results may prove less useful for scholarly research. Similarly, a search may lead you to the most visited site on a topic, but the site's popularity is no guarantee of its authority or accuracy.

If you know at the outset the exact topic you wish to research, you can perform a keyword search, which produces a listing of sites containing the word or words you specify. To avoid long lists containing many irrelevant sites, be as specific as possible in your terms—thus, "human cloning" will yield a shorter, more unified list than "cloning" alone would. Most search tools offer instructions on how to phrase search requests for the best results. You can often use Boolean and other operators to make searches precise (see 1.4.4c and 1.4.5a).

Bookmarking and recording the URL. Whenever you discover what seems a useful document or site, be sure to record its address so that you can easily return to the source for further information or clarification. You can compile a record by using the bookmark feature in your browser, copying URLs and pasting them into a file in your word processor, or using research-management software or sites.

Recording the date of access. Always note the date or dates on which you consult a source. The date of access is important because the material could be revised after you visit the site. You will need the date of access for your working bibliography and your list of works cited.

Internet sources among other sources. Whereas many instructors encourage using Internet sources, few consider a search of the Web alone adequate research for most research papers. Instructors generally require that other materials, including print publications, be sought. Similarly, e-mail discussion lists and online forums are helpful for sharing ideas but are rarely deemed acceptable resources for research papers. (See 1.6 on evaluating source materials.)

1.4.9. SUMMING UP

Your school library is likely to be your most reliable guide when you conduct research. You should therefore become as familiar as possible with the library's electronic and print resources and its various services. Library resources include

- electronic resources (e.g., online catalog of holdings, reference works, bibliographic and full-text databases)
- books and similar publications (e.g., pamphlets)
- print periodicals (e.g., journals, newspapers, magazines)
- additional sources (e.g., sound and video recordings)

Library services may include

- a media center
- photocopying machines
- access to computers

- use of software applications, printers, scanning devices, and other hardware
- interlibrary loans

Useful Web sources are

- sites recommended by instructors and librarians
- gateway sites

1.5. COMPILING A WORKING BIBLIOGRAPHY

1.5.1. Keeping Track of Sources

As you discover information and opinions on your topic, you should keep track of sources that you may use for your paper. A record of such sources is called a *working bibliography*. Your preliminary reading will probably provide the first titles for this list. Other titles will emerge when you consult reference works and the library's central catalog and when you explore the Internet. If you read carefully through the bibliography and notes of each work you consult, more often than not you will discover additional important sources. Your working bibliography will frequently change during your research as you add titles and eliminate those that do not prove useful and as you probe and emphasize some aspects of your subject in preference to others. The working bibliography will eventually evolve into the list of works cited that appears at the end of the research paper.

1.5.2. Creating a Computer File for the Working Bibliography

A computer is particularly useful for compiling the working bibliography. Create a computer file for this purpose, and enter full information about sources into the file as you proceed with your research. Whenever you wish to add new works to the list, to remove works you no longer think helpful, or to correct entries already stored, you retrieve the file, make the changes, and save the revised file for future use. As you research, you can arrange and rearrange your sources however you wish (e.g., in alphabetical order, in chronological order by date of publication, in order of relevance to your topic); you can also divide sources into groups (e.g., those already consulted and those not yet consulted, those most useful and those less so). At any point, you can print the file to review it or to use it for research. Since bibliographic information is essential to researching and writing the paper, be certain to save this file and to keep copies of it on paper and in a backup location.

1.5.3. Recording Essential Publication Information

When you add sources to your working bibliography, be sure you enter all the publication information needed for the works-cited list. The information to be recorded depends on the kind of source used. See chapter 5 for complete guidelines on compiling the works-cited list of the research paper.

1.5.4. Noting Other Useful Information

Besides the data needed for the works-cited list, it is useful to add other information to items in the working bibliography. For example, if you derive a source from a bibliographic work, record where you found the reference, in case you need to recheck it. Also note the library call number, the network address (URL), or other identifying information required to locate each work.

The following entry in a working bibliography contains not only all the facts needed for the final bibliography (author's name, full title, and relevant publication information) but also information useful for research: the origin of the reference (the electronic database of the *MLA International Bibliography*) and the call number (PS374.D4 M38 2000). You will delete reference origins and call numbers when you convert your working bibliography into the list of works cited.

> McCann, Sean. *Gumshoe America: Hard-Boiled Crime Fiction and the Rise and Fall of New Deal Liberalism*. Durham: Duke UP, 2000. [*MLA Bib.*; PS374.D4 M38 2000]

1.5.5. Verifying Publication Information

Whenever you consult a source, carefully verify the publication facts against your records—even if you have printed out or downloaded the data. Add any missing information that you will need for the works-cited list, and correct any part of your records that does not match the data obtained from the work itself. Recording and verifying all the information about your sources when you first consult them will spare you many last-minute problems and frustrations.

1.5.6. Converting the Working Bibliography to the Works-Cited List

Eventually, you will transform your working bibliography into a works-cited list. If your working bibliography is in a computer file, edit the entries to remove unnecessary information (e.g., origin of reference, call number), arrange them alphabetically by author (see 5.3.3 on the arrangement of entries), and title the list "Works Cited" (see 5.3.1 on titles for other kinds of source lists). When you have finished the final draft of your paper, transfer the edited bibliography file to the end of the file containing the paper (see 5.3.2 on the format of the list).

1.5.7. SUMMING UP

If compiled with care and attention, the working bibliography will be invaluable to you throughout the preparation of your paper. It will, on the one hand, function as an efficient tool for finding and acquiring information and ideas and, on the other, provide all the data you will need for your list of works cited.

1.6. EVALUATING SOURCES

All researchers, students as well as professional scholars, need to assess the quality of any work scrupulously before using and citing it. Students writing their first research papers often find it difficult to evaluate sources. Not all sources are equally reliable or of equal quality. In reading and evaluating potential sources, you should not assume that something is truthful or trustworthy just because it appears in print or is on the Internet. Some material may be based on incorrect or outdated information or on poor logic, and the author's knowledge or view of the subject may be biased or too limited. Weigh what you read against your own knowledge and intelligence as well as against other treatments of the subject. Focus particularly on the *authority*, *accuracy*, and *currency* of the sources you use. Following are some criteria to keep in mind when you evaluate sources. If you have doubts about a source, your instructor or a librarian can probably help you.

1.6.1. Authority

Peer Review

Most scholarly journals and academic book publishers are committed to a policy of consultant review—commonly referred to by scholars as "peer review." In peer review, publishers seek the advice of expert readers, or referees, before considering a manuscript for publication. Each consultant reads the work and sends the publisher a report evaluating the manuscript and, in general, either recommending or not recommending it for publication. Readers comment on such matters as the importance of the subject, the originality and soundness of the argument, the accuracy of the facts, and the currency of the research. At most scholarly journals and presses, moreover, there is also an editorial board that similarly reviews the manuscript, along with the readers' reports, before deciding whether to publish the work. Thus, a manuscript submitted to a refereed publication must undergo rigorous scrutiny before it is published.

Internet Sources

Assessing Internet resources is a particular challenge. Whereas the print publications that researchers depend on are generally issued by reputable publishers, like university presses, that accept accountability for the quality and reliability of the works they distribute, relatively few electronic publications currently have comparable authority. Some Internet publications are peer-reviewed, but many are not. Online materials are often self-published, without any outside review.

What to Look For

In evaluating any source, print or electronic, look especially for information on the following aspects. Figure 6 shows how these considerations apply to a specific Web site.

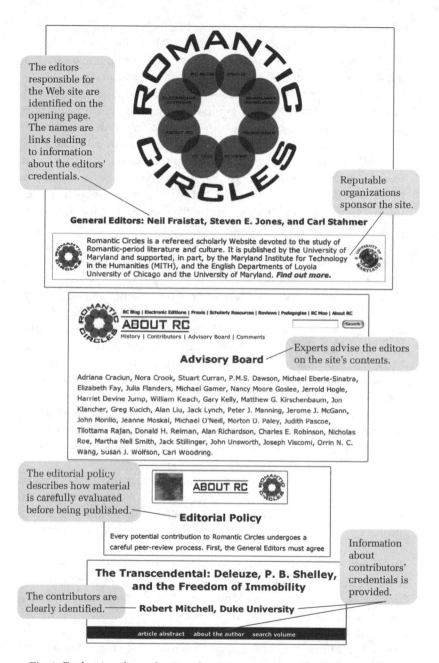

The editors responsible for the Web site are identified on the opening page. The names are links leading to information about the editors' credentials.

Reputable organizations sponsor the site.

General Editors: Neil Fraistat, Steven E. Jones, and Carl Stahmer

Romantic Circles is a refereed scholarly Website devoted to the study of Romantic-period literature and culture. It is published by the University of Maryland and supported, in part, by the Maryland Institute for Technology in the Humanities (MITH), and the English Departments of Loyola University of Chicago and the University of Maryland. *Find out more.*

RC Blog | Electronic Editions | Praxis | Scholarly Resources | Reviews | Pedagogies | RC Moo | About RC

ABOUT RC

History | Contributors | Advisory Board | Comments

Experts advise the editors on the site's contents.

Advisory Board

Adriana Craciun, Nora Crook, Stuart Curran, P.M.S. Dawson, Michael Eberle-Sinatra, Elizabeth Fay, Julia Flanders, Michael Gamer, Nancy Moore Goslee, Jerrold Hogle, Harriet Devine Jump, William Keach, Gary Kelly, Matthew G. Kirschenbaum, Jon Klancher, Greg Kucich, Alan Liu, Jack Lynch, Peter J. Manning, Jerome J. McGann, John Morillo, Jeanne Moskal, Michael O'Neill, Morton D. Paley, Judith Pascoe, Tilottama Rajan, Donald H. Reiman, Alan Richardson, Charles E. Robinson, Nicholas Roe, Martha Nell Smith, Jack Stillinger, John Unsworth, Joseph Viscomi, Orrin N. C. Wang, Susan J. Wolfson, Carl Woodring.

The editorial policy describes how material is carefully evaluated before being published.

ABOUT RC

Editorial Policy

Every potential contribution to Romantic Circles undergoes a careful peer-review process. First, the General Editors must agree

Information about contributors' credentials is provided.

The Transcendental: Deleuze, P. B. Shelley, and the Freedom of Immobility

The contributors are clearly identified.

Robert Mitchell, Duke University

article abstract   about the author   search volume

Fig. 6. Evaluating the authority of an Internet source. The Web site *Romantic Circles* has the characteristics of an authoritative source suitable for scholarly research.

- **Author.** When we consult a printed book or article, we expect to find prominently displayed the name of the author of the work. Whenever you consult a source, print or electronic, make sure that the author of the document or the person or group responsible for the publication or site is identified. Once you establish authorship, consider the authoritativeness of the work. Publications sometimes indicate an author's credentials in the field by including relevant biographical information (e.g., professional title or affiliation, list of publications or other accomplishments). On the Web, you may find the author's credentials by following a link to a home page or to a page (labeled, e.g., "About Us") that lists personnel responsible for the site. You can also search the Internet and other sources to find information about an author. For example, if you are evaluating a book, you might consult *Book Review Index* and *Book Review Digest* to see how experts in the field of study received this book and any others by the author.

- **Text.** If you are working with historical documents or literary texts that exist in various versions, make certain you use reliable editions. For example, versions of Shakespeare's plays published during his lifetime and shortly after his death sometimes differ drastically. The task of a modern scholarly editor is to compare, analyze, and evaluate these variations and produce an edition that is as historically authoritative as possible. Therefore, if you want to use, say, an electronic text of a Shakespeare play, look for one that, at a minimum, clearly states who the editor of the text is and when the electronic edition was published or identifies the printed source that was the basis for the electronic version.

- **Editorial policy.** Take note of the entire work or site you are using even if you are interested only in a particular document within it. In a journal or at a Web site, look for a statement of mission or purpose as well as for evidence that the document underwent consultant review (e.g., the listing of an editorial board).

- **Publisher or sponsoring organization.** Like the name of the author, the name of the publisher is normally evident in print publications. Similarly, the name of the publisher or sponsoring organization of a Web site should be clearly stated, preferably with access to information about the organization (e.g., through a prompt such as "About the Project"). An element at or near the end of the domain name (e.g., the *.org* in "www.npr.org") may indicate the kind of organization from which a Web site emanates—for example, a commercial enterprise (*.com*), an educational institution (*.edu*), a government agency (*.gov*), or a not-for-profit organization (*.org*). There is no guarantee that material from, say, an *.edu* site is reliable; such a site probably includes unsupervised personal pages as well as peer-reviewed scholarly projects. Nonetheless, knowing the organization involved might help you evaluate potential usefulness or shortcomings. For instance, many *.com* sites offer helpful information, but some are no more than advertisements, such as a book company's lavish praise for books that it publishes.

1.6.2. Accuracy and Verifiability

If you are evaluating scholarly material, check to see that the work's sources are indicated, so that its information can be verified. The sources probably appear in a list of works cited. The titles in the list might also tell you something about the breadth of the author's knowledge of the subject and about any possible bias. A Web publication might supply hypertextual links to the sources. Note, too, whether the document or site gives an e-mail address or otherwise tells how you can ask the author or sponsoring organization for further information or clarification.

1.6.3. Currency

The publication date of a print source suggests how current the author's scholarship is. Although online documents and sites have the potential for continual updating, many remain in their original states and, depending on the subject, may be out-of-date. When considering any resource, be sure at least one date is assigned to it. Several dates are sometimes listed for an electronic publication. For example, if a document on the Web had a previous print existence, there could be the date of print publication as well as the date of electronic publication. In addition, there might be the date when the material was last revised or updated. Ideally, a document should record all dates of publication and revision (see 5.6 on including all relevant dates in works-cited-list entries). Finally, scrutinizing the publication dates of works cited in the text also reveals the currency of its scholarship.

1.6.4. SUMMING UP

Evaluate all sources you use for your research. Focus on the authority, accuracy, and currency of the sources. Consider such questions as the following:

- Who is the author of the work, and what are the author's credentials for writing and publishing this work?
- When judged against your previous reading and your understanding of the subject, is the information furnished by the author correct? Is the argument presented logically and without bias?
- Are the author's sources clearly and adequately indicated, so that they can be verified?
- Are the author's sources current, or are they outdated?
- Who is the publisher, or what is the sponsoring organization, of the work?
- Is the work peer-reviewed—that is, has it been read and recommended for publication by experts?

1.7. TAKING NOTES

When you determine that material is reliable and useful, you will want to take notes on it.

1.7.1. Methods of Note-Taking

Although everyone agrees that note-taking is essential to research, probably no two researchers use exactly the same methods. Some prefer to take notes by hand on index cards or sheets of paper. Using a computer might save you time and should improve the accuracy with which you transcribe material, including quotations, from your notes into the text of your paper. However you take notes, set down first the author's full name and the complete title of the source—enough information to enable you to locate the source easily in your working bibliography. If the source is not yet in the working bibliography, record all the publication information you will need for research and for your works-cited list (see 1.5.3–4), and add the source to the working bibliography.

1.7.2. Types of Note-Taking

There are, generally speaking, three types of note-taking:

- **Summary.** Summarize if you want to record only the general idea of large amounts of material.
- **Paraphrase.** If you require detailed notes on specific sentences and passages but do not need the exact wording, you may wish to paraphrase—that is, to restate the material in your own words.
- **Quotation.** When you believe that some sentence or passage in its original wording might make an effective addition to your paper, transcribe that material exactly as it appears, word for word, comma for comma. Whenever you quote verbatim from a work, be sure to use quotation marks scrupulously in your notes to distinguish the quotation from summary and paraphrase. Using electronic materials calls for special vigilance. If you download a text and integrate quotations from it into your paper, check to see that you have placed quotation marks around words taken from the source.

1.7.3. Recording Page or Reference Numbers

In summarizing, paraphrasing, or quoting, keep an accurate record of the pages or other numbered sections (e.g., numbered paragraphs in an electronic text) that you use. When a quotation continues to another page or section, carefully note where the page or section break occurs, since only a small portion of what you transcribe may ultimately find its way into your paper.

1.7.4. Using a Computer for Note-Taking

Using a word processor to store notes is handy, but while you are doing research, you may find yourself in a situation—for example, working in the library—where you do not have access to a computer. Then you will need to write your notes by hand and transfer them into a computer later. Strategies of storing and retrieving notes vary (see 1.9 for using note files during writing). A few common strategies follow:

- For a short paper for which you have taken few notes, you may place all notes in a single file and draw material from it whenever you want.

- For a longer paper that makes use of numerous sources, you may create a new file for each source.
- Another strategy is to write out summaries and paraphrases of the source by hand and to enter into computer files only quotations, which you can electronically copy into your text as you write. At the least, this strategy will eliminate the time and effort and, more important, the possibility of error involved in transcribing quoted words more than once.
- By downloading quotations from a database to your computer, you of course do not need to transcribe them at all.

When you use a computer for note-taking, be certain to save all note files and to keep copies of them on paper and in a backup location.

1.7.5. Amount and Accuracy of Note-Taking

In taking notes, seek to steer a middle course between recording too much and recording too little. In other words, try to be both thorough and concise. Above all, strive for accuracy, not only in copying words for direct quotation but also in summarizing and paraphrasing authors' ideas.

1.7.6. SUMMING UP

The three main types of note-taking are *summary*, *paraphrase*, and *quotation*. There are, however, varying methods and strategies for note-taking. You may take notes by hand or use a computer. If you are using a computer, you can type in or download material, you can create one file for all sources or separate files for different sources, and so forth. Whichever method or strategy you follow, be sure to save and back up all computer files, to set down or verify publication information you will need for research and writing, to keep a careful record of page or other reference numbers, and, most important of all, to take accurate notes. Precise note-taking will help you avoid the problem of plagiarism (see ch. 2).

1.8. OUTLINING

1.8.1. Working Outline

A Useful Intermediate Activity

Some writers like to work from an outline; others do not. For research papers, outlining can be a particularly useful intermediate activity between research and writing. In fact, some instructors require each student to hand in an outline with the final draft. Others require a draft outline earlier, asking the student to submit not only a topic for the paper but also a tentative list of subtopics for research. They then suggest that this working outline be continually revised—items dropped, added, modified—as the research progresses. Instructors who require submission of a research project portfolio (see 1.9.4) sometimes ask that at least one version of the working outline be included in the portfolio in addition to the final outline (see 1.8.3).

An Overall View of the Paper

You may find a series of outlines helpful, whether or not your instructor requires them, especially if you are a beginning writer of research papers. An outline will help you to get an overall view of your paper and, perhaps more important, to figure out how each section of the paper relates to the others. Thus, developing an outline can help you to see the logical progression of your argument. A working outline will also make it easier to keep track of all important aspects of your subject and to focus your research on relevant topics. Continual revision of the working outline, moreover, will encourage you to change your thinking and your approach as new information modifies your understanding of the subject.

Creating a Computer File for Each Version

Word-processing programs commonly have an outlining feature that offers several formats with automatic numbering and lettering. It is probably best to create a different computer file for each version of an outline. For example, when you save the first version, give it a name like "outline 1." When you are ready to revise the outline, open the first version, choose Save As to save a copy of the file, and give the copy a new name (e.g., "outline 2"). The open file is now the copy, which you can revise. The first version remains unchanged. If you become dissatisfied with the way the second draft or a subsequent one is progressing, you can discard it, return to an earlier draft, which is stored untouched on the disk, and begin revising in another direction. Printing out each new version will let you compare it more easily with other versions.

1.8.2. Thesis Statement

An Answer to a Question or Problem

As you get closer to writing, you can begin to shape the information you have at hand into a unified, coherent whole by framing a thesis statement for your paper: a single sentence that formulates both your topic and your point of view. In a sense, the thesis statement is your answer to the central question or problem you have raised. Writing this statement will enable you to see where you are heading and to remain on a productive path as you plan and write. Try out different possibilities until you find a statement that seems right for your purpose. Moreover, since the experience of writing may well alter your original plans, do not hesitate to revise the thesis statement as you write the paper.

Purpose and Audience

Two factors are important to the shaping of a thesis statement—your *purpose* and your *audience*:

* What *purpose* will you try to achieve in the paper? Do you want to describe something, explain something, argue for a certain point of view, or persuade your reader to think or do something?
* What *audience* are you writing for? Is your reader a specialist on the subject? someone likely to agree or disagree with you? someone likely to be interested or uninterested in the subject?

The answers to these questions should to a large extent give your research the appropriate slant or point of view not just in your thesis statement but also in the final outline and the paper itself.

Requirements and Assistance of the Instructor

Many instructors require students to submit thesis statements for approval some two or three weeks before the paper is due. The statement is often included in a research project portfolio (see 1.9.4). If you have difficulty writing a thesis statement, talk with your instructor about the research you have done and about what you want to say; given this information, your instructor can probably help you frame an appropriate thesis statement.

1.8.3. Final Outline

From Working Outline to Final Outline

After you have a satisfactory thesis statement, you can begin transforming your working outline into a final one. This step will help you organize your ideas and the accumulated research into a logical, fluent, and effective paper. Again, many instructors request that final outlines be submitted with papers or included in a research project portfolio (see 1.9.4).

Deleting Irrelevant Material

Start by carefully reviewing all your notes to see how strongly they will support the various points in the working outline. Next, read over your working outline *critically* and delete everything that is irrelevant to the thesis statement or that might weaken your argument.

Eliminating material is often painful since you might have an understandable desire to use everything you have collected and to impress your readers (especially teachers) with all the work you have done and with all you now know on the subject. But you should resist these temptations, for the inclusion of irrelevant or repetitive material will lessen the effectiveness of your paper. Keep your thesis statement and your audience in mind. Include only the ideas and information that will help you accomplish what you have set out to do and that will lead your readers to care about your investigation, your presentation, and your conclusions.

Shaping a Structure for the Paper

As you continue to read, reread, and think about the ideas and information you have decided to use, you will begin to see new connections between items, and patterns of organization will suggest themselves. Bring related material together under general headings, and arrange these sections so that one logically connects with another. Then order the subjects under each heading so that they, too, proceed logically. Finally, plan an effective introduction and a conclusion appropriate to the sequence you have worked out.

Organizing Principles

Common organizing principles include

- **chronology** (useful for historical discussions—e.g., how the Mexican War developed)
- **cause and effect** (e.g., the consequences a scientific discovery will have)
- **process** (e.g., how a politician got elected)
- **deductive logic**, which moves from the general to the specific (e.g., from the problem of violence in the United States to violence involving handguns)
- **inductive logic**, which moves from the specific to the general (e.g., from violence involving handguns to the problem of violence in the United States)

Methods of Development

As you choose an organizational plan, keep in mind the method or methods you will use in developing your paper. For example, which of the following do you plan to accomplish?

- to define, classify, or analyze something
- to use descriptive details or give examples
- to compare or contrast one thing with another
- to argue for a certain point of view

The procedures you intend to adopt will influence the way you arrange your material, and they should be evident in your outline.

Integrating Quotations and Sources

It is also a good idea to indicate in the outline, specifically and precisely, the quotations and sources you will use. All this planning will take a good deal of time and thought, and you may well make several preliminary outlines before arriving at the one you will follow. But the time and thought will be well spent. The more planning you do, the easier and more efficient the writing will be.

Types of Outlines

If the final outline is only for your use, its form will have little importance. If it is to be submitted, your instructor will probably discuss the various forms of outline and tell you which to use. Whatever the form, maintain it consistently. The two most common forms are

- **the topic outline** (which uses only short phrases throughout)
- **the sentence outline** (which uses complete sentences throughout)

Labeling Parts of an Outline

The descending parts of an outline are normally labeled in the following order:

I.
  A.
    1.
      a.
        (1)
          (a)
          (b)
        (2)
      b.
    2.
  B.
II.

Logic requires that there be a *II* to complement a *I*, a *B* to complement an *A*, and so forth.

Creating Computer Files for Major Topics

If you have stored your notes in your computer, a helpful intermediate activity between outlining and writing is to incorporate your notes into your outline. Using this strategy, you should create a separate file for each major topic of your outline and shift relevant material, in appropriate order, from note files into the various topic files. Then, as you write, you can call up the topic files one by one and blend material from them into the text of the paper. Be sure to save and to back up your outline files.

1.8.4. SUMMING UP

- **A working outline** is a useful intermediary document between research and writing. It helps you gain an overview of the paper and keep track of all important aspects of the subject.
- **A thesis statement** is a single sentence that formulates both your topic and your point of view. It is an answer to the central question or problem you have raised. When preparing the thesis statement,

keep in mind your purpose in writing and the audience you are writing for.

- **The final outline** helps you organize your ideas and research into a coherent paper. Organizing principles include chronology, cause and effect, and deductive and inductive logic. The most common forms of outlining are the topic outline and the sentence outline. If you create a separate computer file for each major topic, you can write the paper by calling up each file in turn, following the progression of the outline.

1.9. WRITING DRAFTS

1.9.1. The First Draft

Do not expect your first draft to be the finished product. The successful research paper is usually the culmination of a series of drafts. Habits, capacities, and practices of writers differ widely. Some individuals write more slowly and come close to a final draft the first time through. Others prefer to work in stages and expect to undertake several drafts. In any case, review and rewriting are always necessary. Plan ahead and leave plenty of time for revision.

You might start off by trying to set down all your ideas in the order in which you want them to appear. Do not be concerned if the writing in the first draft is hasty and fairly rough. Attempt to stay focused by following your outline closely. Revise the outline, of course, whenever new ideas occur to you and it no longer works. After you complete a rough draft, read it over and try to refine it.

1.9.2. Subsequent Drafts

In revising, you may add, eliminate, and rearrange material. If a section in the first draft seems unclear or sketchy, you may have to expand it by writing another sentence or two or even a new paragraph. Similarly, to improve the fluency and coherence of the paper, you may need to add transitions between sentences and paragraphs or to define connections or contrasts. Delete any material that is irrelevant, unimportant, repetitive, or dull and dispensable. If the presentation of ideas seems illogical or confusing, you may find that you can clarify by rearranging phrases, clauses, sentences, or paragraphs.

In later drafts you should concern yourself with the more mechanical kinds of revision. For example, strive for more precise and economical wording. Try, in addition, to vary your sentence patterns as well as your choice of words. Finally, correct all technical errors, using a standard writing guide to check punctuation, grammar, and usage and consulting a standard dictionary for the spelling and meaning of words. Your last draft, carefully proofread and corrected, is the text of your research paper.

1.9.3. Writing with a Word Processor

a. Techniques

If you do not own a computer, see whether your school or public library has personal computers available for student use. With a word processor, you can store a first draft—or just a portion of one—and later retrieve and revise it. If you create a different file for each draft, you can return to a preceding draft whenever you wish.

Word processing allows for efficient transitions between the various activities related to the research paper. After developing an outline, for instance, you can copy it into a new file, where the outline can serve as the basis for your writing of the text. Or if you created a file of notes for each major topic in your outline (see 1.8.3), you can copy into the text file each topic file in sequence as you write. If your paper will be short and you have taken few notes, you may choose to copy the entire note file into the text file. Using this approach, you can scroll up and down the file and transfer what you want into the text of the paper. If your paper will be longer and you have created a separate file for each of numerous sources, you can readily transfer material (e.g., an effective quotation) from a note file to the text file. You might find it easier to print out all your notes before writing the paper and to decide in advance which ones you want to use in the text. In this way, when you retrieve note files, you will know exactly what parts you are seeking.

Another way to proceed is to use split windows or multiple windows to read note files as you write the paper. When you have completed your final draft, you can simply add the file containing the works-cited list to the end of the paper. With practice and planning, then, as you write your paper you can use a word processor strategically to draw on outline, note, and bibliography files that you created earlier in the project.

Most word processors have the following features, which you can use profitably in your writing:

- **Global revision.** This feature of word processing permits you to search for and automatically change text. Thus, if you realize you misspelled the same word several times in your draft, you can correct all the misspellings with a single command.
- **Special pasting.** If in a word-processing document you paste text that you copied from another document, the pasted text may keep its original formatting. Most word processors provide the option of special pasting, in which the pasted text takes on the formatting of the new document.
- **Stored phrases.** If you will need to type a complicated phrase repeatedly, store the phrase and assign a shortcut to it. Whenever you type the shortcut, the phrase will be entered.
- **Comparing documents.** Compare two versions of the document and see how they differ.
- **Paragraph formatting.** In each entry in the works-cited list, the first line is flush left, and subsequent lines are indented. The easiest way to achieve this formatting is to highlight the paragraphs that are (or will be) entries and then choose hanging indention in the options for formatting paragraphs.

b. Limitations

Word processing has certain limitations. Since no more than a fixed number of lines of text are visible on a computer screen, you may find it difficult to get a sense of your whole project. Some writers like to print out text regularly to see better how the writing is developing from paragraph to paragraph and from page to page. Use spelling and usage checkers cautiously, for they are only as effective as the dictionaries they contain. On the one hand, a spelling checker will call your attention to words that are correctly spelled if they are not in its dictionary. On the other, it will not point out misspellings that match words in the dictionary—for example, *their* used for *there* or *its* for *it's*.

Finally, in working on a computer file, you run the risk of losing it, through a technical mistake, equipment failure, or a power outage. Be sure to save your work frequently (after writing a page or so), not just when you finish with it or leave the computer. It is also a good idea to keep a paper copy of text you write and to create a backup file in case something happens to the file you are using to prepare the paper. Most important of all, leave yourself ample time to cope with any technical problems that may arise.

1.9.4. The Final Draft and the Research Project Portfolio

All instructors require submission of the final draft of the research paper. Some instructors ask students to prepare and submit a research project portfolio, which documents the evolution of the paper. The portfolio might contain such items as the approved thesis statement, the final outline, an early draft, and the final draft.

1.9.5. SUMMING UP

Research papers are normally composed through a series of drafts. The first draft is usually rough, and subsequent drafts are increasingly refined revisions of the original version. A word processor is useful for writing research papers, although it has some limitations as well. The assignment concludes with the submission of the final draft or of a research project portfolio.

1.10. LANGUAGE AND STYLE

Effective writing depends as much on clarity and readability as on content. The organization and development of your ideas, the coherence of your presentation, and your command of sentence structure, grammar, and diction are all important considerations, as are the mechanics of writing—capitalization, spelling, punctuation, and so on. The key to successful communication is using the right language for the audience you are addressing. In all writing, the challenge is to find the words, phrases, clauses, sentences, and paragraphs that express your thoughts and ideas precisely and that make them interesting to others.

Because good scholarship requires objectivity, careful writers of research papers avoid language that implies unsubstantiated or irrelevant generalizations about such personal qualities as age, disability, economic class, ethnicity, marital status, parentage, political or religious beliefs, race, sex, or sexual orientation. Discussions about this subject have generally focused on wording that could be labeled sexist. For example, many writers no longer use *he*, *him*, or *his* to express a meaning that includes women or girls: "If a young artist is not confident, he can quickly become discouraged." The use of *she*, *her*, and *hers* to refer to a person who may be of either sex can also be distracting and momentarily confusing. Both usages can often be avoided through a revision that recasts the sentence into the plural or that eliminates the pronoun: "If young artists are not confident, they can quickly become discouraged" or "A young artist who is not confident can quickly become discouraged." Another technique is to make the discussion refer to a person who is identified, so that there is a reason to use a specific singular pronoun. *They*, *them*, *their*, and *theirs* cannot logically be applied to a single person, and *he or she* and *her or him* are cumbersome alternatives to be used sparingly. Many authors now also avoid terms that unnecessarily integrate a person's sex with a job or role. For instance, *anchorman*, *policeman*, *stewardess*, and *poetess* are commonly replaced with *anchor*, *police officer*, *flight attendant*, and *poet*. For advice on current practices, consult your instructor or one of the guides to nondiscriminatory language listed in A.3.

2 Plagiarism and Academic Integrity

You have probably read or heard about charges of plagiarism in disputes in the publishing and recording industries. You may also have had classroom discussions about student plagiarism in particular and academic dishonesty in general. Many schools have developed guidelines or procedures regarding plagiarism. Honor codes and other means to promote academic integrity are also common. This section describes ethical considerations in research writing and can help you avoid plagiarism and other unethical acts.

2.1. DEFINITION OF PLAGIARISM

Derived from the Latin word *plagiarius* ("kidnapper"), *to plagiarize* means "to commit literary theft" and to "present as new and original an idea or product derived from an existing source" (*Merriam-Webster's Collegiate Dictionary* [11th ed.; 2003; print]). Plagiarism involves two kinds of wrongs. Using another person's ideas, information, or expressions without acknowledging that person's work constitutes intellectual theft. Passing off another person's ideas, information, or expressions as your own to get a better grade or gain some other advantage constitutes fraud. Plagiarism is sometimes a moral and ethical offense rather than a legal one since some instances of plagiarism fall outside the scope of copyright infringement, a legal offense (see 2.7.4).

2.2. CONSEQUENCES OF PLAGIARISM

A complex society that depends on well-informed citizens strives to maintain high standards of quality and reliability for documents that are publicly circulated and used in government, business, industry, the professions, higher education, and the media. Because research has the power to affect opinions and actions, responsible writers compose their work with great care. They specify when they refer to another author's ideas, facts, and words, whether they want to agree with, object to, or analyze the source. This kind of documentation not only recognizes the work writers do; it also tends to discourage the circulation of error, by inviting readers to determine for themselves whether a reference to another text presents a reasonable account of what that text says. Plagiarists undermine these important public values. Once detected, plagiarism in a work provokes skepticism and even outrage among readers, whose trust in the author has been broken.

The charge of plagiarism is a serious one for all writers. Plagiarists are often seen as incompetent—incapable of developing and expressing their own thoughts—or, worse, dishonest, willing to deceive others for personal gain. When professional writers, such as journalists, are exposed as plagiarists, they are likely to lose their jobs, and they are certain to suffer public embarrassment and loss of prestige. Almost always, the course of a writer's career is permanently affected by a single act of plagiarism. The serious consequences of plagiarism reflect the value the public places on trustworthy information.

Students exposed as plagiarists may suffer severe penalties, ranging from failure in the assignment or in the course to expulsion from school. This is because student plagiarism does considerable harm. For one thing, it damages teachers' relationships with students, turning teachers into detectives instead of mentors and fostering suspicion instead of trust. By undermining institutional standards for assigning grades and awarding degrees, student plagiarism also becomes a matter of significance to the public. When graduates' skills and knowledge fail to match their grades, an institution's reputation is damaged. For example, no one would choose to be treated by a physician who obtained a medical degree by fraud. Finally, students who plagiarize harm themselves. They lose an important opportunity to learn how to write a research paper. Knowing how to collect and analyze information and reshape it in essay form is essential to academic success. This knowledge is also required in a wide range of careers in law, journalism, engineering, public policy, teaching, business, government, and not-for-profit organizations.

Plagiarism betrays the personal element in writing as well. Discussing the history of copyright, Mark Rose notes the tie between our writing and our sense of self—a tie that, he believes, influenced the idea that a piece of writing could belong to the person who wrote it. Rose says that our sense of ownership of the words we write "is deeply rooted in our conception of ourselves as individuals with at least a modest grade of singularity, some degree of personality" (*Authors and Owners: The Invention of Copyright* [Cambridge: Harvard UP, 1993; print; 142]). Gaining skill as a writer opens the door to learning more about yourself and to developing a personal voice and approach in your writing. It is essential for all student writers to understand how to avoid committing plagiarism.

2.3. INFORMATION SHARING TODAY

Innumerable documents on a host of subjects are posted on the Web apparently for the purpose of being shared. The availability of research materials and the ease of transmitting, modifying, and using them have influenced the culture of the Internet, where the free exchange of information is an ideal. In this sea of materials, some students may question the need to acknowledge the authorship of individual documents. Professional writers, however, have no doubt about the matter. They recognize the importance of documentation whether they base their research on print or electronic publications. And so they continue to cite their sources and to mark the passages they quote.

In the culture of the academy, too, the free exchange of information is a long-standing ideal. Under certain circumstances, this ideal is described as academic freedom. But nothing about academic freedom or the free exchange of information implies ignoring authorship. Academic standards require all writers to acknowledge the authors whose work they use when preparing papers and other kinds of studies and reports.

New technologies have made information easier to locate and obtain, but research projects only begin with identifying and collecting source material. The essential intellectual tasks of a research project have not changed. These tasks call for a student to understand the published facts, ideas, and insights about a subject and to integrate them with the student's own views on the topic. To achieve this goal, student writers must rigorously distinguish between what they borrow and what they create.

As information sharing has become easier, so has plagiarism. For instance, on the Internet it is possible to buy and download completed research papers. Some students are misinformed about buying research papers, on the Internet or on campus. They believe that if they buy a paper, it belongs to them, and therefore they can use the ideas, facts, sentences, and paragraphs in it, free from any worry about plagiarism. Buying a paper, however, is the same as buying a book or a magazine. You own the physical copy of the book or magazine, which you may keep in your bookcase, give to a friend, or sell. And you may use whatever you learn from reading it in your own writing. But you are never free from the obligation to let your readers know the source of the ideas, facts, words, or sentences you borrow. Publications are a special kind of property. You can own them physically, but the publisher or author retains rights to the content. You should also know that purchased papers are readily recognizable, and teachers can often trace downloaded materials through an Internet search.

2.4. UNINTENTIONAL PLAGIARISM

The purpose of a research paper is to synthesize previous research and scholarship with your ideas on the subject. Therefore, you should feel free to use other persons' words, facts, and thoughts in your research paper, but the material you borrow must not be presented as if it were your own creation. When you write your research paper, remember that you must document everything that you borrow—not only direct quotations and paraphrases but also information and ideas.

Often plagiarism in student writing is unintentional, as when an elementary school pupil, assigned to do a report on a certain topic, copies down, word for word, everything on the subject in an encyclopedia. Unfortunately, some students continue to take this approach in high school and even in college, not realizing that it constitutes plagiarism. To guard against the possibility of unintentional plagiarism during research and writing, keep careful notes that always distinguish among three types of material: your ideas, your summaries and paraphrases of others' ideas and facts, and exact wording you copy from sources. Plagiarism sometimes happens because researchers do not keep precise records of their reading, and by the time they return to their notes, they have forgotten whether their summaries and paraphrases contain quoted material that is poorly marked or unmarked. Presenting an author's exact wording without marking it as a quotation is plagiarism, even if you cite the source. For this reason, recording only quotations is the most reliable method of note-taking in substantial research projects, especially for beginning students. It is the surest way, when you work with notes, to avoid unintentional plagiarism. Similar problems can occur in notes kept electronically. When you copy and paste passages, make sure that you add quotation marks around them. (See 1.7 for more on note-taking.)

Another kind of unintentional plagiarism happens when students write research papers in a second language. In an effort to avoid grammatical errors, they may copy the structure of an author's sentences. When replicating grammatical patterns, they sometimes inadvertently plagiarize the author's ideas, information, words, and expressions.

If you realize after handing a paper in that you accidentally plagiarized an author's work, you should report the problem to your instructor as soon as possible. In this way you eliminate the element of fraud. You may receive a lower grade than you had hoped for, but getting a lower grade is better than failing a course or being expelled.

2.5. FORMS OF PLAGIARISM

The most blatant form of plagiarism is to obtain and submit as your own a paper written by someone else (see 2.3). Other, less conspicuous forms of plagiarism include the failure to give appropriate acknowledgment when repeating or paraphrasing another's wording, when taking a particularly apt phrase, and when paraphrasing another's argument or presenting another's line of thinking.

Repeating or Paraphrasing Wording

Suppose, for example, that you want to use the material in the following passage, which appears on page 625 of an essay by Wendy Martin in the book *Columbia Literary History of the United States.*

ORIGINAL SOURCE

Some of Dickinson's most powerful poems express her firmly held conviction that life cannot be fully comprehended without an understanding of death.

If you write the following sentence without documentation, you have plagiarized because you borrowed another's wording without acknowledgment, even though you changed its form:

PLAGIARISM

Emily Dickinson firmly believed that we cannot fully comprehend life unless we also understand death.

But you may present the material if you cite your source:

As Wendy Martin has suggested, Emily Dickinson firmly believed that we cannot fully comprehend life unless we also understand death (625).

The source is indicated, in accordance with MLA style, by the name of the author ("Wendy Martin") and by a page reference in parentheses, preferably at the end of the sentence. The name refers the reader to the corresponding entry in the works-cited list, which appears at the end of the paper.

> Martin, Wendy. "Emily Dickinson." *Columbia Literary History of the United States.* Emory Elliott, gen. ed. New York: Columbia UP, 1988. 609-26. Print.

Taking a Particularly Apt Phrase

ORIGINAL SOURCE

Everyone uses the word *language* and everybody these days talks about *culture.* . . . "Languaculture" is a reminder, I hope, of the *necessary* connection between its two parts. . . . (Michael Agar, *Language Shock: Understanding the Culture of Conversation* [New York: Morrow, 1994; print; 60])

If you write the following sentence without documentation, you have committed plagiarism because you borrowed without acknowledgment a term ("languaculture") invented by another writer:

PLAGIARISM

> At the intersection of language and culture lies a concept that we might call "languaculture."

But you may present the material if you cite your source:

> At the intersection of language and culture lies a concept that Michael Agar has called "languaculture" (60).

In this revision, the author's name refers the reader to the full description of the work in the works-cited list at the end of the paper, and the parenthetical documentation identifies the location of the borrowed material in the work.

> Agar, Michael. *Language Shock: Understanding the Culture of Conversation.* New York: Morrow, 1994. Print.

Paraphrasing an Argument or Presenting a Line of Thinking

ORIGINAL SOURCE

Humanity faces a quantum leap forward. It faces the deepest social upheaval and creative restructuring of all time. Without clearly recognizing it, we are engaged in building a remarkable civilization from the ground up. This is the meaning of the Third Wave.

Until now the human race has undergone two great waves of change, each one largely obliterating earlier cultures or civilizations and replacing them with the ways of life inconceivable to those who came before. The First Wave of change—the agricultural revolution— took thousands of years to play itself out. The Second Wave—the rise of industrial civilization—took a mere hundred years. Today history is even more accelerative, and it is likely that the Third Wave will sweep across history and complete itself in a few decades. (Alvin Toffler, *The Third Wave* [1980; New York: Bantam, 1981; print; 10])

If you write the following sentence without documentation, you have committed plagiarism because you borrowed another writer's line of thinking without acknowledgment:

PLAGIARISM

There have been two revolutionary periods of change in history: the agricultural revolution and the industrial revolution. The agricultural revolution determined the course of history for thousands of years; the industrial civilization lasted about a century. We are now on the threshold of a new period of revolutionary change, but this one may last for only a few decades.

But you may present the material if you cite your source:

According to Alvin Toffler, there have been two revolutionary periods of change in history: the agricultural revolution and the industrial revolution. The agricultural revolution determined the course of history for thousands of years; the industrial civilization lasted about a century. We are now on the threshold of a new period of revolutionary change, but this one may last for only a few decades (10).

In this revision, the author's name refers the reader to the full description of the work in the works-cited list at the end of the paper, and the parenthetical documentation identifies the location of the borrowed material in the work.

Toffler, Alvin. *The Third Wave*. 1980. New York: Bantam, 1981. Print.

2.6. WHEN DOCUMENTATION IS NOT NEEDED

In addition to documenting direct quotations and paraphrases, you should consider the status of the information and ideas you glean from sources in relation to your audience and to the scholarly consensus on your topic. In general, information and ideas you deem broadly known by your readers and widely accepted by scholars, such as the basic biography of an author or the dates of a historical event, can be used without documentation. But where readers are likely to seek more guidance or where the facts are in significant dispute among scholars, documentation is needed; you could attribute a disputed fact to the source with which you agree or could document the entire controversy. While direct quotations and paraphrases are always documented, scholars seldom document proverbs, sayings, and clichés. If you have any doubt about whether you are committing plagiarism, cite your source or sources.

2.7. RELATED ISSUES

Other issues related to plagiarism and academic integrity include reusing a research paper, collaborative work, research on human subjects, and copyright infringement.

2.7.1. Reusing a Research Paper

If you must complete a research project to earn a grade in a course, handing in a paper you already earned credit for in another course is deceitful. Moreover, you lose the opportunity to improve your knowledge and skills. If you want to rework a paper that you prepared for another course, ask your current instructor for permission to do so. If you wish to draw on or reuse portions of your previous writing in a new paper, ask your instructor for guidance.

2.7.2. Collaborative Work

An example of collaborative work is a group project you carry out with other students. Joint participation in research and writing is common and, in fact, encouraged in many courses and in many professions. It does not constitute plagiarism provided that credit is given for all contributions. One way to give credit, if roles were clearly demarcated or were unequal, is to state exactly who did what. Another way, especially if roles and contributions were merged and shared, is to acknowledge all concerned equally. Ask your instructor for advice if you are not certain how to acknowledge collaboration.

2.7.3. Research on Human Subjects

Many academic institutions have policies governing research on human subjects. Examples of research involving human subjects include clinical trials of a drug or personal interviews for a psychological study. Institutions usually require that researchers obtain the informed consent of human subjects for such projects. Although research for a paper in high school or college rarely involves human subjects, ask your instructor about your institution's policy if yours does.

2.7.4. Copyright Infringement

Whereas summaries, paraphrases, and brief quotations in research papers are normally permissible with appropriate acknowledgment, reproducing and distributing an entire copyrighted work or significant portions of it without obtaining permission to do so from the copyright holder is an infringement of copyright law and a legal offense, even if the violator acknowledges the source. This is true for works in all media. For a detailed discussion of copyright and other legal issues related to publishing, see chapter 2 of the *MLA Style Manual and Guide to Scholarly Publishing* (3rd ed.; New York: MLA, 2008; print).

2.8. SUMMING UP

You have plagiarized if
- you took notes that did not distinguish summary and paraphrase from quotation and then you presented wording from the notes as if it were all your own.

- while browsing the Web, you copied text and pasted it into your paper without quotation marks or without citing the source.
- you repeated or paraphrased someone's wording without acknowledgment.
- you took someone's unique or particularly apt phrase without acknowledgment.
- you paraphrased someone's argument or presented someone's line of thought without acknowledgment.
- you bought or otherwise acquired a research paper and handed in part or all of it as your own.

You can avoid plagiarism by

- making a list of the writers and viewpoints you discovered in your research and using this list to double-check the presentation of material in your paper.
- keeping the following three categories distinct in your notes: your ideas, your summaries of others' material, and exact wording you copy.
- identifying the sources of all material you borrow—exact wording, paraphrases, ideas, arguments, and facts.
- checking with your instructor when you are uncertain about your use of sources.

3 The Mechanics of Writing

Although the scope of this book precludes a detailed discussion of grammar, usage, style, and related aspects of writing, this chapter addresses mechanical questions that you will likely encounter in writing research papers.

1. Spelling
2. Punctuation
3. Italics
4. Names of persons
5. Numbers
6. Titles of works in the research paper
7. Quotations
8. Capitalization and personal names in languages other than English

3.1. SPELLING

3.1.1. Consistency

Spelling, including hyphenation, should be consistent throughout the research paper—except in quotations, which must retain the spelling of the original, whether correct or incorrect. You can best ensure consistency by using a single dictionary and by always adopting the spelling that it gives first in any entry with variant spellings. (See A.1 for titles of standard dictionaries.)

3.1.2. Word Division

Turn off the automatic-hyphenation option in your word processor. Dividing words at the ends of lines is unnecessary in a research paper, and it has disadvantages. A word divided between lines is harder to read, and the reader sometimes cannot tell whether the hyphen it contains is part of your spelling or part of the spelling in text you are quoting. If you choose to divide a word, consult your dictionary about where the break should occur.

3.1.3. Plurals

The plurals of English words are generally formed by addition of the suffix -s or -es (*laws*, *taxes*), with several exceptions (e.g., *children*, *halves, mice, sons-in-law, bison*). The tendency in American English is to form the plurals of words naturalized from other languages in the standard manner. The plurals *librettos* and *formulas* are therefore more common in American English than *libretti* and *formulae*. But some adopted words, like *alumnus* and *phenomenon*, retain the original plurals (*alumni, phenomena*). Consult a dictionary for guidance. If the dictionary gives more than one plural form for a word (*appendixes, appendices*), use the first listed. (See 3.2.7 for plurals of letters and for possessive forms of plurals.)

3.1.4. Foreign Words

If you quote material in a foreign language, you must reproduce all accents and other marks exactly as they appear in the original (*école, pietà, tête, leçon, Fähre, año*). If you need marks that are not available in your word processor, write them in by hand. On the use of foreign words in an English text, see 3.3.2; on capitalization and personal names in languages other than English, see 3.8.

3.2. PUNCTUATION

3.2.1. The Purpose of Punctuation

The primary purpose of punctuation is to ensure the clarity and readability of writing. Punctuation clarifies sentence structure, separating some words and grouping others. It adds meaning to written words and guides the understanding of readers as they move through sentences. The rules set forth here cover many of the situations you will encounter in writing research papers. For the punctuation of quotations in your text, see 3.7. For the punctuation of parenthetical references and bibliographies, see chapters 5 and 6. See also the individual listings in the index for specific punctuation marks.

3.2.2. Commas

   a. Use a comma before a coordinating conjunction (*and, but, for, nor, or, so,* or *yet*) joining independent clauses in a sentence.

Congress passed the bill, and the president signed it into law.

The poem is ironic, for the poet's meaning contrasts with her words.

But the comma may be omitted when the sentence is short and the connection between the clauses is not open to misreading if unpunctuated.

Wallace sings and Armstrong plays cornet.

b. Use commas to separate words, phrases, and clauses in a series.

WORDS

Boccaccio's tales have inspired plays, films, operas, and paintings.

PHRASES

Alfred the Great established a system of fortified towns, reorganized the military forces, and built a fleet of warships.

CLAUSES

In the Great Depression, millions lost their jobs, businesses failed, and charitable institutions closed their doors.

But use semicolons when items in a series have internal commas.

Pollsters focused their efforts on Columbus, Ohio; Des Moines, Iowa; and Saint Louis, Missouri.

c. Use a comma between coordinate adjectives—that is, adjectives that separately modify the same noun.

Critics praise the novel's unaffected, unadorned style. (The adjectives *unaffected* and *unadorned* each modify *style*.)

but

A famous photo shows Marianne Moore in a black tricornered hat. (The adjective *black* modifies *tricornered hat*.)

d. Use commas to set off a parenthetical comment, or an aside, if it is brief and closely related to the rest of the sentence. (For punctuation of longer, more intrusive, or more complex parenthetical elements, see 3.2.5.)

The Tudors, for example, ruled for over a century.

e. Use commas to set off a nonrestrictive modifier—that is, a modifier that is not essential to the meaning of the sentence. A nonrestrictive modifier, unlike a restrictive one, could be dropped without changing the main sense of the sentence. Modifiers in the following three categories are either nonrestrictive or restrictive. (For the use of parentheses and dashes around complex nonrestrictive modifiers, see 3.2.5b.)

Words in Apposition

NONRESTRICTIVE

Isabel Allende, the Chilean novelist, will appear at the arts forum tonight.

RESTRICTIVE

The Chilean novelist Isabel Allende will appear at the arts forum tonight.

Clauses That Begin with *Who*, *Whom*, *Whose*, *Which*, and *That*

NONRESTRICTIVE

Scientists, who must observe standards of objectivity in their work, can contribute usefully to public-policy debates.

RESTRICTIVE

Scientists who receive the Nobel Prize sometimes contribute usefully to public-policy debates.

Many writers prefer to use *which* to introduce nonrestrictive clauses and *that* to introduce restrictive clauses.

Adverbial Phrases and Clauses

NONRESTRICTIVE

The novel takes place in China, where many languages are spoken.

RESTRICTIVE

The novel takes place in a land where many languages are spoken.

f. Use a comma after a long introductory phrase or clause.

PHRASE

After years of anxiety over the family's finances, Linda Loman looks forward to the day the mortgage will be paid off.

CLAUSE

Although she was virtually unknown in her day, scholars have come to recognize the originality of her work.

g. Use commas to set off alternative or contrasting phrases.

It is Julio, not his mother, who sets the plot in motion.

but

Several cooperative but autonomous republics were formed. (The conjunction *but* links *cooperative* and *autonomous*, making a comma inappropriate.)

h. Do not use a comma between subject and verb.

Many of the characters who dominate the early chapters and then disappear [no comma] are portraits of the author's friends.

i. Do not use a comma between verb and object.

The agent reported to the headquarters staff [no comma] that the documents had been traced to an underground garage.

j. Do not use a comma between the parts of a compound subject, compound object, or compound verb.

COMPOUND SUBJECT

A dozen wooden chairs [no comma] and a window that admits a shaft of light complete the stage setting.

COMPOUND OBJECT

Ptolemy devised a system of astronomy accepted until the sixteenth century [no comma] and a scientific approach to the study of geography.

COMPOUND VERB

He composed several successful symphonies [no comma] but won the most fame for his witticisms.

k. Do not use a comma between two parallel subordinate elements.

She broadens her analysis by exploring the tragic elements of the play [no comma] and by integrating the hunting motif with the themes of death and resurrection.

l. Use a comma in a date whose order is month, day, and year. If such a date comes in the middle of a sentence, include a comma after the year.

> Martin Luther King, Jr., was born on January 15, 1929, and died on April 4, 1968.

But commas are not used with dates whose order is day, month, and year.

> Martin Luther King, Jr., was born on 15 January 1929 and died on 4 April 1968.

m. Do not use a comma between a month and a year or between a season and a year.

> The events of July 1789 are as familiar to the French as those of July 1776 are to Americans.

> I passed my oral exams in spring 2007.

See 3.7.7 for commas with quotations.

3.2.3. Semicolons

a. Use a semicolon between independent clauses not linked by a conjunction.

> The coat is tattered beyond repair; still, Akaky hopes the tailor can mend it.

b. Use semicolons between items in a series when the items contain commas.

> Present at the symposium were Henri Guillaume, the art critic; Sam Brown, the *Daily Tribune* reporter; and Maria Rosa, the conceptual artist.

3.2.4. Colons

The colon is used between two parts of a sentence when the first part creates a sense of anticipation about what follows in the second. Type one space after a colon.

a. Use a colon to introduce a list, an elaboration of what was just said, or the formal expression of a rule or principle.

LIST

The reading list includes three Latin American novels: *The Death of Artemio Cruz*, *One Hundred Years of Solitude*, and *The Green House*.

ELABORATION

The plot is founded on deception: the three main characters have secret identities.

RULE OR PRINCIPLE

Many books would be briefer if their authors followed the logical principle known as Occam's razor: Explanations should not be multiplied unnecessarily. (A rule or principle after a colon should begin with a capital letter.)

But do not use a colon before a list if the list is grammatically essential to the introductory wording.

The novels on the reading list include *The Death of Artemio Cruz*, *One Hundred Years of Solitude*, and *The Green House*. (The list is the object of the verb *include*.)

b. Use a colon to introduce a quotation that is independent from the structure of the main sentence.

In *The Awakening*, Mme Ratignolle exhorts Robert Lebrun to stop flirting with Edna: "She is not one of us; she is not like us."

A quotation that is integral to the sentence structure is generally preceded by no punctuation or, if a verb of saying (*says*, *exclaims*, *notes*, *writes*) introduces the quotation, by a comma. A colon is used after a verb of saying, however, if the verb introduces certain kinds of formal literary quotations, such as long quotations set off from the main text (see 3.7.2–4, 3.7.7). On colons separating titles and subtitles, see 3.6.1.

3.2.5. Dashes and Parentheses

Dashes make a sharper break in the continuity of the sentence than commas do, and parentheses make a still sharper one. To indicate a dash, type two hyphens, with no space before, between, or after. Your word processor may convert the two hyphens into a dash, as seen in the examples below. Your writing will be smoother and more readable if you use dashes and parentheses sparingly. Limit the number of dashes in a sentence to two paired dashes or one unpaired dash.

a. Use dashes or parentheses to enclose a sentence element that interrupts the train of thought.

The "hero" of the play (the townspeople see him as heroic, but he is the focus of the author's satire) introduces himself as a veteran of the war.

b. Use dashes or parentheses to set off a parenthetical element that contains a comma and that might be misread if set off with commas.

The colors of the costume—blue, scarlet, and yellow—acquire symbolic meaning in the story.

c. Use a dash to introduce words that summarize a preceding series.

Ruthlessness and acute sensitivity, greed and compassion—the main character's contradictory qualities prevent any simple interpretation of the film.

A dash may also be used instead of a colon to introduce a list or an elaboration of what was just said (see 3.2.4a).

3.2.6. Hyphens

Compound words of all types—nouns, verbs, adjectives, and so on—are written as separate words (*hard drive, hard labor*), with hyphens (*hard-and-fast, hard-boiled*), and as single words (*hardcover, hardheaded*). The dictionary shows how to write many compounds. A compound not in the dictionary should usually be written as separate words unless a hyphen is needed to prevent readers from misunderstanding the relation between the words. Following are some rules to help you decide whether you need a hyphen in compounds and other terms that may not appear in the dictionary.

a. Use a hyphen in a compound adjective beginning with an adverb such as *better, best, ill, lower, little,* or *well* when the adjective precedes a noun.

better-prepared ambassador

best-known work

ill-informed reporter

lower-priced tickets

well-dressed announcer

But do not use a hyphen when the compound adjective comes after the noun it modifies.

The ambassador was better prepared than the other delegates.

b. Do not use a hyphen in a compound adjective beginning with an adverb ending in -ly or with too, very, or much.

thoughtfully presented thesis

too hasty judgment

very contrived plot

much maligned performer

c. Use a hyphen in a compound adjective ending with the present participle (e.g., loving) or the past participle (e.g., inspired) of a verb when the adjective precedes a noun.

sports-loving throng

fear-inspired loyalty

d. Use a hyphen in a compound adjective formed by a number and a noun when the adjective precedes a noun.

early-thirteenth-century architecture

e. Use hyphens in other compound adjectives before nouns to prevent misreading.

Portuguese-language student   (The hyphen makes it clear that the term refers to a student who is studying Portuguese and not to a language student who is Portuguese.)

f. Do not use hyphens in familiar unhyphenated compound terms, such as social security, high school, liberal arts, and show business, when they appear before nouns as modifiers.

social security tax

high school reunion

g. Use hyphens to join coequal nouns.

scholar-athlete

writer-critic

author-chef

But do not use a hyphen in a pair of nouns in which the first noun modifies the second.

opera lover

father figure

h. In general, do not use hyphens after prefixes (e.g., *anti-*, *co-*, *multi-*, *non-*, *over-*, *post-*, *pre-*, *re-*, *semi-*, *sub-*, *un-*, *under-*).

antiwar	overpay	semiretired
coworker	postwar	subsatellite
multinational	prescheduled	unambiguous
nonjudgmental	reinvigorate	underrepresented

But sometimes a hyphen is called for after a prefix.

post-Victorian   (Use a hyphen before a capital letter.)

re-cover   (The hyphen distinguishes this verb, meaning "cover again," from *recover*, meaning "get back" or "recuperate.")

anti-icing   (Without the hyphen, the doubled vowel would make the term hard to recognize.)

3.2.7. Apostrophes

A principal function of apostrophes is to indicate possession. They are also used in contractions (*can't, wouldn't*), which are rarely acceptable in research papers, and the plurals of the letters of the alphabet (*p's and q's, three A's*).

a. To form the possessive of a singular noun, add an apostrophe and an *s*.

a poem's meter

b. To form the possessive of a plural noun ending in *s*, add only an apostrophe.

firefighters' trucks

c. To form the possessive of an irregular plural noun not ending in *s*, add an apostrophe and an *s*.

women's studies

d. To form the possessive of nouns in a series, add a single apostrophe and an *s* if the ownership is shared.

Palmer and Colton's book on European history

But if the ownership is separate, place an apostrophe and an *s* after each noun.

Palmer's and Colton's books on European history

e. To form the possessive of any singular proper noun, add an apostrophe and an *s*.

Venus's beauty

Dickens's reputation

f. To form the possessive of a plural proper noun, add only an apostrophe.

the Vanderbilts' estate

the Dickenses' economic woes

g. Do not use an apostrophe to form the plural of an abbreviation or a number.

PhDs   1990s
MAs   fours
TVs   SAT score in the 1400s

On using apostrophes to abbreviate dates, see 3.5.5.

3.2.8. Quotation Marks

a. Place quotation marks around a word or phrase given in someone else's sense or in a special sense or purposefully misused.

A silver dome concealed the robot's "brain."

Their "friend" brought about their downfall.

If introduced unnecessarily, this device can make writing heavy-handed. Quotation marks are not needed after *so-called*.

Their so-called friend brought about their downfall.

b. Use quotation marks for a translation of a foreign word or phrase.

The first idiomatic Spanish expression I learned was *irse todo en humo* ("to go up in smoke").

You may use single quotation marks for a translation that follows the original directly, without intervening words or punctuation.

The word *text* derives from the Latin verb *texere* 'to weave.'

On quotation marks with titles, see 3.6.3–4. On quotation marks with quotations and with translations of quotations, see 3.7.7 and 3.7.8, respectively.

3.2.9. Square Brackets

Use square brackets around a parenthesis within a parenthesis, so that the levels of subordination can be easily distinguished.

The sect known as the Jansenists (after Cornelius Jansen [1585-1638]) faced opposition from both the king and the pope.

For square brackets around an ellipsis or an interpolation in a quotation, see 3.7.5 and 3.7.6, respectively. For square brackets around missing, unverified, or interpolated data in documentation, see 5.5.2, 5.5.22, and 5.5.24.

3.2.10. Slashes

The slash, or diagonal, is rarely necessary in formal prose. Other than in quotations of poetry (see 3.7.3), the slash has a place mainly between two terms paired as opposites or alternatives and used together as a noun.

The writer discussed how fundamental oppositions like good/evil,
East/West, and aged/young affect the way cultures view historical events.

But use a hyphen when such a compound precedes and modifies a
noun.

nature-nurture conflict

East-West relations

3.2.11. Periods, Question Marks, and Exclamation Points

A sentence can end with a period, a question mark, or an exclamation point. Periods end declarative sentences. (For the use of periods
with ellipsis points, see 3.7.5.) Question marks follow interrogative
sentences. Except in direct quotation, avoid exclamation points in
research writing.

Place a question mark inside a closing quotation mark if a question mark occurs there in the quoted passage. But if the quotation
ends a sentence that is a question, place a question mark outside
the quotation. If a question mark occurs where a comma or period
would normally be required, omit the comma or period. Note the use
of the question mark and other punctuation marks in the following
sentences:

Whitman asks, "Have you felt so proud to get at the meaning of poems?"

Where does Whitman speak of "the meaning of poems"?

"Have you felt so proud to get at the meaning of poems?" Whitman asks.

3.2.12. Spacing after Concluding Punctuation Marks

In an earlier era, writers using a typewriter commonly left two spaces
after a period, a question mark, or an exclamation point. Publications
in the United States today usually have the same spacing after concluding punctuation marks as between words on the same line. Since
word processors make available the same fonts used by typesetters
for printed works, many writers, influenced by the look of typeset
publications, now leave only one space after a concluding punctuation mark. In addition, some publishers' guidelines for preparing a
manuscript's electronic files ask professional authors to type only the

spaces that are to appear in print. Because it is increasingly common for papers and manuscripts to be prepared with a single space after all concluding punctuation marks, this spacing is shown in the examples in this handbook.

As a practical matter, however, there is nothing wrong with using two spaces after concluding punctuation marks unless an instructor requests that you do otherwise. Whichever spacing you choose, be sure to use it consistently in all parts of your paper—the works-cited list as well as the main text. By contrast, internal punctuation marks, such as a colon, a comma, and a semicolon, should always be followed by one space.

3.3. ITALICS

Italic is a style of type in which the characters slant to the right (*Casablanca*). More visually pleasing than underlining if sometimes less distinctive, italicization is commonly acceptable in research papers. It is assumed in the examples in this handbook. In material that will be graded, edited, or typeset, the clarity of every detail of text is important. Choose a type font in which the italic style contrasts clearly with the regular style.

In electronic environments that do not permit italicization, it is common to place one underline before and after each word or group of words that would be italicized in print.

Casablanca

Life Is a Dream

The rest of this section discusses using italics for words and letters referred to as words and letters (3.3.1), foreign words in an English text (3.3.2), and emphasis (3.3.3). (See 3.6.2 for the italicizing of titles.)

3.3.1. Words and Letters Referred to as Words and Letters

Italicize words and letters that are referred to as words and letters.

Shaw spelled *Shakespeare* without the final *e*.

The word *albatross* probably derives from the Spanish and Portuguese word *alcatraz*.

3.3.2. Foreign Words in an English Text

In general, italicize foreign words used in an English text.

The Renaissance courtier was expected to display *sprezzatura*, or nonchalance, in the face of adversity.

The numerous exceptions to this rule include quotations entirely in another language ("Julius Caesar said, 'Veni, vidi, vici' "); non-English titles of works published within larger works (poems, stories, essays, articles), which are placed in quotation marks and not italicized ("El sueño," the title of a poem by Quevedo); proper nouns (the Entente Cordiale), except when italicized through another convention (SS *Normandie* [see 3.6.2]); and foreign words anglicized through frequent use. Since American English rapidly naturalizes foreign words, use a dictionary to decide whether a foreign expression requires italics. Following are some adopted foreign words, abbreviations, and phrases commonly not italicized:

ad hoc	et al.	laissez-faire
cliché	etc.	lieder
concerto	genre	raison d'être
e.g.	hubris	versus

3.3.3. Emphasis

Italics for emphasis ("Booth *does* concede, however . . .") is a device that rapidly becomes ineffective. It is rarely appropriate in research writing.

3.4. NAMES OF PERSONS

3.4.1. First and Subsequent Uses of Names

In general, the first time you use a person's name in the text of your research paper, state it fully and accurately, exactly as it appears in your source.

Arthur George Rust, Jr.

Victoria M. Sackville-West

Do not change Arthur George Rust, Jr., to Arthur George Rust, for example, or drop the hyphen in Victoria M. Sackville-West. In subsequent references to the person, you may give the last name only (Rust, Sackville-West)—unless, of course, you refer to two or more persons with the same last name—or you may give the most common form of the name (e.g., Garcilaso for Garcilaso de la Vega). In casual references to the very famous—say, Mozart, Shakespeare, or Michelangelo—it is not necessary to give the full name initially.

In some languages (e.g., Chinese, Hungarian, Japanese, Korean, and Vietnamese), surnames precede given names; consult the *MLA Style Manual and Guide to Scholarly Publishing* (3rd ed.; New York: MLA, 2008; print; 3.6.7, 3.6.12) and other relevant reference works for guidance on these names. For rules concerning names of persons in other languages, see 3.8.

3.4.2. Titles of Persons

In general, do not use formal titles (Mr., Mrs., Miss, Ms., Dr., Professor, Reverend) in referring to men or women, living or dead (Churchill, not Mr. Churchill; Einstein, not Professor Einstein; Hess, not Dame Myra; Montagu, not Lady Montagu). A few women in history are traditionally known by their titles as married women (e.g., Mrs. Humphry Ward, Mme de Staël). Treat other women's names the same as men's.

FIRST USE	SUBSEQUENT USES
Emily Dickinson	Dickinson (not Miss Dickinson)
Harriet Beecher Stowe	Stowe (not Mrs. Stowe)
Margaret Mead	Mead (not Ms. Mead)

The appropriate way to refer to persons with titles of nobility can vary. For example, the full name and title of Henry Howard, earl of Surrey, should be given at first mention, and thereafter Surrey alone may be used. In contrast, for Benjamin Disraeli, first earl of Beaconsfield, it is sufficient to give Benjamin Disraeli initially and Disraeli subsequently. Follow the example of your sources in citing titles of nobility.

3.4.3. Names of Authors and Fictional Characters

It is common and acceptable to use simplified names of famous authors (Vergil for Publius Vergilius Maro, Dante for Dante Alighieri). Also acceptable are pseudonyms of authors.

Molière (Jean-Baptiste Poquelin)

George Eliot (Mary Ann Evans)

Mark Twain (Samuel Clemens)

Stendhal (Marie-Henri Beyle)

Refer to fictional characters in the same way that the work of fiction does. You need not always use their full names, and you may retain titles (Dr. Jekyll, Mme Defarge).

3.5. NUMBERS

3.5.1. Arabic Numerals

Although there are still a few well-established uses for roman numerals (see 3.5.7), virtually all numbers not spelled out are commonly represented today by arabic numerals.

3.5.2. Use of Words or Numerals

If you are writing about literature or another subject that involves infrequent use of numbers, you may spell out numbers written in one or two words and represent other numbers by numerals (*one, thirty-six, ninety-nine, one hundred, fifteen hundred, two thousand, three million*, but *2½, 101, 137, 1,275*). To form the plural of a spelled-out number, treat the word like an ordinary noun (*sixes, sevens*).

If your project is one that calls for frequent use of numbers—say, a paper on a scientific subject or a study of statistical findings—use numerals for all numbers that precede technical units of measurement (*16 amperes, 5 milliliters*). In such a project, also use numerals for numbers that are presented together and that refer to similar things, such as in comparisons or reports of experimental data. Spell out other numbers if they can be written in one or two words. In the following example of statistical writing, neither "ten years" nor "six-state region" is presented with related figures, so the numbers are spelled out, unlike the other numbers in the sentence.

> In the ten years covered by the study, the number of participating institutions in the United States doubled, reaching 90, and membership in the six-state region rose from 4 to 15.

But do not begin a sentence with a numeral.

> Two thousand four was an election year in the United States.

Except at the beginning of a sentence, always use numerals in the following instances:

WITH ABBREVIATIONS OR SYMBOLS

6 lbs.	4:20 p.m.	3%
8 KB	$9	2"

IN ADDRESSES

4401 13th Avenue

IN DATES

1 April 2007

April 1, 2007

IN DECIMAL FRACTIONS

8.3

IN DIVISIONS

page 7

year 3 of the study

For large numbers, you may use a combination of numerals and words.

> 4.5 million

Express related numbers in the same style.

> only 5 of the 250 delegates
> exactly 3 automobiles and 129 trucks
> from 1 billion to 1.2 billion

3.5.3. Commas in Numbers

Commas are usually placed between the third and fourth digits from the right, the sixth and seventh, and so on.

1,000

20,000

7,654,321

Following are some of the exceptions to this practice:

PAGE AND LINE NUMBERS

on page 1014

ADDRESSES

at 4132 Broadway

FOUR-DIGIT YEAR NUMBERS

in 1999

But commas are added in year numbers of five or more figures.

in 20,000 BC

3.5.4. Percentages and Amounts of Money

Treat percentages and amounts of money like other numbers: use numerals with the appropriate symbols.

1%	$5.35	68¢
45%	$35	
100%	$2,000	

In discussions involving infrequent use of numbers, you may spell out a percentage or an amount of money if you can do so in three words or fewer (*five dollars, forty-five percent, two thousand dollars, sixty-eight cents*). Do not combine spelled forms of numbers with symbols.

3.5.5. Dates and Times of the Day

Be consistent in writing dates: use either the day-month-year style (*22 July 2008*) or the month-day-year style (*July 22, 2008*) but not both. If you begin with the month, be sure to add a comma after the day and also after the year, unless another punctuation mark goes there, such as a period or a question mark. Do not use a comma between month and year (*August 1998*).

Spell out centuries in lowercase letters.

the twentieth century

Hyphenate centuries when they are used as adjectives before nouns.

eighteenth-century thought

nineteenth- and twentieth-century literature

Decades are usually written out without capitalization (*the nineties*), but it is acceptable to express them in figures (*the 1990s, the '60s*). Whichever form you use, be consistent.

The abbreviation *BC* follows the year, but *AD* precedes it.

19 BC

AD 565

Instead of *BC* and *AD*, some writers prefer to use *BCE*, "before the common era," and *CE*, "common era," both of which follow the year.

Numerals are used for most times of the day (*2:00 p.m., the 6:20 flight*). Exceptions include time expressed in quarter and half hours and in hours followed by *o'clock*.

a quarter to twelve

half past ten

five o'clock

3.5.6. Inclusive Numbers

In a range of numbers, give the second number in full for numbers through ninety-nine.

2-3	21-48
10-12	89-99

For larger numbers, give only the last two digits of the second number, unless more are necessary.

96-101	923-1,003
103-04	1,003-05
395-401	1,608-774

In a range of years beginning in AD 1000 or later, omit the first two digits of the second year if they are the same as the first two digits of the first year. Otherwise, write both years in full.

2000-03

1898-1901

In a range of years beginning from AD 1 through 999, follow the rules for inclusive numbers in general.

73-76

600-62

Do not abbreviate ranges of years that begin before AD 1.

748-742 BC

143 BC-AD 149

On the use of commas in numbers, see 3.5.3.

3.5.7. Roman Numerals

Use capital roman numerals for the primary divisions of an outline (see 1.8) and after the names of persons in a series.

Elizabeth II

John D. Rockefeller IV

John Paul II

Use lowercase roman numerals for citing pages of a book that are so numbered (e.g., the pages in a preface). Write out inclusive roman numerals in full: *xxv–xxvi*, *xlvi–xlix*. Your instructor may prefer that you use roman numerals to designate acts and scenes of plays (see 6.4.8, on citing common literature).

3.6. TITLES OF WORKS IN THE RESEARCH PAPER

3.6.1. Capitalization and Punctuation

Whenever you cite the title of a published work in your research paper, take the title from the title page, not, for example, from the cover or from a running head at the top of a page. Do not reproduce any unusual typographic characteristics, such as special capitalization or lowercasing of all letters. A title page may present a title designed like one of the following examples:

> MODERNISM & NEGRITUDE

> **READING SITES**
> Social Difference and Reader Response

> Turner's early sketchbooks

These titles should appear in a research paper as follows:

Modernism and Negritude

Reading Sites: Social Difference and Reader Response

Turner's Early Sketchbooks

The rules for capitalizing titles are strict. In a title or a subtitle, capitalize the first word, the last word, and all principal words, including those that follow hyphens in compound terms. Therefore, capitalize the following parts of speech:

- Nouns (e.g., *flowers*, as in *The Flowers of Europe*)
- Pronouns (e.g., *our*, as in *Save Our Children*; *that*, as in *The Mouse That Roared*)
- Verbs (e.g., *watches*, as in *America Watches Television*; *is*, as in *What Is Literature?*)
- Adjectives (e.g., *ugly*, as in *The Ugly Duckling*; *that*, as in *Who Said That Phrase?*)
- Adverbs (e.g., *slightly*, as in *Only Slightly Corrupt*; *down*, as in *Go Down, Moses*)

- Subordinating conjunctions (e.g., *after, although, as if, as soon as, because, before, if, that, unless, until, when, where, while,* as in *One If by Land* and *Anywhere That Chance Leads*)

Do not capitalize the following parts of speech when they fall in the middle of a title:

- Articles (*a, an, the,* as in *Under the Bamboo Tree*)
- Prepositions (e.g., *against, as, between, in, of, to,* as in *The Merchant of Venice* and "A Dialogue between the Soul and Body")
- Coordinating conjunctions (*and, but, for, nor, or, so, yet,* as in *Romeo and Juliet*)
- The *to* in infinitives (as in *How to Play Chess*)

Use a colon and a space to separate a title from a subtitle, unless the title ends in a question mark or an exclamation point. Include other punctuation only if it is part of the title or subtitle.

The following examples illustrate how to capitalize and punctuate a variety of titles. For a discussion of which titles to italicize and which to place in quotation marks, see 3.6.2–3.

The Teaching of Spanish in English-Speaking Countries

Storytelling and Mythmaking: Images from Film and Literature

Life As I Find It

The Artist as Critic

Whose Music? A Sociology of Musical Language

"Italian Literature before Dante"

"What Americans Stand For"

"Why Fortinbras?"

"Marcel Proust: Archetypal Music—an Exercise in Transcendence"

When the first line of a poem serves as the title of the poem, reproduce the line exactly as it appears in the text.

Dickinson's poem "I heard a Fly buzz—when I died—" contrasts the everyday and the momentous.

For rules concerning capitalization of titles in languages other than English, see 3.8. See 3.6.4 for titles and quotations within titles.

3.6.2. Italicized Titles

Italicize the names of books, plays, poems published as books, pamphlets, periodicals (newspapers, magazines, and journals), Web sites, online databases, films, television and radio broadcasts, compact discs, audiocassettes, record albums, dance performances, operas and other long musical compositions (except those identified simply by form, number, and key; see 3.6.5), works of visual art, ships, aircraft, and spacecraft.

The Awakening (book)

The Importance of Being Earnest (play)

The Waste Land (poem published as a book)

New Jersey Driver Manual (pamphlet)

Wall Street Journal (newspaper)

Time (magazine)

PMLA (journal)

Stanford Encyclopedia of Philosophy (Web site)

LexisNexis Academic (online database)

It's a Wonderful Life (film)

Star Trek (television broadcast)

What's the Word? (radio broadcast)

Sgt. Pepper's Lonely Hearts Club Band (compact disc, audiocassette, record album)

The Nutcracker (dance performance)

Rigoletto (opera)

Berlioz's *Symphonie fantastique* (long musical composition identified by name)

Chagall's *I and My Village* (painting)

French's *The Minute Man* (sculpture)

USS *Arizona* (ship)

Spirit of St. Louis (aircraft)

Challenger (spacecraft)

3.6.3. Titles in Quotation Marks

Use quotation marks for the titles of articles, essays, stories and poems published within larger works, chapters of books, pages in Web
sites, individual episodes of television and radio broadcasts, and
short musical compositions (e.g., songs). Also use quotation marks
for unpublished works, such as lectures and speeches.

"Literary History and Sociology" (journal article)

"Sources of Energy in the Next Decade" (magazine article)

"Etruscan" (encyclopedia article)

"The Fiction of Langston Hughes" (essay in a book)

"The Lottery" (story)

"Kubla Khan" (poem)

"The American Economy before the Civil War" (chapter in a book)

"Philosophy of Economics" (page in a Web site)

"The Trouble with Tribbles" (episode of the television broadcast *Star Trek*)

"Mood Indigo" (song)

"Preparing for a Successful Interview" (lecture)

3.6.4. Titles and Quotations within Titles

Italicize a title normally indicated by italics when it appears within a
title enclosed in quotation marks.

"*Romeo and Juliet* and Renaissance Politics" (an article about a play)

"Language and Childbirth in *The Awakening*" (an article about a novel)

Enclose in single quotation marks a title normally indicated by quotation marks when it appears within another title requiring quotation
marks.

"Lines after Reading 'Sailing to Byzantium'" (a poem about a poem)

"The Uncanny Theology of 'A Good Man Is Hard to Find'" (an article about
  a story)

Also place single quotation marks around a quotation that appears
within a title requiring quotation marks.

"Emerson's Strategies against 'Foolish Consistency'" (an article with a
  quotation in its title)

Use quotation marks around a title normally indicated by quotation marks when it appears within an italicized title.

"The Lottery" and Other Stories (a book of stories)

New Perspectives on "The Eve of St. Agnes" (a book about a poem)

If a period is required after an italicized title that ends with a quotation mark, place the period before the quotation mark.

The study appears in *New Perspectives on "The Eve of St. Agnes."*

There are two common methods for identifying a normally italicized title when it appears within an italicized title. In one practice, the title within is neither italicized nor enclosed in quotation marks. This method is preferred in publications of the Modern Language Association.

Approaches to Teaching Murasaki Shikibu's The Tale of Genji (a book about a novel)

From The Lodger *to* The Lady Vanishes*: Hitchcock's Classic British Thrillers* (a book about films)

In the other method, all titles within italicized titles are placed in quotation marks and italicized.

Approaches to Teaching Murasaki Shikibu's "The Tale of Genji"

From "The Lodger" to "The Lady Vanishes": Hitchcock's Classic British Thrillers

Each approach has advantages and disadvantages. In the first method, the titles of works published independently and the material containing them are always given opposite treatments. This practice has the advantage of consistency, but it can lead to ambiguity: it is sometimes hard to tell where a title like *Approaches to Teaching Murasaki Shikibu's* The Tale of Genji ends and where the adjacent text begins.

The second method prevents confusion between titles and the adjacent text. However, it treats titles of works published independently two ways: they receive quotation marks in italicized titles but nowhere else. In addition, within italicized titles this method abandons the distinction between works that are published independently and those that are not.

Whichever practice you choose or your instructor requires, follow it consistently throughout your paper.

3.6.5. Exceptions

The convention of using italics and quotation marks to indicate titles does not generally apply to the names of scriptural writings (including all books and versions of the Bible); of laws, acts, and similar political documents; of musical compositions identified by form, number, and key; of series, societies, buildings, and monuments; and of conferences, seminars, workshops, and courses. These terms all appear without italics or quotation marks.

SCRIPTURE

Bible	Talmud
Old Testament	Koran
Genesis	Upanishads
Gospels	

But italicize titles of individual published editions of scriptural writings (*The Interlinear Bible*, *The Talmud of the Land of Israel: A Preliminary Translation and Explanation*, *The Upanishads: A Selection for the Modern Reader*) and treat the editions in the works-cited list like any other published book.

LAWS, ACTS, AND SIMILAR POLITICAL DOCUMENTS

Magna Carta

Declaration of Independence

MUSICAL COMPOSITIONS IDENTIFIED BY FORM, NUMBER, AND KEY

Beethoven's Symphony no. 7 in A, op. 92

SERIES

University of North Carolina Studies in Comparative Literature

SOCIETIES

American Medical Association

BUILDINGS AND MONUMENTS

Sears Tower

Arch of Constantine

CONFERENCES, SEMINARS, WORKSHOPS, AND COURSES

Strengthening the Cooperative Effort in Biomedical Research: A National
    Conference for Universities and Industry
Introduction to Calculus
Anthropology 102

Words designating the divisions of a work are also not italicized or
put within quotation marks, nor are they capitalized when used in
the text ("The author says in her preface . . . ," "In canto 32 Ariosto
writes . . .").

preface	scene 7
introduction	stanza 20
list of works cited	chapter 2
appendix	

3.6.6. Shortened Titles

If you cite a title often in the text of your paper, you may, after stating
the title in full at least once, use a shortened form, preferably a familiar or obvious one (e.g., "Nightingale" for "Ode to a Nightingale"), or
an abbreviation (for standard abbreviated titles of common literature,
see 7.7).

3.7. QUOTATIONS

3.7.1. Use and Accuracy of Quotations

Quotations are effective in research papers when used selectively.
Quote only words, phrases, lines, and passages that are particularly
interesting, vivid, unusual, or apt, and keep all quotations as brief as
possible. Overquotation can bore your readers and might lead them
to conclude that you are neither an original thinker nor a skillful
writer.

The accuracy of quotations in research writing is extremely important. They must reproduce the original sources exactly. Unless indicated in brackets or parentheses (see 3.7.6), changes must not be
made in the spelling, capitalization, or interior punctuation of the

source. You must construct a clear, grammatically correct sentence that allows you to introduce or incorporate a quotation with complete accuracy. Alternatively, you may paraphrase the original and quote only fragments, which may be easier to integrate into the text. If you change a quotation in any way, make the alteration clear to the reader, following the rules and recommendations below.

3.7.2. Prose

If a prose quotation runs no more than four lines and requires no special emphasis, put it in quotation marks and incorporate it into the text.

> "It was the best of times, it was the worst of times," wrote Charles
> Dickens of the eighteenth century.

You need not always reproduce complete sentences. Sometimes you may want to quote just a word or phrase as part of your sentence.

> For Charles Dickens the eighteenth century was both "the best of times"
> and "the worst of times."

You may put a quotation at the beginning, middle, or end of your sentence or, for the sake of variety or better style, divide it by your own words.

> Joseph Conrad writes of the company manager in *Heart of Darkness*, "He
> was obeyed, yet he inspired neither love nor fear, nor even respect."

or

> "He was obeyed," writes Joseph Conrad of the company manager in *Heart
> of Darkness*, "yet he inspired neither love nor fear, nor even respect."

If a quotation ending a sentence requires a parenthetical reference, place the sentence period after the reference. (For more information on punctuating quotations, see 3.7.7.)

> For Charles Dickens the eighteenth century was both "the best of times"
> and "the worst of times" (35).

> "He was obeyed," writes Joseph Conrad of the company manager in *Heart
> of Darkness*, "yet he inspired neither love nor fear, nor even respect" (87).

If a quotation extends to more than four lines when run into the text, set it off from your text by beginning a new line, indenting one inch from the left margin, and typing it double-spaced, without adding quotation marks. A colon generally introduces a quotation displayed in this way, though sometimes the context may require a different mark of punctuation or none at all. If you quote only a single paragraph or part of one, do not indent the first line more than the rest. A parenthetical reference for a prose quotation set off from the text follows the last line of the quotation.

> At the conclusion of *Lord of the Flies*, Ralph and the other boys realize the horror of their actions:
>
> > The tears began to flow and sobs shook him. He gave himself up to them now for the first time on the island; great, shuddering spasms of grief that seemed to wrench his whole body. His voice rose under the black smoke before the burning wreckage of the island; and infected by that emotion, the other little boys began to shake and sob too. (186)

If you need to quote two or more paragraphs, indent the first line of each paragraph an additional quarter inch. If the first sentence quoted does not begin a paragraph in the source, however, do not indent it the additional amount. Indent only the first lines of the successive paragraphs.

> In *Moll Flanders* Defoe maintains the pseudoautobiographical narration typical of the picaresque tradition:
>
> > My true name is so well known in the records, or registers, at Newgate and in the Old Bailey, and there are some things of such consequence still depending there relating to my particular conduct, that it is not to be expected I should set my name or the account of my family to this work. . . .
> >
> > It is enough to tell you, that . . . some of my worst comrades, who are out of the way of doing me harm . . . know me by the name of Moll Flanders. . . . (1)

On omitting words within quotations, see 3.7.5. For translations of quotations, see 3.7.8.

3.7.3. Poetry

If you quote part or all of a single line of verse that does not require special emphasis, put it in quotation marks within your text. You may also incorporate two or three lines in this way, using a slash with a space on each side (/) to separate them.

> Bradstreet frames the poem with a sense of mortality: "All things within this fading world hath end" (1).

> Reflecting on the "incident" in Baltimore, Cullen concludes, "Of all the things that happened there / That's all that I remember" (11-12).

Verse quotations of more than three lines should begin on a new line. Unless the quotation involves unusual spacing, indent each line one inch from the left margin and double-space between lines, adding no quotation marks that do not appear in the original. A parenthetical reference for a verse quotation set off from the text follows the last line of the quotation (as in quotations of prose); a parenthetical reference that will not fit on the line should appear on a new line, flush with the right margin of the page.

> Elizabeth Bishop's "In the Waiting Room" is rich in evocative detail:
>> It was winter. It got dark
>> early. The waiting room
>> was full of grown-up people,
>> arctics and overcoats,
>> lamps and magazines. (6-10)

A line that is too long to fit within the right margin should be continued on the next line and the continuation indented an additional quarter inch. You may reduce the indention of the quotation to less than one inch from the left margin if doing so will eliminate the need for such continuations. If the spatial arrangement of the original lines, including indention and spacing within and between them, is unusual, reproduce it as accurately as possible.

> E. E. Cummings concludes the poem with this vivid description of a carefree scene, reinforced by the carefree form of the lines themselves:
>> it's
>> spring

and

    the

        goat-footed

balloonMan   whistles

far

and

wee (16-24)

When a verse quotation begins in the middle of a line, the partial line should be positioned where it is in the original and not shifted to the left margin.

> In "I Sit and Sew," by Alice Dunbar-Nelson, the speaker laments that social convention compels her to sit uselessly while her male compatriots lie in need on the battlefield:
>
> > My soul in pity flings
> > Appealing cries, yearning only to go
> > There in that holocaust of hell, those fields of woe—
> > But—I must sit and sew. (11-14)

For translations of quotations, see 3.7.8.

3.7.4. Drama

If you quote dialogue between two or more characters in a play, set the quotation off from your text. Begin each part of the dialogue with the appropriate character's name indented one inch from the left margin and written in all capital letters: HAMLET. Follow the name with a period, and start the quotation. Indent all subsequent lines in that character's speech an additional quarter inch. When the dialogue shifts to another character, start a new line indented one inch from the left margin. Maintain this pattern throughout the entire quotation.

> Marguerite Duras's screenplay for *Hiroshima mon amour* suggests at the outset the profound difference between observation and experience:
>
> > HE. You saw nothing in Hiroshima. Nothing.
> > SHE. I saw *everything. Everything.* . . . The hospital, for instance, I saw it. I'm sure I did. There is a hospital in Hiroshima. How could I help seeing it?

> HE. You did not see the hospital in Hiroshima. You saw nothing
>   in Hiroshima. (2505-06)

A short time later Lear loses the final symbol of his former power, the
soldiers who make up his train:

> GONERIL.   Hear me, my lord.
>   What need you five-and-twenty, ten or five,
>   To follow in a house where twice so many
>   Have a command to tend you?
> REGAN.   What need one?
> LEAR. O, reason not the need! (2.4.254-58)

In general, stage directions are treated like other quoted text: they
should be reproduced exactly as they appear in the original source
(see 3.7.1). When stage directions interrupt the grammatical sense of
your sentence, they may be replaced with an ellipsis (see 3.7.5). For
the other aspects of formatting, follow the recommendations above
for quoting prose and poetry (3.7.2–3).

3.7.5. Ellipsis

Whenever you wish to omit a word, a phrase, a sentence, or more from
a quoted passage, you should be guided by two principles: fairness
to the author quoted and the grammatical integrity of your writing.
A quotation should never be presented in a way that could cause a
reader to misunderstand the sentence structure of the original source.
If you quote only a word or a phrase, it will be obvious that you left
out some of the original sentence.

> In his inaugural address, John F. Kennedy spoke of a "new frontier."

But if omitting material from the original sentence or sentences leaves
a quotation that appears to be a sentence or a series of sentences, you
must use ellipsis points, or three spaced periods, to indicate that your
quotation does not completely reproduce the original. Whenever you
omit words from a quotation, the resulting passage—your prose and
the quotation integrated into it—should be grammatically complete
and correct.

For an ellipsis within a sentence, use three periods with a space
before each and a space after the last (. . .).

ORIGINAL

Medical thinking, trapped in the theory of astral influences, stressed air as the communicator of disease, ignoring sanitation or visible carriers. (Barbara W. Tuchman, *A Distant Mirror: The Calamitous Fourteenth Century* [1978; New York: Ballantine, 1979; print; 101–02])

QUOTATION WITH AN ELLIPSIS IN THE MIDDLE

In surveying various responses to plagues in the Middle Ages, Barbara W. Tuchman writes, "Medical thinking . . . stressed air as the communicator of disease, ignoring sanitation or visible carriers" (101-02).

When the ellipsis coincides with the end of your sentence, use three periods with a space before each following a sentence period—that is, four periods, with no space before the first or after the last.

QUOTATION WITH AN ELLIPSIS AT THE END

In surveying various responses to plagues in the Middle Ages, Barbara W. Tuchman writes, "Medical thinking, trapped in the theory of astral influences, stressed air as the communicator of disease. . . ."

If a parenthetical reference follows the ellipsis at the end of your sentence, however, use three periods with a space before each, and place the sentence period after the final parenthesis.

QUOTATION WITH AN ELLIPSIS AT THE END FOLLOWED BY A PARENTHETICAL REFERENCE

In surveying various responses to plagues in the Middle Ages, Barbara W. Tuchman writes, "Medical thinking, trapped in the theory of astral influences, stressed air as the communicator of disease . . ." (101-02).

In a quotation of more than one sentence, an ellipsis in the middle can indicate the omission of any amount of text.

ORIGINAL

Presidential control reached its zenith under Andrew Jackson, the extent of whose attention to the press even before he became a candidate is suggested by the fact that he subscribed to twenty newspapers. Jackson was never content to have only one organ grinding out his tune. For a time, the *United States Telegraph* and the *Washington Globe* were almost equally favored as party organs, and there were fifty-seven journalists on the government payroll. (William L. Rivers, *The Mass Media: Reporting, Writing, Editing* [2nd ed.; New York: Harper, 1975; print; 7])

QUOTATION OMITTING A SENTENCE

In discussing the historical relation between politics and the press, William
L. Rivers notes:

> Presidential control reached its zenith under Andrew Jackson, the
> extent of whose attention to the press even before he became a
> candidate is suggested by the fact that he subscribed to twenty
> newspapers. . . . For a time, the *United States Telegraph* and the
> *Washington Globe* were almost equally favored as party organs,
> and there were fifty-seven journalists on the government payroll. (7)

QUOTATION WITH AN OMISSION FROM THE MIDDLE OF ONE
SENTENCE TO THE END OF ANOTHER

In discussing the historical relation between politics and the press, William
L. Rivers notes, "Presidential control reached its zenith under Andrew
Jackson. . . . For a time, the *United States Telegraph* and the *Washington
Globe* were almost equally favored as party organs, and there were
fifty-seven journalists on the government payroll" (7).

QUOTATION WITH AN OMISSION FROM THE MIDDLE OF ONE
SENTENCE TO THE MIDDLE OF ANOTHER

In discussing the historical relation between politics and the press, William L.
Rivers notes that when presidential control "reached its zenith under Andrew
Jackson, . . . there were fifty-seven journalists on the government payroll" (7).

The omission of words and phrases from quotations of poetry is also
indicated by three or four spaced periods (as in quotations of prose).

ORIGINAL

In Worcester, Massachusetts,
I went with Aunt Consuelo
to keep her dentist's appointment
and sat and waited for her
in the dentist's waiting room.
It was winter. It got dark
early. The waiting room
was full of grown-up people,
arctics and overcoats,
lamps and magazines.
(Elizabeth Bishop, "In the Waiting Room" [*Poets.org*; Acad. of Amer.
Poets, n.d.; Web; 30 May 2008; lines 1–10])

QUOTATION WITH AN ELLIPSIS AT THE END

Elizabeth Bishop's "In the Waiting Room" is rich in evocative detail:

> In Worcester, Massachusetts,
> I went with Aunt Consuelo
> to keep her dentist's appointment
> and sat and waited for her
> in the dentist's waiting room.
> It was winter. It got dark
> early. The waiting room
> was full of grown-up people. . . . (1-8)

The omission of a line or more in the middle of a poetry quotation that is set off from the text is indicated by a line of spaced periods approximately the length of a complete line of the quoted poem.

QUOTATION OMITTING A LINE OR MORE IN THE MIDDLE

Elizabeth Bishop's "In the Waiting Room" is rich in evocative detail:

> In Worcester, Massachusetts,
> I went with Aunt Consuelo
> to keep her dentist's appointment
>
> . . . .
> It was winter. It got dark
> early. (1-3, 6-7)

In this example, the quotation ends in the middle of a line and at the end of a sentence. You do not need to indicate with an ellipsis that more material appears on the line in the original.

If the author you are quoting uses ellipsis points, you should distinguish them from your ellipses by putting square brackets around the ones you add or by including an explanatory phrase in parentheses after the quotation.

ORIGINAL

"We live in California, my husband and I, Los Angeles. . . . This is beautiful country; I have never been here before." (N. Scott Momaday, *House Made of Dawn* [1968; New York: Perennial-Harper, 1977; print; 29])

QUOTATION WITH AN ADDED ELLIPSIS

In N. Scott Momaday's *House Made of Dawn*, when Mrs. St. John arrives at

the rectory, she tells Father Olguin, "We live in California, my husband and
I, Los Angeles. . . . This is beautiful country [. . .]" (29).

or

In N. Scott Momaday's *House Made of Dawn*, when Mrs. St. John arrives at
the rectory, she tells Father Olguin, "We live in California, my husband and
I, Los Angeles. . . . This is beautiful country . . ." (29; 1st ellipsis in orig.).

3.7.6. Other Alterations of Sources

Occasionally, you may decide that a quotation will be unclear or confusing to your reader unless you provide supplementary information.
For example, you may need to insert material missing from the original, to add *sic* (from the Latin for "thus" or "so") to assure readers
that the quotation is accurate even though the spelling or logic might
make them think otherwise, or to italicize words for emphasis. While
such contributions to a quotation are permissible, you should keep
them to a minimum and make sure to distinguish them from the original, usually by explaining them in parentheses after the quotation or
by putting them in square brackets within the quotation.

A comment or an explanation that immediately follows the closing
quotation mark appears in parentheses.

Shaw admitted, "Nothing can extinguish my interest in Shakespear" (sic).

Lincoln specifically advocated a government "*for* the people" (emphasis
added).

A comment or an explanation that goes inside the quotation must
appear within square brackets, not parentheses.

He claimed he could provide "hundreds of examples [of court decisions]
to illustrate the historical tension between church and state."

Milton's Satan speaks of his "study [pursuit] of revenge."

Similarly, if a pronoun in a quotation seems unclear, you may add an
identification in square brackets.

In the first act he soliloquizes, "Why she would hang on him [Hamlet's
father] / As if increase of appetite had grown / By what it fed on. . . ."

3.7.7. Punctuation with Quotations

Whether set off from the text or run into it, quoted material is usually preceded by a colon if the quotation is formally introduced and by a comma or no punctuation if the quotation is an integral part of the sentence structure.

> Shelley held a bold view: "Poets are the unacknowledged legislators of the World" (794).

> Shelley thought poets "the unacknowledged legislators of the World" (794).

> "Poets," according to Shelley, "are the unacknowledged legislators of the World" (794).

Do not use opening and closing quotation marks to enclose quotations set off from the text, but reproduce any quotation marks that are in the passage quoted.

> In "Memories of West Street and Lepke," Robert Lowell, a conscientious objector (or "C.O."), recounts meeting a Jehovah's Witness in prison:
>> I was so out of things, I'd never heard
>> of the Jehovah's Witnesses.
>> "Are you a C.O.?" I asked a fellow jailbird.
>> "No," he answered, "I'm a J.W." (36-39)

Use double quotation marks around quotations incorporated into the text, single quotation marks around quotations within those quotations.

> In "Memories of West Street and Lepke," Robert Lowell, a conscientious objector (or "C.O."), recounts meeting a Jehovah's Witness in prison: "'Are you a C.O.?' I asked a fellow jailbird. / 'No,' he answered, 'I'm a J.W.'" (38-39).

When a quotation consists entirely of material enclosed by quotation marks in the source work, usually one pair of double quotation marks is sufficient, provided that the introductory wording makes clear the special character of the quoted material.

> Meeting a fellow prisoner, Lowell asks, "Are you a C.O.?" (38).

Except for changing internal double quotation marks to single ones when you incorporate quotations into your text, you should reproduce internal punctuation exactly as in the original. The closing punctuation, though, depends on where the quoted material appears in your sentence. Suppose, for example, that you want to quote the following sentence: "You've got to be carefully taught." If you begin your sentence with this line, you have to replace the closing period with a punctuation mark appropriate to the new context.

"You've got to be carefully taught," wrote Oscar Hammerstein II about how racial prejudice is perpetuated.

If the quotation ends with a question mark or an exclamation point, however, the original punctuation is retained, and no comma is required.

"How can I describe my emotions at this catastrophe, or how delineate the wretch whom with such infinite pains and care I had endeavoured to form?" wonders the doctor in Mary Shelley's *Frankenstein* (42).

"What a wonderful little almanac you are, Celia!" Dorothea Brooke responds to her sister (7).

By convention, commas and periods that directly follow quotations go inside the closing quotation marks, but a parenthetical reference should intervene between the quotation and the required punctuation. Thus, if a quotation ends with a period, the period appears after the reference.

N. Scott Momaday's *House Made of Dawn* begins with an image that also concludes the novel: "Abel was running" (7).

If a quotation ends with both single and double quotation marks, the comma or period precedes both.

"The poem alludes to Stevens's 'Sunday Morning,'" notes Miller.

All other punctuation marks—such as semicolons, colons, question marks, and exclamation points—go outside a closing quotation mark, except when they are part of the quoted material.

ORIGINAL

I believe taxation without representation is tyranny!

QUOTATIONS

He attacked "taxation without representation" (32).

Did he attack "taxation without representation"?

What dramatic events followed his attack on "taxation without representation"!

but

He declared, "I believe taxation without representation is tyranny!"

If a quotation ending with a question mark or an exclamation point concludes your sentence and requires a parenthetical reference, retain the original punctuation within the quotation mark and follow with the reference and the sentence period outside the quotation mark.

In Mary Shelley's *Frankenstein*, the doctor wonders, "How can I describe my emotions at this catastrophe, or how delineate the wretch whom with such infinite pains and care I had endeavoured to form?" (42).

Dorothea Brooke responds to her sister, "What a wonderful little almanac you are, Celia!" (7).

3.7.8. Translations of Quotations

If you believe that a significant portion of your audience will not be familiar with the language of a quotation you present, you should add a translation. If the translation is not yours, give its source in addition to the source of the quotation. In general, the translation should immediately follow the quotation whether they are run into or set off from the text, although their order may be reversed if most readers will not likely be able to read the original. If the quotation is run into the text, use double quotation marks around a translation placed in parentheses following the quotation but single quotation marks around a translation that immediately follows without intervening punctuation.

At the opening of Dante's *Inferno*, the poet finds himself in "una selva oscura" ("a dark wood"; 1.2; Ciardi 28).

At the opening of Dante's *Inferno*, the poet finds himself in "una selva oscura" 'a dark wood' (1.2; Ciardi 28).

Do not use quotation marks around quotations and translations set off from the text.

> Dante's *Inferno* begins literally in the middle of things:
>
> Nel mezzo del cammin di nostra vita
>
> mi ritrovai per una selva oscura,
>
> ché la diritta via era smarrita.
>
> Ahi quanto a dir qual era è cosa dura
>
> esta selva selvaggia e aspra e forte
>
> che nel pensier rinova la paura! (1.1-6)
>
> Midway in our life's journey, I went astray
>
> from the straight road and woke to find myself
>
> alone in a dark wood. How shall I say
>
> what wood that was! I never saw so drear,
>
> so rank, so arduous a wilderness!
>
> Its very memory gives a shape to fear. (Ciardi 28)

See also 3.2.8b for guidelines on translating a foreign word or phrase within a sentence.

3.8. CAPITALIZATION AND PERSONAL NAMES IN LANGUAGES OTHER THAN ENGLISH

The following section contains recommendations for writing personal names and for capitalizing in French, German, Italian, Spanish, and Latin. If you need such rules for other languages or if you need information on romanizing from languages that do not use the Latin alphabet, such as Russian or Chinese, consult the *MLA Style Manual and Guide to Scholarly Publishing* (3rd ed.; New York: MLA, 2008; print; 3.6–7, 3.11).

3.8.1. French

Personal Names

With some exceptions, especially in English-language contexts, French *de* following a first name or a title such as *Mme* or *duc* is not used with the last name alone.

La Boétie (Étienne de La Boétie)

Maupassant (Guy de Maupassant)

Nemours (Louis-Charles d'Orléans, duc de Nemours)

but

De Quincey (Thomas De Quincey)

When the last name has only one syllable, however, *de* is usually retained.

de Gaulle (Charles de Gaulle)

The preposition also remains, in the form *d'*, when it elides with a last name beginning with a vowel.

d'Arcy (Pierre d'Arcy)

The forms *du* and *des*—combinations of *de* with *le* and *les*—are always used with last names and are capitalized.

Des Périers (Bonaventure Des Périers)

Du Bos (Charles Du Bos)

A hyphen is frequently used between French given names, as well as between their initials (Marie-Joseph Chénier, M.-J. Chénier). Note that *M.* and *P.* before names may be abbreviations for the titles *Monsieur* 'Mr.' and *Père* 'Father' (M. René Char, P. J. Reynard).

Capitalization

In prose and verse, French capitalization is the same as English except that the following terms are not capitalized in French unless they begin sentences or, sometimes, lines of verse: (1) the subject pronoun *je* 'I,' (2) the names of months and days of the week, (3) the names of languages, (4) adjectives derived from proper nouns, (5) titles preceding personal names, and (6) the words meaning "street," "square," "lake," "mountain," and so on, in most place-names.

Un Français m'a parlé anglais près de la place de la Concorde.

Hier j'ai vu le docteur Maurois qui conduisait une voiture Ford.

Le capitaine Boutillier m'a dit qu'il partait pour Rouen le premier jeudi d'avril avec quelques amis normands.

There are two widely accepted methods of capitalizing French titles and subtitles of works. One method is to capitalize the first word in titles and subtitles and all proper nouns in them. This method is normally followed in publications of the Modern Language Association.

La chambre claire: Note sur la photographie

Du côté de chez Swann

La guerre de Troie n'aura pas lieu

Nouvelle revue d'onomastique

In the other method, when a title or subtitle begins with an article, the first noun and any preceding adjectives are also capitalized.

La Chambre claire: Note sur la photographie

Du côté de chez Swann

La Guerre de Troie n'aura pas lieu

In this system, all major words in titles of series and periodicals are sometimes capitalized.

Nouvelle Revue d'Onomastique

Whichever practice you choose or your instructor requires, follow it consistently throughout your paper.

3.8.2. German

Personal Names

German *von* is generally not used with the last name alone, but there are some exceptions, especially in English-language contexts, where the *von* is firmly established by convention.

Droste-Hülshoff (Annette von Droste-Hülshoff)

Kleist (Heinrich von Kleist)

but

Von Braun (Wernher Von Braun)

Von Trapp (Maria Von Trapp)

In alphabetizing a German name with an umlaut (the mark over the vowel in *ä, ö, ü*), Germanists treat the umlauted vowel as if it were followed by an *e*; thus, *Götz* would be alphabetized as *Goetz* and would precede *Gott* in an alphabetical listing. Nonspecialists, however, and many libraries in English-speaking countries alphabetize such names without regard to the umlaut; in this practice, *Götz* would be alphabetized as *Gotz* and would therefore follow *Gott* in an alphabetical listing. Whichever practice you choose or your instructor requires, follow it consistently throughout your paper.

Capitalization

In prose and verse, German capitalization differs considerably from English. Always capitalized in German are all nouns—including adjectives, infinitives, pronouns, prepositions, and other parts of speech used as nouns—as well as the pronoun *Sie* 'you' and its possessive, *Ihr* 'your,' and their inflected forms. Generally not capitalized unless they begin sentences or, usually, lines of verse are (1) the subject pronoun *ich* 'I,' (2) the names of languages and of days of the week used as adjectives, adverbs, or complements of prepositions, and (3) adjectives and adverbs formed from proper nouns, except when the proper nouns are names of persons and the adjectives and adverbs refer to the persons' works or deeds.

> Ich glaube an das Gute in der Welt.
>
> Er schreibt, nur um dem Auf und Ab der Buch-Nachfrage zu entsprechen.
>
> Fahren Sie mit Ihrer Frau zurück?
>
> Ein französischer Schriftsteller, den ich gut kenne, arbeitet sonntags immer an seinem neuen Buch über die platonische Liebe.
>
> *Der Staat* ist eine der bekanntesten Platonischen Schriften.

In letters and ceremonial writings, the pronouns *du* and *ihr* 'you' and their derivatives are capitalized.

In a title or a subtitle, capitalize the first word and all words normally capitalized.

> *Thomas Mann und die Grenzen des Ich*
>
> *Ein treuer Diener seines Herrn*
>
> *Zeitschrift für vergleichende Sprachforschung*

3.8.3. Italian

Personal Names

The names of many Italians who lived before or during the Renaissance are alphabetized by first name.

> Dante Alighieri
>
> Leonardo da Vinci
>
> Michelangelo Buonarroti

But other names of the period follow the standard practice.

> Boccaccio, Giovanni
>
> Cellini, Benvenuto
>
> Stampa, Gaspara

The names of members of historic families are also usually alphabetized by last name.

> Este, Beatrice d'
>
> Medici, Lorenzo de'

In modern times, Italian *da, de, del, della, di,* and *d'* are usually capitalized and used with the last name alone.

> D'Annunzio (Gabriele D'Annunzio)
>
> Da Ponte (Lorenzo Da Ponte)
>
> Del Buono (Oreste Del Buono)
>
> Della Robbia (Andrea Della Robbia)
>
> De Sica (Vittorio De Sica)
>
> Di Costanzo (Angelo Di Costanzo)

Capitalization

In prose and verse, Italian capitalization is the same as English except that in Italian centuries and other large divisions of time are capitalized (*il Seicento*) and the following terms are not capitalized unless they begin sentences or, usually, lines of verse: (1) the subject pronoun *io* 'I,' (2) the names of months and days of the week, (3) the names of languages and nationalities, (4) nouns, adjectives, and adverbs derived from proper nouns, (5) titles preceding personal names, and (6) the words meaning "street," "square," and so on, in most place-names.

Un italiano parlava francese con uno svizzero in piazza di Spagna.

Il dottor Bruno ritornerà dall'Italia giovedì otto agosto e io partirò il nove.

In a title or a subtitle, capitalize only the first word and all words normally capitalized.

L'arte tipografica in Urbino

Bibliografia della critica pirandelliana

Collezione di classici italiani

Dizionario letterario Bompiani

Studi petrarcheschi

3.8.4. Spanish

Personal Names

Spanish *de* is not used before the last name alone.

Las Casas (Bartolomé de Las Casas)

Madariaga (Salvador de Madariaga)

Rueda (Lope de Rueda)

Timoneda (Juan de Timoneda)

Spanish *del*, formed from the fusion of the preposition *de* and the definite article *el*, is capitalized and used with the last name alone.

Del Río (Ángel Del Río)

A Spanish surname may include both the paternal name and the maternal name, with or without the conjunction *y*. The surname of a married woman usually includes her paternal surname and her husband's paternal surname, connected by *de*. Alphabetize Spanish names by the full surnames (consult your sources or a biographical dictionary for guidance in distinguishing surnames and given names).

Carreño de Miranda, Juan

Cervantes Saavedra, Miguel de

Díaz del Castillo, Bernal

García Márquez, Gabriel

Larra y Sánchez de Castro, Mariano José

López de Ayala, Pero

Matute, Ana María

Ortega y Gasset, José

Quevedo y Villegas, Francisco Gómez de

Sinués de Marco, María del Pilar

Zayas y Sotomayor, María de

Even persons commonly known by the maternal portions of their surnames, such as Galdós and Lorca, should be alphabetized by their full surnames.

García Lorca, Federico

Pérez Galdós, Benito

Capitalization

In prose and verse, Spanish capitalization is the same as English except that the following terms are not capitalized in Spanish unless they begin sentences or, sometimes, lines of verse: (1) the subject pronoun *yo* 'I,' (2) the names of months and days of the week, (3) the names of languages and nationalities, (4) nouns and adjectives derived from proper nouns, (5) titles preceding personal names, and (6) the words meaning "street," "square," and so on, in most place-names.

El francés hablaba inglés en la plaza Colón.

Ayer yo vi al doctor García en un coche Ford.

Me dijo don Jorge que iba a salir para Sevilla el primer martes de abril con unos amigos neoyorquinos.

In a title or a subtitle, capitalize only the first word and words normally capitalized.

Breve historia del ensayo hispanoamericano

Extremos de América

La gloria de don Ramiro

Historia verdadera de la conquista de la Nueva España

Revista de filología española

Trasmundo de Goya

Some instructors follow other rules. In titles of series and periodicals, they capitalize all major words: *Revista de Filología Española*.

3.8.5. Latin

Personal Names

Roman male citizens generally had three names: a praenomen (given name), a nomen (clan name), and a cognomen (family or familiar name). Men in this category are usually referred to by nomen, cognomen, or both; your source or a standard reference book such as *The Oxford Classical Dictionary* will provide guidance.

Brutus   (Marcus Iunius Brutus)

Calpurnius Siculus   (Titus Calpurnius Siculus)

Cicero   (Marcus Tullius Cicero)

Lucretius   (Titus Lucretius Carus)

Plautus   (Titus Maccius Plautus)

Roman women usually had two names—a nomen (the clan name in the feminine form) and a cognomen (often derived from the father's cognomen): Livia Drusilla (daughter of Marcus Livius Drusus). Sometimes a woman's cognomen indicates her chronological order among the daughters of the family: Antonia Minor (younger daughter of Marcus Antonius). Most Roman women are referred to by nomen: Calpurnia, Clodia, Octavia, Sulpicia. Some, however, are better known by cognomen: Agrippina (Vipsania Agrippina).

When citing Roman names, use the forms most common in English.

Horace   (Quintus Horatius Flaccus)

Julius Caesar   (Gaius Iulius Caesar)

Livy   (Titus Livius)

Ovid   (Publius Ovidius Naso)

Vergil   (Publius Vergilius Maro)

Finally, some medieval and Renaissance figures are best known by their adopted or assigned Latin names.

Albertus Magnus   (Albert von Bollstädt)

Comenius   (Jan Amos Komenský)

Copernicus   (Niklas Koppernigk)

Paracelsus   (Theophrastus Bombast von Hohenheim)

Capitalization

Although practice varies, Latin most commonly follows the English rules for capitalization, except that *ego* 'I' is not capitalized.

Semper ego auditor tantum? Numquamne reponam / Vexatus totiens rauci Theseide Cordi?

Quidquid id est, timeo Danaos et dona ferentes.

Nil desperandum.

Quo usque tandem abutere, Catilina, patientia nostra?

In a title or a subtitle, however, capitalize only the first word and all words normally capitalized.

De senectute

Liber de senectute

Pro Marcello

4 The Format of the Research Paper

If your instructor has specific requirements for the format of a research paper, check them before preparing your final draft. The recommendations presented in this chapter are the most common. They assume that you will prepare your paper using a word processor. When you submit your paper, be sure to keep a printout of it as well as electronic copies in at least two places.

4.1. MARGINS

Except for page numbers, leave margins of one inch at the top and bottom and on both sides of the text. (For placement of page numbers, see 4.4.) If you lack 8½-by-11-inch paper and use a larger size, do not print the text in an area greater than 6½ by 9 inches. Indent the first word of a paragraph one-half inch from the left margin. Indent set-off quotations one inch from the left margin. (For examples, see 3.7.)

4.2. TEXT FORMATTING

Always choose an easily readable typeface (e.g., Times New Roman) in which the regular type style contrasts clearly with the italic, and set it to a standard size (e.g., 12 points). Do not justify the lines of text at the right margin; turn off your word processor's automatic hyphenation feature. Set your word processor to double-space the entire research paper, including quotations, notes, and the list of works cited. Leave one space after a period or other concluding punctuation mark, unless your instructor prefers two spaces.

4.3. HEADING AND TITLE

A research paper does not need a title page. Instead, beginning one inch from the top of the first page and flush with the left margin, type your name, your instructor's name, the course number, and the date on separate lines, double-spacing between the lines. Double-space again and center the title. Double-space also between the lines of the title, and double-space between the title and the first line of the text

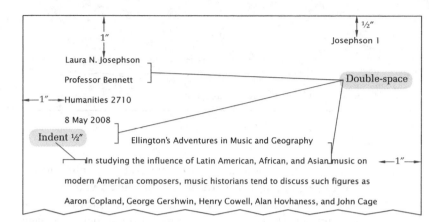

Fig. 7. The top of the first page of a research paper.

(see fig. 7). Do not italicize or underline your title, put it in quotation marks or boldface, or type it in all capital letters. Follow the rules for capitalization in 3.6.1, and italicize only the words that you would italicize in the text (see 3.3 and 3.6.2).

Local Television Coverage of International News Events

The Attitude toward Violence in *A Clockwork Orange*

The Use of the Words *Fair* and *Foul* in Shakespeare's *Macbeth*

Romanticism in England and the *Scapigliatura* in Italy

Do not use a period after your title or after any heading in the paper (e.g., *Works Cited*).

If your teacher requires a title page, format it according to the instructions you are given.

4.4. PAGE NUMBERS

Number all pages consecutively throughout the research paper in the upper right-hand corner, one-half inch from the top and flush with the right margin. Type your last name before the page number, as a precaution in case of misplaced pages (fig. 8). Automatic page

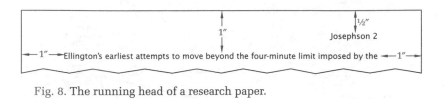

Fig. 8. The running head of a research paper.

numbering by your word processor will save you the time and effort of numbering every page. A word processor allows you to create
a running head that consists of your last name followed by a space
and the page number. Do not use the abbreviation *p.* before a page
number or add a period, a hyphen, or any other mark or symbol. The
word processor may automatically insert your running head on every
page of your paper if you do not specify otherwise. Some teachers,
however, prefer that no number appear on the first page. Follow your
teacher's preference.

4.5. TABLES AND ILLUSTRATIONS

Place tables and illustrations as close as possible to the parts of the
text to which they relate. A table is usually labeled *Table*, given an
arabic numeral, and titled. Type both label and title flush left on separate lines above the table, and capitalize them as titles (do not use all
capital letters). Give the source of the table and any notes immediately below the table in a caption. To avoid confusion between notes
to the text and notes to the table, designate notes to the table with
lowercase letters rather than with numerals. Double-space throughout; use dividing lines as needed (see fig. 9).

Any other type of illustrative visual material—for example, a photograph, map, line drawing, graph, or chart—should be labeled *Figure*
(usually abbreviated *Fig.*), assigned an arabic numeral, and given a
caption: "Fig. 1. Mary Cassatt, *Mother and Child*, Wichita Museum,
Wichita." A label and caption ordinarily appear directly below the illustration and have the same one-inch margins as the text of the paper
(see fig. 10). If the caption of a table or illustration provides complete
information about the source and the source is not cited in the text,
no entry for the source in the works-cited list is necessary.

Table 1

Degrees in Modern Foreign Languages and Literatures Conferred by
Degree-Granting Institutions of Higher Education in the United States[a]

Year	Bachelor's Degrees	Master's Degrees	Doctor's Degrees
1996-97	13,053	2,470	793
1997-98	13,618	2,367	819
1998-99	14,163	2,267	757
1999-2000	14,186	2,228	804
2000-01	14,292	2,244	818
2001-02	14,236	2,284	780
2002-03	14,854	2,256	749
2003-04	15,408	2,307	743
2004-05	16,008	2,517	762
2005-06	16,762	2,637	777

Source: United States, Dept. of Educ., Inst. of Educ. Sciences, Natl. Center
for Educ. Statistics; *Digest of Education Statistics 2007*; US Dept. of
Educ., Mar. 2008; Web; 11 June 2008; table 297.

a. These figures include degrees conferred in a single language or a
combination of modern foreign languages and exclude degrees in linguistics,
Latin, classics, ancient and Middle and Near Eastern biblical and Semitic
languages, ancient and classical Greek, Sanskrit and classical Indian
languages, and sign language and sign language interpretation.

Fig. 9. A table in a research paper.

If your research papers have many illustrations, you will probably
want to become familiar with the various kinds of software for the
creation of tables, graphs, drawings, and so forth. These programs
automatically number tables and illustrations, set them appropriately
into the text, and generate a listing of all tables and illustrations created for the paper.

Fig. 1. Manticore, woodcut from Edward Topsell, *The History of Four-Footed Beasts and Serpents . . .* (London, 1658; 344); rpt. in Konrad Gesner, *Curious Woodcuts of Fanciful and Real Beasts* (New York: Dover, 1971; print; 8).

Fig. 10. A figure in a research paper.

Ex. 1. Ludwig van Beethoven, Symphony no. 3 in E flat, op. 55 (*Eroica*), first movement, opening.

Fig. 11. A musical example in a research paper.

Musical illustrations are labeled *Example* (usually abbreviated *Ex.*), assigned an arabic numeral, and given a caption: "Ex. 1. Pyotr Ilich Tchaikovsky, Symphony no. 6 in B, op. 74 (*Pathétique*), finale." A label and caption ordinarily appear directly below the example and have the same one-inch margins as the text of the paper (see fig. 11).

4.6. PAPER AND PRINTING

Use only white, 8½-by-11-inch paper of good quality. If you lack 8½-by-11-inch paper, use the closest size available. Use a high-quality printer. Most instructors prefer papers printed on a single side, but some instructors encourage printing on both sides as a means of conserving paper.

4.7. CORRECTIONS AND INSERTIONS

Proofread and correct your research paper carefully before submitting it. If you find a mistake in the final copy, reopen the word-processing file, make the appropriate revisions, and reprint the corrected page or pages. Be sure to save the changed file. Some writers find such software as spelling checkers and usage checkers helpful when used with caution (see 1.9.3). If your instructor permits brief corrections on the printout, write them neatly and legibly in ink directly above the lines involved, using carets (∧) to indicate where they go. Do not use the margins or write a change below the line it affects. If corrections on any page are numerous or substantial, revise your file and reprint the page.

4.8. BINDING

Pages of your research paper may get misplaced or lost if they are left unattached or merely folded down at a corner. Although a plastic folder or some other kind of binder may seem an attractive finishing touch, most instructors find such devices a nuisance in reading and commenting on students' work. Many prefer that a paper be secured with a simple paper or binder clip, which can be easily removed and restored. Others prefer the use of staples.

4.9. ELECTRONIC SUBMISSION

There are at present no commonly accepted standards for the electronic submission of research papers. If you are asked to submit your paper electronically, obtain from your teacher guidelines for formatting, mode of submission (e.g., by e-mail, on a Web site), and so forth, and follow them closely.

To facilitate discussion of your work, you should incorporate reference markers in the paper if it does not include page numbers. Paragraphs are sometimes numbered in electronic publications. If you use this system, place the appropriate number, in square brackets—"[12]"—and followed by a space, at the beginning of each paragraph.

5 Documentation: Preparing the List of Works Cited

5.1. DOCUMENTING SOURCES

Nearly all research builds on previous research. Researchers commonly begin a project by studying past work on their topics and deriving relevant information and ideas from their predecessors. This process is largely responsible for the continual expansion of human knowledge. In presenting their work, researchers generously acknowledge their debts to predecessors by carefully documenting each source, so that earlier contributions receive appropriate credit and readers can evaluate the basis for claims and conclusions.

As you prepare your paper, you should similarly seek to build on the work of previous writers and researchers. And whenever you draw on another's work, you must also document your source by indicating what you borrowed—whether facts, opinions, or quotations—and where you borrowed it from. Through documentation, you will provide your readers with a description of key features of each source (such as its authorship and its medium of publication). Documentation also assists readers in locating the sources you used. Cite only the sources you have consulted directly. If you have not already done so, read carefully the earlier section on plagiarism (ch. 2) to learn what you must document in your paper.

5.2. MLA STYLE

In MLA documentation style, you acknowledge your sources by keying brief parenthetical citations in your text to an alphabetical list of works that appears at the end of the paper. The parenthetical citation that concludes the following sentence is typical of MLA style.

> The aesthetic and ideological orientation of jazz underwent considerable scrutiny in the late 1950s and early 1960s (Anderson 7).

The citation "(Anderson 7)" tells readers that the information in the sentence was derived from page 7 of a work by an author named Anderson. If readers want more information about this source, they can turn to the works-cited list, where, under the name Anderson, they would find the following information.

126

Anderson, Iain. *This Is Our Music: Free Jazz, the Sixties, and American Culture*. Philadelphia: U of Pennsylvania P, 2007. Print. The Arts and Intellectual Life in Mod. Amer.

This entry states that the work's author is Iain Anderson and its title is *This Is Our Music: Free Jazz, the Sixties, and American Culture*. The remaining information relates, in shortened form, that the work was produced in Philadelphia by the University of Pennsylvania Press in 2007 as a print publication in a book series called The Arts and Intellectual Life in Modern America. Using the abbreviations listed in chapter 7 makes an entry in MLA style concise yet readable. Similarly, when the name of a contributor to a work appears more than once in an entry, only the last name appears after the initial occurrence (for examples, see 5.5.8).

A citation in MLA style contains only enough information to enable readers to find the source in the works-cited list. If the author's name is mentioned in the text, only the page number appears in the citation: "(7)." If more than one work by the author is in the list of works cited, a shortened version of the title is given. "(Anderson, *This* 7)." (See ch. 6 for a fuller discussion of parenthetical citations in MLA style.)

MLA style is not the only way to document sources. Many disciplines have their own documentation systems. MLA style is widely used in the humanities. Although generally simpler and more concise than other documentation styles, it shares with most others its central feature: parenthetical citations keyed to a works-cited list. If you learn MLA documentation style at an early stage in your school career, you will probably have little difficulty in adapting to other styles.

Documentation styles differ according to discipline because they are shaped by the kind of research and scholarship undertaken. For example, in the sciences, where timeliness of research is crucial, the date of publication is usually given prominence. Thus, in the style recommended by the American Psychological Association (APA), a typical citation includes the date of publication (as well as the abbreviation *p.* before the page number). Compare APA and MLA parenthetical citations for the same source.

APA

(Anderson, 2007, p. 7)

MLA

(Anderson 7)

In the humanities, where most important scholarship remains relevant for a substantial period, publication dates receive less attention: though normally stated in the works-cited list, they are omitted in parenthetical references. An important reason for this omission is that many humanities scholars like to keep their texts as readable and as free of disruptions as possible.

In an entry for a book in an APA-style works-cited list, the date (in parentheses) immediately follows the name of the author (whose first name is written only as an initial), just the first word of the title is capitalized, and the publisher's full name is generally provided.

APA

Anderson, I. (2007). *This is our music: Free jazz, the sixties, and American culture.* Philadelphia: University of Pennsylvania Press.

By contrast, in an MLA-style entry, the author's name appears as given in the work (normally in full), every important word of the title is capitalized, some words in the publisher's name are abbreviated, the publication date follows the publisher's name, and the medium of publication is recorded. The book in this example is part of a series, and the title of the series is included in the entry. In both styles, the first line of the entry is flush with the left margin, and the second and subsequent lines are indented.

MLA

Anderson, Iain. *This Is Our Music: Free Jazz, the Sixties, and American Culture.* Philadelphia: U of Pennsylvania P, 2007. Print. The Arts and Intellectual Life in Mod. Amer.

As you conduct your research, you should note the provenance, or origin, of the sources you use. What are the available editions of a work? If a work is available in several media, which version did you consult and why? What are the differences between a live performance and a recording? Attention to such questions will assist you in creating a persuasive and authoritative research paper. If, after following the correct format for an entry in the list of works cited, you want to communicate additional information about the work, you may expand your description of it in your text or in a note (for the use of content notes, see 6.5.1).

Chapters 5 and 6 offer an authoritative and comprehensive presentation of MLA style.

5.3. THE LIST OF WORKS CITED

5.3.1. Introduction

MLA style provides a flexible, modular format for recording key features of works cited or consulted in the preparation of your research paper. This chapter describes several sequences of elements that can be combined to form entries in lists of works. In building an entry, you should know which elements to look for in the source. Not all elements will be present in a given source. Moreover, since MLA style is flexible about the inclusion of some information and even about the ordering of the elements, you should understand how your choice relates to your research project. For example, as noted in 5.7.3, a research paper on the work of a film director may list the director's name first, while a research paper on the work of a film actor may list the performer's name first (the guidelines for citing editions [5.5.10] and translations [5.5.11] are similarly flexible). While it is tempting to think that every source has only one complete and correct format for its entry in a list of works cited, in truth there are often several options for recording key features of a work. For this reason, software programs that generate entries are not likely to be useful. You may need to improvise when the type of scholarly project or the publication medium of a source is not anticipated by this handbook. Be consistent in your formatting throughout your work. Choose the format that is appropriate to your research paper and that will satisfy your readers' needs.

Although the list of works cited appears at the end of your paper, you need to draft the section in advance, so that you will know what information to give in parenthetical references as you write. For example, you have to include shortened titles if you cite two or more works by the same author, and you have to add initials or first names if two of the cited authors have the same last name: "(K. Roemer 123–24)," "(M. Roemer 67)." This chapter therefore explains how to prepare a list of works cited, and the next chapter demonstrates how to document sources where you use them in your text.

As the heading *Works Cited* indicates, this list contains all the works that you will cite in your text. The list simplifies documentation by permitting you to make only brief references to these works in the text. For example, when you have the following entry in your list of works cited, a citation such as "(Harbord 32–35)" fully identifies your source to readers (provided that you cite no other work by an author with the same last name).

> Harbord, Janet. *The Evolution of Film: Rethinking Film Studies*. Cambridge:
> Polity, 2007. Print.

Other names for such a listing are *Bibliography* (literally, "description of books") and *Literature Cited*. Usually, however, the broader title *Works Cited* is most appropriate, since research papers often draw not only on printed books and articles but also on films, recordings, Web publications, and other nonprint sources.

Titles used for other kinds of source lists include *Annotated Bibliography*, *Works Consulted*, and *Selected Bibliography*. An annotated bibliography, also called *Annotated List of Works Cited*, contains descriptive or evaluative comments on the sources. (For more information on such listings, see James L. Harner, *On Compiling an Annotated Bibliography* [2nd ed.; New York: MLA, 2000; print].)

> Harbord, Janet. *The Evolution of Film: Rethinking Film Studies*. Cambridge:
> Polity, 2007. Print. A synthesis of classic film theory and an
> examination of the contemporary situation of film studies that draws
> on recent scholarship in philosophy, anthropology, and media
> studies.

The title *Works Consulted* indicates that the list is not confined to works cited in the paper. The headings *Selected Bibliography, Selected List of Works Consulted*, and *Suggestions for Further Reading* are appropriate for lists that suggest readings.

5.3.2. Placement of the List of Works Cited

The list of works cited appears at the end of the paper. Begin the list on a new page and number each page, continuing the page numbers of the text. For example, if the text of your research paper ends on page 10, the works-cited list begins on page 11. The page number appears in the upper right-hand corner, half an inch from the top and

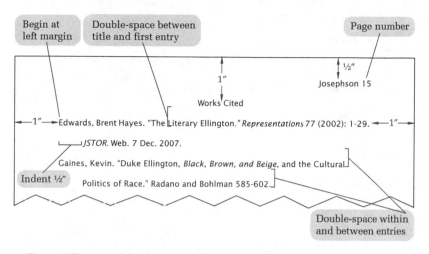

Fig. 12. The top of the first page of a works-cited list.

flush with the right margin (see fig. 12). Center the title, *Works Cited*, an inch from the top of the page. Double-space between the title and the first entry. Begin each entry flush with the left margin; if an entry runs more than one line, indent the subsequent line or lines one-half inch from the left margin. This format is sometimes called *hanging indention*, and you can set your word processor to create it automatically for a group of paragraphs. Hanging indention makes alphabetical lists easier to use. Double-space the entire list, both between and within entries. Continue the list on as many pages as necessary.

5.3.3. Arrangement of Entries

Entries in a works-cited list are arranged in alphabetical order, which helps the reader to find the entry corresponding to a citation in the text. In general, alphabetize entries in the list of works cited by the author's last name, using the letter-by-letter system. In this system, the order of names is determined by the letters before the commas that separate last names and first names. Spaces and other punctuation marks are ignored. The letters following the commas are considered only when two or more last names are identical. The following examples are alphabetized letter by letter. (For more information on alphabetizing foreign names, see 3.8.)

Descartes, René
De Sica, Vittorio

MacDonald, George
McCullers, Carson

Morris, Robert
Morris, William
Morrison, Toni

Saint-Exupéry, Antoine de
St. Denis, Ruth

If two or more entries citing coauthors begin with the same name, alphabetize by the last names of the second authors listed.

Scholes, Robert, and Robert Kellogg
Scholes, Robert, Carl H. Klaus, and Michael Silverman
Scholes, Robert, and Eric S. Rabkin

If the author's name is unknown, alphabetize by the title, ignoring any initial *A*, *An*, or *The* or the equivalent in another language. For example, the title *An Encyclopedia of the Latin American Novel* would be alphabetized under *e* rather than *a*, the title *Le théâtre en France au Moyen Âge* under *t* rather than *l*. If the title begins with a numeral, alphabetize the title as if the numeral were spelled out. For instance, *1914: The Coming of the First World War* should be alphabetized as if it began "Nineteen-Fourteen. . . ." (But see 5.7.14 on alphabetizing titles from the United States Code.)

If the name of an author whose works you used appears in various spellings in the works (e.g., Virgil, Vergil), consolidate all the entries for the sources under the preferred variant in your works-cited list. If your sources include works published under both an author's real name and a pseudonym, either consolidate the entries under the better-known name or list them separately, with a cross-reference at the real name and with the real name in square brackets after the pseudonym (see 5.3.6 on cross-references). If works by a woman are published under both her natal and her married names, list them separately, with cross-references at both names.

Bakhtin, M. M. (*see also* Vološinov, V. N.). *The Dialogic Imagination: Four Essays*. Ed. Michael Holquist. Trans. Caryl Emerson and Holquist. Austin: U of Texas P, 1981. *Google Book Search*. Web. 3 Dec. 2007.

Penelope, Julia (*see also* Stanley, Julia P.). "John Simon and the 'Dragons of Eden.'" *College English* 44.8 (1982): 848-54. *JSTOR*. Web. 3 Dec. 2007.

Stanley, Julia P. (*see also* Penelope, Julia). "'Correctness,' 'Appropriateness,' and the Uses of English." *College English* 41.3 (1979): 330-35. *JSTOR*. Web. 3 Dec. 2007.

Vološinov, V. N. [M. M. Bakhtin]. *Marxism and the Philosophy of Language*. Trans. Ladislav Matejka and I. R. Titunik. Cambridge: Harvard UP, 1986. *Google Book Search*. Web. 3 Dec. 2007.

Other kinds of bibliographies may be arranged differently. An annotated list, a list of works consulted, or a list of selected readings for a historical study, for example, may be organized chronologically by publication date. Some bibliographies are divided into sections and the items alphabetized in each section. A list may be broken down into primary and secondary sources or into different research media or genres (books, articles, films). Alternatively, it may be arranged by subject matter (literature and law, law in literature, law as literature), by period (classical utopia, Renaissance utopia), or by area (Egyptian mythology, Greek mythology, Norse mythology).

5.3.4. Two or More Works by the Same Author

To cite two or more works by the same author, give the name in the first entry only. Thereafter, in place of the name, type three hyphens, followed by a period and the title. The three hyphens stand for exactly the same name as in the preceding entry. If the person named edited, translated, or compiled the work, place a comma (not a period) after the three hyphens, and write the appropriate abbreviation (*ed.*, *trans.*, or *comp.*) before giving the title. If the same person served as, say, the editor of two or more works listed consecutively, the abbreviation *ed.* must be repeated with each entry. This sort of label does not affect the order in which entries appear; works listed under the same name are alphabetized by title.

Borroff, Marie. *Language and the Poet: Verbal Artistry in Frost, Stevens, and Moore.* Chicago: U of Chicago P, 1979. Print.

---, trans. *Pearl.* New York: Norton, 1977. Print.

---. "Sound Symbolism as Drama in the Poetry of Robert Frost." *PMLA* 107.1 (1992): 131-44. *JSTOR.* Web. 13 May 2008.

---, ed. *Wallace Stevens: A Collection of Critical Essays.* Englewood Cliffs: Prentice, 1963. Print.

If a single author cited in an entry is also the first of multiple authors in the following entry, repeat the name in full; do not substitute three hyphens. Repeat the name in full whenever you cite the same person as part of a different authorship. The three hyphens are never used in combination with persons' names.

Tannen, Deborah. *Talking Voices: Repetition, Dialogue, and Imagery in Conversational Discourse.* 2nd ed. New York: Cambridge UP, 2007. Print. Studies in Interactional Sociolinguistics 26.

---. *You're Wearing That? Understanding Mothers and Daughters in Conversation.* New York: Ballantine-Random, 2006. Print.

Tannen, Deborah, and Roy O. Freedle, eds. *Linguistics in Context: Connecting Observation and Understanding.* Norwood: Ablex, 1988. Print.

Tannen, Deborah, and Muriel Saville-Troike, eds. *Perspectives on Silence.* Norwood: Ablex, 1985. Print.

5.3.5. Two or More Works by the Same Authors

To cite two or more works by the same authors, give the names in the first entry only. Thereafter, in place of the names, type three hyphens, followed by a period and the title. The three hyphens stand for exactly the same names, in the same order, as in the preceding entry. Authors' names whose order in the source work is different from that of the previously listed names should be listed in the same order as in the work and alphabetized appropriately.

Gilbert, Sandra M., and Susan Gubar, eds. *The Female Imagination and the Modernist Aesthetic.* New York: Gordon, 1986. Print.

---. "Sexual Linguistics: Gender, Language, Sexuality." *New Literary History* 16.3 (1985): 515-43. *JSTOR.* Web. 26 June 2007.

5.3.6. Cross-References

To avoid unnecessary repetition in citing two or more works from the same collection, you may create a complete entry for the collection and cross-reference individual pieces to the entry. In a cross-reference, state the author and the title of the piece, the last name of the editor or editors of the collection, and the inclusive page or reference numbers. If the piece is a translation, add the name of the translator after the title, unless one person translated the entire collection.

Agee, James. "Knoxville: Summer of 1915." Oates and Atwan 171-75.

Atwan, Robert. Foreword. Oates and Atwan x-xvi.

Kingston, Maxine Hong. "No Name Woman." Oates and Atwan 383-94.

Oates, Joyce Carol, and Robert Atwan, eds. *The Best American Essays of the Century.* Boston: Houghton, 2000. Print.

Rodriguez, Richard. "Aria: A Memoir of a Bilingual Childhood." Oates and Atwan 447-66.

Walker, Alice. "Looking for Zora." Oates and Atwan 395-411.

If you list two or more works under the editor's name, however, add the title (or a shortened version of it) to the cross-reference.

Angelou, Maya. "Pickin Em Up and Layin Em Down." Baker, *Norton Book* 276-78.

Baker, Russell, ed. *The Norton Book of Light Verse.* New York: Norton, 1986. Print.

---, ed. *Russell Baker's Book of American Humor.* New York: Norton, 1993. Print.

Hurston, Zora Neale. "Squinch Owl Story." Baker, *Russell Baker's Book* 458-59.

Lebowitz, Fran. "Manners." Baker, *Russell Baker's Book* 556-59.

Lennon, John. "The Fat Budgie." Baker, *Norton Book* 357-58.

5.4. CITING PERIODICAL PRINT PUBLICATIONS

5.4.1. Introduction

Print periodicals—newspapers, magazines, journals—appear regularly at fixed intervals. Unlike newspapers and magazines, which typically appear daily, weekly, or monthly and include varied forms of writing on diverse topics, journals are usually issued no more than four times a year and address a discrete domain of scholarly, professional, or aesthetic concern through critical or creative writing. Also unlike newspapers and magazines, most journals are paginated continuously throughout each annual volume—that is, if the first issue for a year ends on page 130, the second issue begins on page 131 and so forth. Some scholarly journals do not number pages continuously throughout an annual volume but begin each issue on page 1. Include the issue number, whenever available, along with the volume number in a citation for any journal, since the issue number is essential for identifying issues paginated separately in annual volumes and is useful even for specifying consecutively paginated issues (e.g., in retrievals by interlibrary loan or from online databases). The volume and issue numbers of newspapers and magazines are not cited.

Entries for publications in print periodicals consist of several elements in a prescribed sequence. This list shows most of the possible components of an entry for an article in a print periodical and the order in which they are normally arranged:

1. Author's name (for more than one author, see 5.5.4; for a corporate author, see 5.5.5; for an anonymous work, see 5.5.9)
2. Title of the article (in quotation marks)
3. Name of the periodical (italicized)
4. Series number or name (if relevant; see 5.4.4)
5. Volume number (for a scholarly journal)
6. Issue number (if available, for a scholarly journal)
7. Date of publication (for a scholarly journal, the year; for other periodicals, the day, month, and year, as available)
8. Inclusive page numbers
9. Medium of publication consulted (*Print*)
10. Supplementary information (see esp. 5.4.12)

Section 5.4.2 explains how to formulate the entry for the most common kind of periodical print publication, an article in a scholarly journal. The rest of 5.4 explains how to cite additional items. For information on citing periodical publications accessed through the Web, see 5.6.3–4. For a Web site sponsored by a newspaper or magazine, see 5.6.2b.

5.4.2. An Article in a Scholarly Journal

Since printed journals have been and continue to be fundamental outlets for scholarship, articles in them will be among the most common sources in the works-cited lists you compile. The works-cited-list entry for an article in a printed scholarly journal has three main divisions:

Author's name. "Title of the article." Publication information.

Here is an example:

Piper, Andrew. "Rethinking the Print Object: Goethe and the Book of Everything." *PMLA* 121.1 (2006). 124-38. Print.

Author's Name

Take the author's name from the beginning or the end of the article (see fig. 13). Reverse the name for alphabetizing, adding a comma after the last name. Put a period after the complete name.

Piper, Andrew.

Apart from reversing the order, give the author's name as it appears in the article. Never abbreviate a name given in full. If, for example, the journal lists the author as "Carleton Brown," do not enter the name as "Brown, C." But use initials if the journal does. For additional advice on this topic, see 5.5.2.

Title of the Article

In general, follow the recommendations for titles given in 3.6. State the full title of the article, enclosed in quotation marks (not italicized). Unless the title has its own concluding punctuation (e.g., a question mark), put a period before the closing quotation mark (see fig. 13).

Piper, Andrew. "Rethinking the Print Object: Goethe and the Book of Everything."

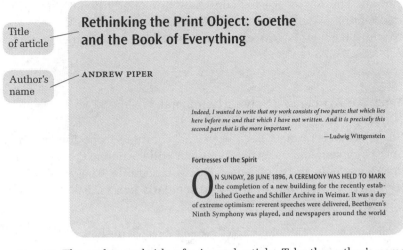

Title of article

Author's name

Fig. 13. The author and title of a journal article. Take the author's name and the title from the article itself, not from the journal cover or the table of contents.

Publication Information

In general, after the title of the article, give the journal title (italicized), the volume number, a period, the issue number, the year of publication (in parentheses), a colon, the inclusive page numbers, a period, the medium of publication consulted, and a period.

Piper, Andrew. "Rethinking the Print Object: Goethe and the Book of
    Everything." *PMLA* 121.1 (2006): 124-38. Print.

Take these facts directly from the journal, not from a source such as a bibliography. Publication information usually appears on the cover or title page of a journal (see fig. 14). Omit any introductory article in the title of an English-language journal (*William and Mary Quarterly*, not *The William and Mary Quarterly*), but retain articles before titles of non-English-language journals (*La rivista dalmatica*). For newspaper titles, see 5.4.5.

The journal's cover or title page usually displays a volume number and may include an issue number ("Number 3") or a month or season before the year ("January 1998," "Fall 2006"). In general, the issues of a journal published in a single year compose one volume. Volumes are usually numbered in continuous sequence—each new volume is

Fig. 14. The publication information for a scholarly journal. Take the information—the journal title, volume number, issue number, and year of publication—from the cover or title page of the journal. Omit any introductory *A*, *An*, or *The* in the journal title, and italicize the journal title. Place a period between the volume and issue numbers. A colon, the inclusive page numbers for the entire article, and the medium of publication consulted normally conclude the citation: "*Critical Inquiry* 34.2 (2008): 313–35. Print."

numbered one higher than its predecessor—while the numbering of issues starts over with 1 in each new volume. Most printed scholarly journals are paginated continuously throughout each annual volume. Then, at the end of the year, the issues in the volume are bound together and shelved in the library by year number. If you are looking for the print version of the article by Andrew Piper cited above, for example, which was published in 2006 in an issue of the scholarly journal *PMLA*, you will likely locate it in your library in what appears to be a book with "*PMLA* 2006" printed on the spine. In that volume, you will find all the issues of *PMLA* published during 2006, and the page numbering of the volume will be continuous, from page 1 of the first issue through to the final page of the last issue published in the year.

In your entry, the volume number follows the title of the journal; do not precede the volume number with the word *volume* or the abbreviation *vol*. Add a period and the issue number directly after the volume number, without any intervening space: "14.2" signifies volume 14, issue 2; "10.3–4," volume 10, issues 3 and 4 combined. Some scholarly journals use issue numbers alone, without volume numbers; on citing articles in such journals, see 5.4.3. Annuals, which are published only once a year, are usually numbered in sequence. Some annuals, such as *Profession*, are not numbered; instead, each issue's place in the series is identified by the year of publication. Entries for newspapers and magazines do not require volume and issue numbers (see 5.4.5–6). Your instructor or a librarian will help you if you are uncertain whether a periodical is a magazine or a scholarly journal. If any doubt remains, include the volume number.

The inclusive page numbers cited should encompass the complete article, not just the portion you used. (Specific page references appear parenthetically at appropriate places in your text; see ch. 6.) Follow the rules for writing inclusive numbers in 3.5.6. Write the page reference for the first page exactly as shown in the source ("198–232," "A32–34," "TV-15–18," "lxii–lxv"). If an article is not printed on consecutive pages—if, for example, after beginning on page 6 it skips to page 10—write only the first page number and a plus sign, leaving no intervening space: "6+." (See examples in 5.4.5–6.)

Here are additional examples of the basic entry for an article printed in a scholarly journal:

Barthelme, Frederick. "Architecture." *Kansas Quarterly* 13.3-4 (1981): 77-80. Print.

Brueggeman, Brenda Jo, and Debra A. Moddelmog. "Coming-Out Pedagogy: Risking Identity in Language and Literature Classrooms." *Pedagogy* 2.3 (2002): 311-35. Print.

Hernández-Reguant, Ariana. "Copyrighting Che: Art and Authorship under Cuban Late Socialism." *Public Culture* 16.1 (2004): 1-29. Print.

MLA Committee on the Status of Women in the Profession. "Women in the Profession, 2000." *Profession* (2000): 191-217. Print.

Tibullus, Albius. "How to Be Tibullus." Trans. David Wray. *Chicago Review* 48.4 (2002-03): 102-06. Print.

Williams, Linda. "Of Kisses and Ellipses: The Long Adolescence of American Movies." *Critical Inquiry* 32.2 (2006): 288-340. Print.

5.4.3. An Article in a Scholarly Journal That Uses Only Issue Numbers

Some scholarly journals do not use volume numbers at all, numbering issues only. Cite the issue numbers of such journals alone.

Kafka, Ben. "The Demon of Writing: Paperwork, Public Safety, and the Reign of Terror." *Representations* 98 (2007): 1-24. Print.

Litvak, Lily. "La Buena Nueva: Cultura y prensa anarquista (1880-1913)." *Revista de Occidente* 304 (2006): 5-18. Print.

5.4.4. An Article in a Scholarly Journal with More Than One Series

Some scholarly journals have been published in more than one series. In citing a journal with numbered series, write the number (an arabic digit with the appropriate ordinal suffix: *2nd*, *3rd*, *4th*, etc.) and the abbreviation *ser.* between the journal title and the volume number.

> Striner, Richard. "Political Newtonism: The Cosmic Model of Politics in
>
> Europe and America." *William and Mary Quarterly* 3rd ser. 52.4
>
> (1995): 583-608. Print.

For a journal divided into a new series and an original series, indicate the series with *ns* or *os* before the volume number.

> Helmling, Steven. "A Martyr to Happiness: Why Adorno Matters." *Kenyon*
>
> *Review* ns 28.4 (2006): 156-72. Print.

5.4.5. An Article in a Newspaper

To cite an English-language newspaper, give the name as it appears on the masthead but omit any introductory article (*New York Times*, not *The New York Times*). Retain articles before the names of non-English-language newspapers (*Le monde*). If the city of publication is not included in the name of a locally published newspaper, add the city in square brackets, not italicized, after the name: "*Star-Ledger* [Newark]." For nationally published newspapers (e.g., *Wall Street Journal*, *Chronicle of Higher Education*), you need not add the city of publication. Next give the complete date—day, month, and year. Abbreviate the names of all months except May, June, and July (see 7.2). Do not give the volume and issue numbers even if they are listed. If an edition is named on the masthead, add a comma after the date and specify the edition (e.g., *natl. ed.*, *late ed.*), because different editions of the same issue of a newspaper contain different material. Follow the edition—or the date if there is no edition—with a colon and the page number or numbers. Then state the medium of publication consulted. For sections labeled with letters and paginated separately, the section letter is sometimes part of each page number: "A1," "B1," "C5," "D3." Copy the page number or numbers exactly. Here are examples illustrating how an article appeared in different sections of two editions of the *New York Times* on the same day:

> Jeromack, Paul. "This Once, a David of the Art World Does Goliath a Favor." *New York Times* 13 July 2002, late ed.: B7+. Print.

> Jeromack, Paul. "This Once, a David of the Art World Does Goliath a Favor." *New York Times* 13 July 2002, New England ed.: A13+. Print.

Sometimes a section is paginated separately and given a section number or letter, but the section designation is not part of the page numbers. In this case, put a comma after the date (or after the edition, if any) and add the abbreviation *sec.*, the appropriate letter or number, a colon, the page number or numbers, and the medium of publication.

> Haughney, Christine. "Women Unafraid of Condo Commitment." *New York Times* 10 Dec. 2006, late ed., sec. 11: 1+. Print.

For sections paginated separately and designated only by title, not by number or letter, give the title before the abbreviation *sec.*

> Dwyer, Jim. "Yeats Meets the Digital Age, Full of Passionate Intensity." *New York Times* 20 July 2008, early ed., Arts and Leisure sec.: 1+. Print.

Newspaper articles are often not printed on consecutive pages—for example, an article might begin on page 1, then skip to page 16. For such articles, write only the first page number and a plus sign, leaving no intervening space: "6+," "C3+." The parenthetical reference in the text tells readers the exact page from which material was used.

Here are additional examples from newspapers:

> Alaton, Salem. "So, Did They Live Happily Ever After?" *Globe and Mail* [Toronto] 27 Dec. 1997: D1+. Print.

> McKay, Peter A. "Stocks Feel the Dollar's Weight." *Wall Street Journal* 4 Dec. 2006: C1+. Print.

> Perrier, Jean-Louis. "La vie artistique de Budapest perturbée par la loi du marché." *Le monde* 26 Feb. 1997: 28. Print.

For a Web site sponsored by a newspaper, see 5.6.2b.

5.4.6. An Article in a Magazine

To cite a magazine published every week or every two weeks, give the complete date (beginning with the day and abbreviating the month,

Volume 255		July 7,	Month, day,
Number 27	**PW**	2008	and year of
ISSN 0000-0019	PUBLISHERS WEEKLY®		publication

Fig. 15. The publication information for a magazine. When you document works in a magazine, do not cite the volume and issue numbers, even if they are printed in the issue. Give the full date or the month or months and year. The entry for a magazine article ends with a colon, the page-number range of the article, and the medium of publication consulted: "*Publishers Weekly* 7 July 2008: 30–31. Print."

except for May, June, and July; see 7.2), followed by a colon, the inclusive page numbers of the article, and the medium of publication consulted. If the article is not printed on consecutive pages, write only the first page number and a plus sign, leaving no intervening space. Do not give the volume and issue numbers even if they are listed (see fig. 15).

McEvoy, Dermot. "Little Books, Big Success." *Publishers Weekly* 30 Oct.

2006: 26-28. Print.

Weintraub, Arlene, and Laura Cohen. "A Thousand-Year Plan for Nuclear

Waste." *Business Week* 6 May 2002: 94-96. Print.

To cite a magazine published every month or every two months, give the month or months and year. If the article is not printed on consecutive pages, write only the first page number and a plus sign, leaving no intervening space. Do not give the volume and issue numbers even if they are listed.

Kates, Robert W. "Population and Consumption: What We Know, What We

Need to Know." *Environment* Apr. 2000: 10-19. Print.

Laskin, Sheldon H. "Jena: A Missed Opportunity for Healing." *Tikkun* Nov.-

Dec. 2007: 29+. Print.

Wood, Jason. "Spellbound." *Sight and Sound* Dec. 2005: 28-30. Print.

For a Web site sponsored by a magazine, see 5.6.2b.

5.4.7. A Review

To cite a review, give the reviewer's name and the title of the review (if there is one); then write *Rev. of* (neither italicized nor enclosed in quotation marks), the title of the work reviewed, a comma, the word *by*, and the name of the author. If the work of someone other than an author—say, an editor, a translator, or a director—is under review, use the appropriate abbreviation, such as *ed.*, *trans.*, or *dir.*, instead of *by*. For a review of a performance, add pertinent information about the production (see the sample entry for Tommasini). If more than one work is under review, list titles and authors in the order given at the beginning of the review (see the entry for Bordewich). Conclude the entry with the name of the periodical and the rest of the publication information.

If the review is titled but unsigned, begin the entry with the title of the review and alphabetize by that title (see the entry for "Racial Stereotype Busters"). If the review is neither titled nor signed, begin the entry with *Rev. of* and alphabetize under the title of the work reviewed (see the entry for *Oxford Bible Atlas*).

Bordewich, Fergus M. Rev. of *Once They Moved like the Wind: Cochise, Geronimo, and the Apache Wars*, by David Roberts, and *Brave Are My People: Indian Heroes Not Forgotten*, by Frank Waters. *Smithsonian* Mar. 1994: 125-31. Print.

Mendelsohn, Daniel. "September 11 at the Movies." Rev. of *United 93*, dir. Paul Greengrass, and *World Trade Center*, dir. Oliver Stone. *New York Review of Books* 21 Sept. 2006: 43-46. Print.

Rev. of *Oxford Bible Atlas*, 4th ed., by Adrian Curtis. *Kirkus Reviews* 1 Sept. 2007: 4. Print.

"Racial Stereotype Busters: Black Scientists Who Made a Difference." Rev. of *American Science Leaders. Journal of Blacks in Higher Education* 25 (1999): 133-34. Print.

Tommasini, Anthony. "A Feminist Look at Sophocles." Rev. of *Jocasta*, by Ruth Schonthal and Hélène Cixous. Voice and Vision Theater Company, Cornelia Connelly Center for Educ., New York. *New York Times* 11 June 1998, late ed.: E5. Print.

5.4.8. An Abstract in an Abstracts Journal

An abstracts journal publishes summaries of journal articles and of other literature. If you are citing an abstract, begin the entry with the publication information for the original work. Then add the relevant information for the journal from which you derived the abstract—title (italicized), volume number, issue number, year (in parentheses, followed by a colon and a space), item number or, when the abstract is not numbered, inclusive page numbers, and medium of publication. Place a period between the volume and issue numbers. Precede an item number with the word *item*. If the title of the journal does not make clear that you are citing an abstract, add the word *Abstract*, neither italicized nor in quotation marks, immediately after the original publication information.

Dissertation Abstracts International (*DAI*) has a long and complex history that might affect the way you cite an abstract in it. Before volume 30 (1969), *Dissertation Abstracts International* was titled *Dissertation Abstracts* (*DA*). From volume 27 to volume 36, *DA* and *DAI* were paginated in two series: A, for humanities and social sciences, and B, for sciences and engineering. With volume 37, *DAI* added a third separately paginated section, C, for abstracts of European dissertations; in 1989 this section expanded its coverage to include institutions throughout the world. The abstracts in *DAI* are available from ProQuest. (For recommendations on citing dissertations themselves, see 5.5.25–26. On citing dissertation abstracts in an online database, see 5.6.4.)

> Pineda, Marcela. "Desire in Postmodern Discourse: An Analysis of the Poetry of Cristina Peri Rossi." Diss. Indiana U, 2004. *DAI* 65.12 (2005): item DA3156288. Print.

5.4.9. An Anonymous Article

If no author's name is given for the article you are citing, begin the entry with the title. Ignore any initial *A*, *An*, or *The* when you alphabetize the entry. Do not include the name of a wire service or news bureau.

> "It Barks! It Kicks! It Scores!" *Newsweek* 30 July 2001: 12. Print.

> "Where Angels No Longer Fear to Tread." *Economist* 22 Mar. 2008: 89+. Print.

5.4.10. An Editorial

If you are citing a signed editorial, begin with the author's name, give the title, and then add the descriptive label *Editorial*, neither italicized nor enclosed in quotation marks. Conclude with the appropriate publication information. If the editorial is unsigned, begin with the title and continue in the same way.

Gergen, David. "A Question of Values." Editorial. *US News and World Report* 11 Feb. 2002: 72. Print.

"It's Subpoena Time." Editorial. *New York Times* 8 June 2007, late ed.: A28. Print.

5.4.11. A Letter to the Editor

To identify a letter to the editor, add the descriptive label *Letter* after the name of the author, but do not italicize the word or place it in quotation marks.

Safer, Morley. Letter. *New York Times* 31 Oct. 1993, late ed., sec. 2: 4. Print.

Schlesinger, Arthur, Jr. Letter. *New York Review of Books* 8 Apr. 2004: 84. Print.

Identify a published response to a letter as "Reply to letter of . . . ," adding the name of the writer of the initial letter. Do not italicize this phrase or place it in quotation marks.

Shih, Shu-mei. Reply to letter of Sabarimuthu Carlos. *PMLA* 119.3 (2004): 555-56. Print.

5.4.12. A Serialized Article

To cite a serialized article or a series of related articles published in more than one issue of a periodical, include all bibliographic information in one entry if each installment has the same author and title.

Sedgwick, Eve Kosofsky. "Epistemology of the Closet." *Raritan* 7.4 (1988): 39-69; 8.1 (1988): 102-30. Print.

If the installments bear different titles, list each one separately. You may include a brief supplementary description at the end of the entry to indicate that the article is part of a series.

> Gellman, Barton, and Jo Becker. "'A Different Understanding with the
> President.'" *Washington Post* 24 June 2007, district ed.: A1+. Print.
> Pt. 1 of a series, Angler: The Cheney Vice Presidency.
>
> ---. "Leaving No Tracks." *Washington Post* 27 June 2007, district final ed.:
> A1+. Print. Pt. 4 of a series, Angler: The Cheney Vice Presidency,
> begun 24 June 2007.
>
> ---. "A Strong Push from Backstage." *Washington Post* 26 June 2007,
> district final ed.: A1+. Print. Pt. 3 of a series, Angler: The Cheney
> Vice Presidency, begun 24 June 2007.
>
> ---. "The Unseen Path to Cruelty." *Washington Post* 25 June 2007, district
> and Maryland final ed.: A1+. Print. Pt. 2 of a series, Angler: The
> Cheney Vice Presidency, begun 24 June 2007.

5.4.13. A Special Issue

To cite an entire special issue of a journal, begin the entry with the name of the person or persons who edited the issue (if given on the title page), followed by a comma and the abbreviation *ed.* or *eds.* Next give the title of the special issue (italicized) and a period, followed by *Spec. issue of* and the name of the journal (the name is italicized). Conclude the entry with the journal's volume and issue numbers (separated by a period: "9.1"), the year of publication (in parentheses), a colon, a space, the complete pagination of the issue, a period, the medium of publication consulted, and a period. (To cite a book that is a reprint of a special issue of a journal, see 5.5.16.)

> Appiah, Kwame Anthony, and Henry Louis Gates, Jr., eds. *Identities*. Spec.
> issue of *Critical Inquiry* 18.4 (1992): 625-884. Print.
>
> Perret, Delphine, and Marie-Denise Shelton, eds. *Maryse Condé*. Spec.
> issue of *Callaloo* 18.3 (1995): 535-711. Print.
>
> *Symposium Issue: Race, Ethnicity, and Civic Identity in the Americas*. Spec.
> issue of *American Literary History* 17.3 (2005): 419-644. Print.

If you are citing one article from a special issue and wish to indicate complete publication information about the issue, use the following form:

> Makward, Christiane. "Reading Maryse Condé's Theater." *Maryse Condé.*
>   Ed. Delphine Perret and Marie-Denise Shelton. Spec. issue of *Callaloo*
>   18.3 (1995): 681-89. Print.

5.5. CITING NONPERIODICAL PRINT PUBLICATIONS

5.5.1. Introduction

Entries for nonperiodical print publications, such as books and pamphlets, consist of several elements in a prescribed sequence. This list shows most of the possible components of a book entry and the order in which they are normally arranged:

1. Name of the author, editor, compiler, or translator (for more than one author, see 5.5.4; for a corporate author, see 5.5.5; for an anonymous work, see 5.5.9)
2. Title of the work (italicized)
3. Edition used (see 5.5.13)
4. Number(s) of the volume(s) used (see 5.5.14)
5. City of publication, name of the publisher, and year of publication
6. Medium of publication consulted (*Print*)
7. Supplementary bibliographic information and annotation (see esp. 5.5.15)

Section 5.5.2 explains how to formulate the entry for the most common kind of nonperiodical print publication, a book by a single author. The rest of 5.5 explains how to cite additional items.

5.5.2. A Book by a Single Author

One of the most common items in students' works-cited lists is the entry for a book by a single author. Such an entry characteristically has three main divisions:

Author's name. *Title of the book.* Publication information.

Here is an example:

> Franke, Damon. *Modernist Heresies: British Literary History, 1883-1924.*
> Columbus: Ohio State UP, 2008. Print.

Author's Name

Reverse the author's name for alphabetizing, adding a comma after the last name (e.g., Porter, Katherine Anne). Put a period after the complete name (see fig. 16).

> Franke, Damon.

Apart from reversing the order, give the author's name as it appears on the title page. Never abbreviate a name given in full. If, for example, the title page lists the author as "Carleton Brown," do not enter the name as "Brown, C." But use initials if the title page does.

> Rowling, J. K.
> Washington, Booker T.

You may spell out a name abbreviated on the title page if you think the additional information will be helpful to readers. Put square brackets around the material you add.

> Rowling, J[oanne] K[athleen].
> Tolkien, J[ohn] R[onald] R[euel].

Similarly, you may give the real name of an author listed under a pseudonym, enclosing the added name in square brackets.

> Eliot, George [Mary Ann Evans].
> Le Carré, John [David Cornwell].

In general, omit titles, affiliations, and degrees that precede or follow names.

ON TITLE PAGE	IN WORKS-CITED LIST
Anthony T. Boyle, PhD	Boyle, Anthony T.
Sister Jean Daniel	Daniel, Jean.
Gerard Manley Hopkins, SJ	Hopkins, Gerard Manley.
Lady Mary Wortley Montagu	Montagu, Mary Wortley.
Sir Philip Sidney	Sidney, Philip.
Saint Teresa de Jesús	Teresa de Jesús.

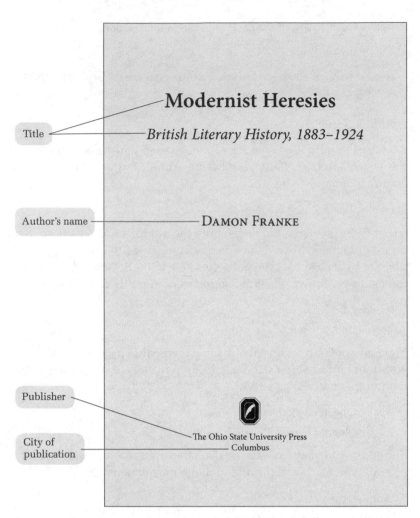

Fig. 16. The title page of a book, with full title, author's name, publisher, and city of publication. Give the author's name as on the title page. Reverse the name for alphabetizing: "Franke, Damon." Place a colon between a main title and a subtitle (unless the main title ends in a question mark or an exclamation point). Follow the capitalization rules in 3.6.1 regardless of how the title is printed on the title page: *Modernist Heresies: British Literary History, 1883–1924*. Shorten the publisher's name, following the guidelines in 7.5: "Columbus: Ohio State UP." See fig. 17 for the publication date of this book.

A suffix that is an essential part of the name—like *Jr.* or a roman numeral—appears after the given name, preceded by a comma.

Rockefeller, John D., IV.

Rust, Arthur George, Jr.

Title of the Book

In general, follow the recommendations for titles provided in 3.6. State the full title of the book, including any subtitle, as given on the title page of the book (see fig. 16). If the book has a subtitle, put a colon directly after the main title, unless the main title ends in a question mark or an exclamation point. Place a period after the entire title (including any subtitle), unless it ends in another punctuation mark. Italicize the entire title, including any colon, subtitle, and punctuation in the title.

Franke, Damon. *Modernist Heresies: British Literary History, 1883-1924.*

Publication Information

In general, give the city of publication, the publisher's name, the year of publication, and the medium of publication consulted. Take these facts directly from the book, not from a source such as a bibliography or a library catalog. The publisher's name that appears on the title page is generally the name to cite. The name may be accompanied there by the city and date. Any publication information not available on the title page (see fig. 16) can usually be found on the copyright page (i.e., the reverse of the title page; see fig. 17) or, particularly in books published outside the United States, on a page at the back of the book. Use a colon between the city of publication and the publisher, a comma between the publisher and the date, and a period after the date. Add the medium of publication consulted, followed by a period.

Franke, Damon. *Modernist Heresies: British Literary History, 1883-1924.*
Columbus: Ohio State UP, 2008. Print.

If several cities are listed in the book, give only the first (see fig. 18). It is not necessary to identify a state, province, or country after the city name. Shorten the publisher's name, following the guidelines in 7.5. If the year of publication is not recorded on the title page, use the latest copyright date.

Date of publication

Copyright © 2008 by The Ohio State University.
All rights reserved.

Library of Congress Cataloging-in-Publication Data
Franke, Damon, 1968–
Modernist heresies : British literary history, 1883–1924 / Damon Franke.
    p. cm.
Includes bibliographical references and index.
ISBN-13: 978-0-8142-1074-1 (cloth : alk. paper)
ISBN-13: 978-0-8142-9151-1 (CD-ROM)
1. Modernism (Literature)—Great Britain. 2. English literature—20th century—History and criticism. 3. English literature—19th century—History and criticism. 4. Religion and literature—Great Britain—History—20th century. 5. Religion and literature—Great Britain—History—19th century. 6. Great Britain—Intellectual life—20th century. 7. Great Britain—Intellectual life—19th century. 8. Heretics, Christian—Great Britain—History. 9. Heresies, Christian, in literature. 10. Paganism in literature. I. Title.
PR478.M6F73 2008
820.9'112—dc22

Fig. 17. The year of publication (2008). If no year appears on the title page, look on the copyright page. Usually the latest copyright date should be cited.

Here are additional examples of the basic book entry. (For citing books in languages other than English, see 5.5.22.)

Johnson, Roberta. *Gender and Nation in the Spanish Modernist Novel.*
    Nashville: Vanderbilt UP, 2003. Print.

Kirby, David. *What Is a Book?* Athens: U of Georgia P, 2002. Print.

Kurlansky, Mark. *Salt: A World History.* New York: Walker, 2002. Print.

Le Carré, John [David Cornwell]. *The Constant Gardener.* New York:
    Scribner's, 2001. Print.

Rowling, J[oanne] K[athleen]. *Harry Potter and the Goblet of Fire.* New
    York: Levine-Scholastic, 2000. Print.

Tatar, Maria. *Off with Their Heads! Fairy Tales and the Culture of
    Childhood.* Princeton: Princeton UP, 1992. Print.

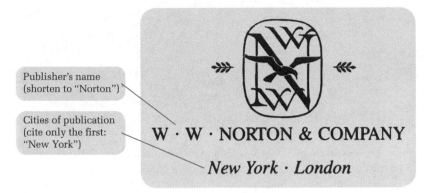

Publisher's name (shorten to "Norton")

Cities of publication (cite only the first: "New York")

W · W · NORTON & COMPANY

New York · London

Fig. 18. More than one city of publication. If several cities are listed, give only the first: "New York: Norton."

Yousef, Nancy. *Isolated Cases: The Anxieties of Autonomy in Enlightenment Philosophy and Romantic Literature.* Ithaca: Cornell UP, 2004. Print.

5.5.3. An Anthology or a Compilation

To cite an anthology or a compilation (e.g., a bibliography) that was edited or compiled by someone whose name appears on the title page, begin your entry with the name of the editor or compiler, followed by a comma and the abbreviation *ed.* or *comp.* If the person named performed more than one function—serving, say, as editor and translator—give both roles in the order in which they appear on the title page (see fig. 19).

Davis, Anita Price, comp. *North Carolina during the Great Depression: A Documentary Portrait of a Decade.* Jefferson: McFarland, 2003. Print.

Kepner, Susan Fulop, ed. and trans. *The Lioness in Bloom: Modern Thai Fiction about Women.* Berkeley: U of California P, 1996. Print.

Shell, Marc, ed. *American Babel: Literatures of the United States from Abnaki to Zuni.* Cambridge: Harvard UP, 2002. Print.

Spafford, Peter, comp. and ed. *Interference: The Story of Czechoslovakia in the Words of Its Writers.* Cheltenham: New Clarion, 1992. Print.

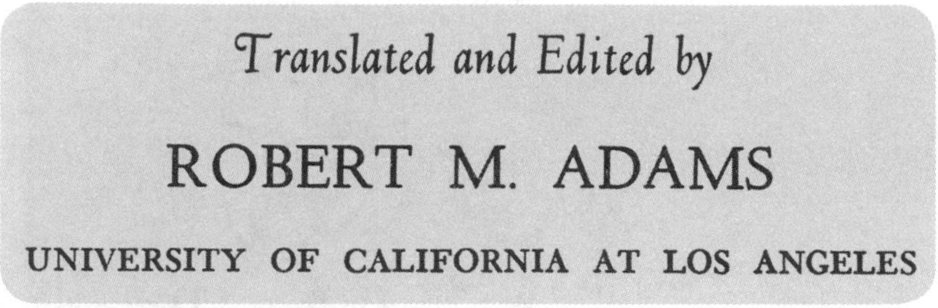

> Translated and Edited by
>
> # ROBERT M. ADAMS
>
> UNIVERSITY OF CALIFORNIA AT LOS ANGELES

Fig. 19. More than one role. If someone is credited with more than one role on the title page, cite the roles in the order in which they are listed: "Trans. and ed. Robert M. Adams."

Weisser, Susan Ostrov, ed. *Women and Romance: A Reader*. New York: New York UP, 2001. Print.

See also the sections on works in an anthology (5.5.6); introductions, prefaces, and similar parts of books (5.5.8); scholarly editions (5.5.10); and translations (5.5.11).

5.5.4. A Book by Two or More Authors

To cite a book by two or three authors, give their names in the same order as on the title page—not necessarily in alphabetical order. Reverse only the name of the first author, add a comma, and give the other name or names in normal form (Deleuze, Gilles, and Félix Guattari). Place a period after the last name. Even if the authors have the same last name, state each name in full (Lee, Matt, and Ted Lee). If the persons listed on the title page are editors, translators, or compilers, place a comma (not a period) after the final name and add the appropriate abbreviation (*eds.*, *trans.*, or *comps.* for "editors," "translators," or "compilers").

Booth, Wayne C., Gregory G. Colomb, and Joseph M. Williams. *The Craft of Research*. 2nd ed. Chicago: U of Chicago P, 2003. Print.

Broer, Lawrence R., and Gloria Holland. *Hemingway and Women: Female Critics and the Female Voice*. Tuscaloosa: U of Alabama P, 2002. Print.

Hutcheon, Linda, and Michael Hutcheon. *Bodily Charm: Living Opera*. Lincoln: U of Nebraska P, 2000. Print.

MacLaury, Robert E., Galina V. Paramei, and Don Dedrick, eds.
  Anthropology of Color: Interdisciplinary Multilevel Modeling.
  Amsterdam: Benjamins, 2007. Print.

If there are more than three authors, you may name only the first and
add *et al.* ("and others"), or you may give all names in full in the order
in which they appear on the title page (see fig. 20).

Fig. 20. More than three authors. Give either the first author's name only,
followed by *et al.* ("and others")—"Plag, Ingo, et al."—or all names in
full in the order in which they appear on the title page: "Plag, Ingo, Maria
Braun, Sabine Lappe, and Mareile Schramm."

Plag, Ingo, et al. *Introduction to English Linguistics.* Berlin: Mouton, 2007.
   Print.

or

Plag, Ingo, Maria Braun, Sabine Lappe, and Mareile Schramm. *Introduction
   to English Linguistics.* Berlin: Mouton, 2007. Print.

5.5.5. A Book by a Corporate Author

A corporate author may be a commission, an association, a committee, or any other group whose individual members are not identified
on the title page. Omit any initial article (*A, An, The*) in the name of
the corporate author (see fig. 21), and do not abbreviate its name. Cite
the book by the corporate author, even if the corporate author is the
publisher. (On citing government publications, see 5.5.20.)

National Research Council. *Beyond Six Billion: Forecasting the World's
   Population.* Washington: Natl. Acad., 2000. Print.

Fig. 21. A corporate author. In citing a book by a corporate author, omit any
initial *A, An,* or *The* in the name of the group. The entry for this publication
would begin "American Philosophical Association."

> Urban Land Institute. *Cities Post-9/11*. Washington: Urban Land Inst.,
> 2002. Print.

5.5.6. A Work in an Anthology

If you are citing an essay, a short story, a poem, or another work that appears within an anthology or some other book collection, you need to add the following information to the basic book entry (5.5.2).

Author, title, and (if relevant) translator of the part of the book being cited. Begin the entry with the author and title of the piece, normally enclosing the title in quotation marks.

> Allende, Isabel. "Toad's Mouth."

But if the work was originally published independently (as, e.g., autobiographics, plays, and novels generally are), italicize its title instead (see the sample entry below for Douglass). Follow the title of the part of the book with a period. If the anthology contains the work of more than one translator, give the translator's name next, preceded by the abbreviation *Trans.* ("Translated by").

> Allende, Isabel. "Toad's Mouth." Trans. Margaret Sayers Peden.

Then state the title of the anthology (italicized).

> Allende, Isabel. "Toad's Mouth." Trans. Margaret Sayers Peden. *A Hammock*
> *beneath the Mangoes: Stories from Latin America.*

Name of the editor, translator, or compiler of the book being cited. If all the works in the collection have the same translator or if the book has an editor or compiler, write *Trans., Ed.,* or *Comp.* ("Translated by," "Edited by," or "Compiled by"), as appropriate, after the book title and give that person's name. If the editor or compiler is also the person named earlier in the entry as the author of the work, use only the last name after *Ed.* or *Comp.*

> Allende, Isabel. "Toad's Mouth." Trans. Margaret Sayers Peden. *A Hammock*
> *beneath the Mangoes: Stories from Latin America.* Ed. Thomas Colchie.

If someone served in more than one role—say, as editor and translator—state the roles in the order in which they appear on the title page (e.g., "Ed. and trans."; see the entry below for Hanzlík). Similarly, if more than one person served in different roles, give the names in the order in which they appear on the title page: "Trans. Jessie Coulson. Ed. George Gibian."

Page numbers of the cited piece. Give the inclusive page numbers of the piece you are citing. Be sure to provide the page numbers for the entire piece, not just for the material you used. Inclusive page numbers follow the publication date and a period (on writing inclusive numbers, see 3.5.6). (If the book has no page numbers, see 5.5.24.) The entry concludes with the medium of publication consulted.

> Allende, Isabel. "Toad's Mouth." Trans. Margaret Sayers Peden. *A Hammock beneath the Mangoes: Stories from Latin America*. Ed. Thomas Colchie. New York: Plume, 1992. 83-88. Print.

Here are additional sample entries for works in anthologies:

> Bordo, Susan. "The Moral Content of Nabokov's *Lolita*." *Aesthetic Subjects*. Ed. Pamela R. Matthews and David McWhirter. Minneapolis: U of Minnesota P, 2003. 125-52. Print.
>
> Eno, Will. *Tragedy: A Tragedy*. *New Downtown Now: An Anthology of New Theater from Downtown New York*. Ed. Mac Wellman and Young Jean Lee. Introd. Jeffrey M. Jones. Minneapolis: U of Minnesota P, 2006. 49-71. Print.
>
> Fagih, Ahmed Ibrahim al-. *The Singing of the Stars*. Trans. Leila El Khalidi and Christopher Tingley. *Short Arabic Plays: An Anthology*. Ed. Salma Khadra Jayyusi. New York: Interlink, 2003. 140-57. Print.
>
> Hanzlík, Josef. "Vengeance." Trans. Ewald Osers. *Interference: The Story of Czechoslovakia in the Words of Its Writers*. Comp. and ed. Peter Spafford. Cheltenham: New Clarion, 1992. 54. Print.
>
> More, Hannah. "The Black Slave Trade: A Poem." *British Women Poets of the Romantic Era*. Ed. Paula R. Feldman. Baltimore: Johns Hopkins UP, 1997. 472-82. Print.
>
> "A Witchcraft Story." *The Hopi Way: Tales from a Vanishing Culture*. Comp. Mando Sevillano. Flagstaff: Northland, 1986. 33-42. Print.

Often the works in anthologies have been published before. If you wish to inform your reader of the date when a previously published piece other than a scholarly article first appeared, you may follow the title of the piece with the year of original publication and a period. You do not need to record the medium of previous publication.

Douglass, Frederick. *Narrative of the Life of Frederick Douglass, an American Slave, Written by Himself.* 1845. *Classic American Autobiographies.* Ed. William L. Andrews and Henry Louis Gates, Jr. New York: Lib. of Amer., 2000. 267-368. Print.

Franklin, Benjamin. "Emigration to America." 1782. *The Faber Book of America.* Ed. Christopher Ricks and William L. Vance. Boston: Faber, 1992. 24-26. Print.

To cite a previously published scholarly article in a collection, give the complete data for the earlier publication and then add *Rpt. in* ("Reprinted in"), the title of the collection, and the new publication facts. (On citing articles in print periodicals, see 5.4; on citing articles accessed through the Web, see 5.6.3–4.)

Appadurai, Arjun. "Disjuncture and Difference in the Global Cultural Economy." *Public Culture* 2.2 (1990): 1-24. Rpt. in *Colonial Discourse and Post-colonial Theory: A Reader.* Ed. Patrick Williams and Laura Chrisman. New York: Columbia UP, 1994. 324-39. Print.

Frye, Northrop. "Literary and Linguistic Scholarship in a Postliterate Age." *PMLA* 99.5 (1984): 990-95. Rpt. in *Myth and Metaphor: Selected Essays, 1974-88.* Ed. Robert D. Denham. Charlottesville: UP of Virginia, 1990. 18-27. Print.

Holladay, Hillary. "Narrative Space in Ann Petry's *Country Place.*" *Xavier Review* 16.1 (1996): 21-35. Rpt. in *Twentieth-Century Literary Criticism.* Ed. Linda Pavlovski and Scott Darga. Vol. 112. Detroit: Gale, 2002. 356-62. Print.

If the article was originally published under a different title, first state the new title and publication facts, followed by *Rpt. of* ("Reprint of"), the original title, and the original publication facts.

Bromwich, David. "Literature and Theory." *Beyond Poststructuralism: The Speculations of Theory and the Experience of Reading.* Ed. Wendell V. Harris. University Park: Pennsylvania State UP, 1996. 203-33. Print. Rpt. of "Recent Work in Literary Criticism." *Social Research* 53.3 (1986): 411-48.

Some anthologies reprint excerpts from previously published material. If the work you are citing is an excerpt, use *Excerpt from* instead of *Rpt. of.*

If you refer to more than one piece from the same collection, you may wish to cross-reference each citation to a single entry for the book (see 5.3.6). On citing articles in reference books, see 5.5.7. On citing introductions, prefaces, and the like, see 5.5.8. On citing a piece in a multivolume anthology, see 5.5.14.

5.5.7. An Article in a Reference Book

Treat an encyclopedia article or a dictionary entry as you would a piece in a collection (5.5.6). If the article is signed, give the author's name first (often articles in reference books are signed with initials identified elsewhere in the work); if it is unsigned, give the title first.

When citing widely used reference books, especially those that frequently appear in new editions, do not give full publication information. For such works, list only the edition (if stated), the year of publication, and the medium of publication consulted.

> "Azimuthal Equidistant Projection." *Merriam-Webster's Collegiate Dictionary*. 11th ed. 2003. Print.
>
> "Ginsburg, Ruth Bader." *Who's Who in America*. 62nd ed. 2008. Print.
>
> "Japan." *The Encyclopedia Americana*. 2004 ed. Print.

If you are citing a specific entry among several for the same word, add *Entry* and the appropriate designation (e.g., number).

> "Manual." Entry 2. *Webster's Third New International Dictionary*. 1981. Print.

If you are citing a specific definition among several, add the abbreviation *Def.* ("Definition") and the appropriate designation (e.g., number, letter).

> "Noon." Def. 4b. *The Oxford English Dictionary*. 2nd ed. 1989. Print.

When citing specialized reference works, however, especially those that have appeared in only one edition, give full publication information, omitting inclusive page numbers for the article if the dictionary or encyclopedia is arranged alphabetically. (On multivolume works, see 5.5.14.)

> Allen, Anita L. "Privacy in Health Care." *Encyclopedia of Bioethics*. Ed. Stephen G. Post. 3rd ed. Vol. 4. New York: Macmillan-Thomson, 2004. Print.

Jödicke, Ansgar. "Alchemy." *Religion Past and Present: Encyclopedia of Theology and Religion.* Ed. Hans Dieter Betz, Don S. Browning, Bernd Janowski, and Eberhard Jüngel. Vol. 1. Leiden: Brill, 2007. Print.

5.5.8. An Introduction, a Preface, a Foreword, or an Afterword

To cite an introduction, a preface, a foreword, or an afterword, begin with the name of its author and then give the name of the part being cited, capitalized but neither italicized nor enclosed in quotation marks (*Introduction, Preface, Foreword, Afterword*). Cite the author of the complete work after its title, giving the full name, in normal order, preceded by the word *By.* If the author of the complete work is also the writer of the introduction, preface, foreword, or afterword, use only the last name after *By* (see 5.2). Continue with full publication information (including the name of any editor or translator of the complete work), the inclusive page numbers, and, finally, the medium of publication consulted. If the complete work is by a single author and is not edited by someone else, do not create an entry for an introduction, a preface, or another part by the author. Instead, create an entry for the work as a whole.

Borges, Jorge Luis. Foreword. *Selected Poems, 1923-1967.* By Borges. Ed. Norman Thomas Di Giovanni. New York: Delta-Dell, 1973. xv xvi. Print.

Coetzee, J. M. Introduction. *The Confusions of Young Törless.* By Robert Musil. Trans. Shaun Whiteside. New York: Penguin, 2001. v-xiii. Print.

Felstiner, John. Preface. *Selected Poems and Prose of Paul Celan.* By Paul Celan. Trans. Felstiner. New York: Norton, 2001. xix-xxxvi. Print.

Hamill, Pete. Introduction. *The Brooklyn Reader: Thirty Writers Celebrate America's Favorite Borough.* Ed. Andrea Wyatt Sexton and Alice Leccese Powers. New York: Harmony, 1994. xi-xiv. Print.

Marsalis, Wynton. Foreword. *Beyond Category: The Life and Genius of Duke Ellington.* By John Edward Hasse. New York: Simon, 1993. 13-14. Print.

Sears, Barry. Afterword. *The Jungle.* By Upton Sinclair. New York: Signet, 2001. 343-47. Print.

> White, Colin. Foreword. *The Patrick O'Brian Muster Book: Persons,*
> *Animals, Ships, and Cannon in the Aubrey-Maturin Sea Novels.* By
> Anthony Gary Brown. 2nd ed. Jefferson: McFarland, 2007. 1-2. Print.

If the introduction, preface, foreword, or afterword has a title, give
the title, enclosed in quotation marks, immediately before the name
of the part.

> Hadot, Pierre. "Prologue at Ephesus: An Enigmatic Saying." Preface. *The*
> *Veil of Isis: An Essay on the History of the Idea of Nature.* By Hadot.
> Trans. Michael Chase. Cambridge: Belknap-Harvard UP, 2006. 1-3.
> Print.
>
> Wallach, Rick. "Cormac McCarthy's Canon as Accidental Artifact."
> Introduction. *Myth, Legend, Dust: Critical Responses to Cormac*
> *McCarthy.* Ed. Wallach. New York: Manchester UP, 2000. xiv-xvi. Print.

5.5.9. An Anonymous Book

If a book has no author's or editor's name on the title page, begin the
entry with the title. Do not use *Anonymous* or *Anon.* Alphabetize
the entry by the title, ignoring any initial *A, An,* or *The.* (Note in the
sample entries that *The Holy Bible* is alphabetized under *h.*)

> *American Heritage Guide to Contemporary Usage and Style.* Boston:
> Houghton, 2005. Print.
>
> *The Holy Bible.* Wheaton: Crossway-Good News, 2003. Print. Eng. Standard
> Vers.
>
> *New York Public Library American History Desk Reference.* New York:
> Macmillan, 1997. Print.

5.5.10. A Scholarly Edition

A scholarly edition (or edition, for short) is a work prepared for publication by someone other than the author—by an editor. For example,
for a 2008 publication of Shakespeare's *Hamlet,* an editor would have
selected a version of the play from the various versions available, decided on any changes in spelling or punctuation, and perhaps added

STEPHEN CRANE

Author's name

THE RED BADGE OF COURAGE

Title

An Episode of
the American Civil War

Editor's name

EDITED BY
FREDSON BOWERS
LINDEN KENT PROFESSOR OF ENGLISH AT
THE UNIVERSITY OF VIRGINIA

Fig. 22. An edition. Unless you primarily cite the work of the editor, begin with the author's name, and give the editor's name, preceded by *Ed.*, after the title. If you wish to give the original publication date, place the year immediately after the title: "Crane, Stephen. *The Red Badge of Courage: An Episode of the American Civil War*. 1895. Ed. Fredson Bowers."

explanatory notes or written an introduction. The editor's name would most likely appear on the title page along with Shakespeare's.

To cite a scholarly edition, begin with the author's name (or the title, for an anonymous work) if you refer primarily to the text itself; give the editor's name, preceded by the abbreviation *Ed.* ("Edited by"), after the title. If for clarity you wish to indicate the original date of publication, place the year directly after the title (see the entry for Crane and fig. 22).

Austen, Jane. *Sense and Sensibility*. Ed. Claudia Johnson. New York: Norton, 2001. Print.

Crane, Stephen. *The Red Badge of Courage: An Episode of the American Civil War*. 1895. Ed. Fredson Bowers. Charlottesville: UP of Virginia, 1975. Print.

Edgeworth, Maria. Castle Rackrent *and* Ennui. Ed. Marilyn Butler. London: Penguin, 1992. Print.

Henderson, George Wylie. *Harlem Calling: The Collected Stories of George Wylie Henderson: An Alabama Writer of the Harlem Renaissance*. Ed. David G. Nicholls. Ann Arbor: U of Michigan P, 2006. Print.

> *Octovian.* Ed. Frances McSparran. London: Oxford UP, 1986. Print. Early
> English Text Soc. 289.

If your citations are generally to the work of the editor (e.g., the introduction, the notes, or editorial decisions regarding the text), begin the entry with the editor's name, followed by a comma and the abbreviation *ed.* ("editor"), and give the author's name, preceded by the word *By*, after the title.

> Bowers, Fredson, ed. *The Red Badge of Courage: An Episode of the
> American Civil War.* By Stephen Crane. 1895. Charlottesville: UP of
> Virginia, 1975. Print.

If the edition is based on a named version of the text, as editions of the Bible usually are, then the name of the version can be recorded at the end of the entry, as supplementary bibliographic information.

> *The Bible.* Introd. and notes by Robert Carroll and Stephen Prickett.
> Oxford: Oxford UP, 1998. Print. Oxford World's Classics. Authorized
> King James Vers.

Consult 5.5.14 if you are citing more than one volume of a multivolume work or if the book is a part of a multivolume edition—say, *The Works of Mark Twain*—and you wish to give supplementary information about the entire project.

5.5.11. A Translation

To cite a translation, state the author's name first if you refer primarily to the work itself; give the translator's name, preceded by *Trans.* ("Translated by"), after the title. If the book has an editor as well as a translator, give the names, with appropriate abbreviations, in the order in which they appear on the title page (see the sample entry for *Beowulf*).

> *Beowulf.* Trans. E. Talbot Donaldson. Ed. Nicholas Howe. New York:
> Norton, 2001. Print.
> Hildegard of Bingen. *Selected Writings.* Trans. Mark Atherton. New York:
> Penguin, 2001. Print.
> Homer. *The Odyssey.* Trans. Robert Fagles. New York: Viking, 1996. Print.

Mankell, Henning. *Firewall*. Trans. Ebba Segerberg. New York: Vintage-
Random, 2003. Print.

Murasaki Shikibu. *The Tale of Genji*. Trans. Edward G. Seidensticker. New
York: Knopf, 1976. Print.

If your citations are mostly to the translator's comments or choice
of wording, begin the entry with the translator's name, followed by
a comma and the abbreviation *trans.* ("translator"), and give the author's name, preceded by the word *By*, after the title. (On citing anthologies of translated works by different authors, see 5.5.6.)

Seidensticker, Edward G., trans. *The Tale of Genji*. By Murasaki Shikibu.
New York: Knopf, 1976. Print.

Although not required, some or all of the original publication facts
may be added as supplementary information at the end of the entry.

Genette, Gérard. *The Work of Art: Immanence and Transcendence*. Trans.
G. M. Goshgarian. Ithaca: Cornell UP, 1997. Print. Trans. of *L'œuvre
d'art: Immanence et transcendence*. Paris: Seuil, 1994.

Levi, Primo. *Survival in Auschwitz: The Nazi Assault on Humanity*. Trans.
Stuart Woolf. New York: Collier-Macmillan, 1987. Print. Trans. of *Se
questo è un uomo*. Torino: Einaudi, 1958.

On citing a book in a language other than English, see 5.5.22.

5.5.12. An Illustrated Book or a Graphic Narrative

Illustrations serve a range of functions in nonperiodical print publications. For a volume in which illustrations supplement the written
text, such as an illustrated edition of a literary work, give the illustrator's name, preceded by the abbreviation *Illus.* ("Illustrated by"), after
the title. If another contributor (e.g., an editor or a translator) is also
cited after the title, place the names in the order in which they appear
on the title page.

Baum, L. Frank. *The Wonderful Wizard of Oz*. Introd. Regina Barreca. Illus.
W. W. Denslow. New York: Signet-Penguin, 2006. Print.

If you refer mainly to the illustrator's work instead of the author's, begin
the entry with the illustrator's name, followed by *illus.* ("illustrator"),
and give the author's name, preceded by the word *By*, after the title.

Denslow, W. W., illus. *The Wonderful Wizard of Oz.* By L. Frank Baum.

Introd. Regina Barreca. New York: Signet-Penguin, 2006. Print.

In a graphic narrative, text and illustrations are intermingled. Format the works-cited-list entry for a graphic narrative entirely created by one person like that for any other nonperiodical print publication.

Spiegelman, Art. *Maus: A Survivor's Tale.* 2 vols. New York: Pantheon-

Random, 1986-91. Print.

Many graphic narratives are created through collaboration. Begin the entry for such a work with the name of the person whose contribution is most relevant to your research, following it with a label identifying the person's role. List other collaborators after the title in the order in which they appear on the title page, also with labels identifying their roles (see fig. 23).

Benoit, Ted, adapt. *Playback: A Graphic Novel.* By Raymond Chandler. Illus.

François Ayroles. Introd. Philippe Garnier. New York: Arcade, 2006.

Print.

Pekar, Harvey, writer. *The Quitter.* Art by Dean Haspiel. Gray tones by Lee

Loughridge. Letters by Pat Brosseau. New York: Vertigo-DC Comics,

2005. Print.

Fig. 23. A graphic narrative created collaboratively. Begin the entry with the name of the person whose contribution is most relevant to your research topic. The names of the other collaborators are listed in the order given on the title page. Label the contributors' roles using terms provided in the source: "Pekar, Harvey, writer. *The Quitter.* Art by Dean Haspiel. Gray tones by Lee Loughridge. Letters by Pat Brosseau."

If the graphic narrative is part of a multivolume work, you may add information about the series following the medium of publication. (See 5.5.14 for more guidance on citing a multivolume work.)

> Yabuki, Kentaro, writer and artist. *Showdown at the Old Castle*. Eng.
> adapt. by Kelly Sue DeConnick. Trans. JN Productions. Touch-up art
> and lettering by Gia Cam Luc. San Francisco: Viz, 2007. Print. Vol. 9
> of *Black Cat*.

For additional guidelines on citing visual art, see 5.7.6 and 5.7.9.

5.5.13. A Book Published in a Second or Subsequent Edition

A book with no edition number or name on its title page is usually a first edition. Unless informed otherwise, readers assume that bibliographic entries refer to first editions. When you use a later edition of a work, identify the edition in your entry by number (*2nd ed., 3rd ed., 4th ed.*), by name (*Rev. ed.*, for "Revised edition"; *Abr. ed.*, for "Abridged edition"), or by year (*2008 ed.*)—whichever the title page indicates (see fig. 24). The specification of edition comes after the name of the editor, translator, or compiler, if there is one, or otherwise after the title of the book. (On citing encyclopedias, dictionaries, and similar works revised regularly, see 5.5.7.)

> Baker, Nancy L., and Nancy Huling. *A Research Guide for Undergraduate
> Students: English and American Literature*. 6th ed. New York: MLA,
> 2006. Print.

A Reader's Guide to
Contemporary Literary Theory
Third Edition
Raman Selden and Peter Widdowson

Fig. 24. A second or other edition. In the works-cited list, include any label that identifies the edition on the title page. The title of this book would be followed by "3rd ed."

Cavafy, C. P. *Collected Poems*. Trans. Edmund Keeley and Philip Sherrard.
Ed. George Savidis. Rev. ed. Princeton: Princeton UP, 1992. Print.

Cheyfitz, Eric. *The Poetics of Imperialism: Translation and Colonization
from* The Tempest *to* Tarzan. Expanded ed. Philadelphia: U of
Pennsylvania P, 1997. Print.

Murasaki Shikibu. *The Tale of Genji*. Trans. Edward G. Seidensticker. Abr.
ed. New York: Vintage-Random, 1985. Print.

Newcomb, Horace, ed. *Television: The Critical View*. 7th ed. New York:
Oxford UP, 2007. Print.

5.5.14. A Multivolume Work

If you are using two or more volumes of a multivolume work, cite
the total number of volumes in the work ("5 vols."). This information
comes after the title—or after any editor's name or identification of
edition—and before the publication information. Specific references
to volume and page numbers ("3: 212–13") belong in the text. (See ch.
6 for parenthetical documentation.)

Blanco, Richard L., ed. *The American Revolution, 1775-1783: An
Encyclopedia*. 2 vols. Hamden: Garland, 1993. Print.

Lauter, Paul, et al., eds. *The Heath Anthology of American Literature*.
5th ed. 5 vols. Boston: Houghton, 2006. Print.

Rampersad, Arnold. *The Life of Langston Hughes*. 2nd ed. 2 vols. New
York: Oxford UP, 2002. Print.

Sadie, Stanley, ed. *The New Grove Dictionary of Music and Musicians*.
2nd ed. 29 vols. New York: Grove, 2001. Print.

Schlesinger, Arthur M., Jr., gen. ed. *History of U.S. Political Parties*. 4 vols.
New York: Chelsea, 1973. Print.

If the volumes of the work were published over a period of years,
give the inclusive dates at the end of the citation ("1952–70"). If the
work is still in progress, write *to date* after the number of volumes
("3 vols. to date") and leave a space after the hyphen that follows the
beginning date ("1982– ").

Cassidy, Frederic, and Joan Houston Hall, eds. *Dictionary of American Regional English*. 4 vols. to date. Cambridge: Belknap-Harvard UP, 1985- . Print.

Lawrence, D. H. *The Letters of D. H. Lawrence*. Ed. James T. Boulton. 8 vols. New York: Cambridge UP, 1979-2000. Print.

Wellek, René. *A History of Modern Criticism, 1750-1950*. 8 vols. New Haven: Yale UP, 1955-92. Print.

If you are using only one volume of a multivolume work, state the number of the volume in the bibliographic entry ("Vol. 2") and give publication information for that volume alone; then you need give only page numbers when you refer to that work in the text.

Lawrence, D. H. *The Letters of D. H. Lawrence*. Ed. James T. Boulton. Vol. 8. New York: Cambridge UP, 2000. Print.

Stowe, Harriet Beecher. "Sojourner Truth, the Libyan Sibyl." 1863. *The Heath Anthology of American Literature*. Ed. Paul Lauter et al. 5th ed. Vol. B. Boston: Houghton, 2006. 2601-09. Print.

Wellek, René. *A History of Modern Criticism, 1750-1950*. Vol. 5. New Haven: Yale UP, 1986. Print.

Although not required, the complete number of volumes may be added as supplementary information at the end of the listing, after the medium of publication consulted, along with other relevant publication facts, such as inclusive dates of publication if the volumes were published over a period of years (see the sample entry for Wellek).

Stowe, Harriet Beecher. "Sojourner Truth, the Libyan Sibyl." 1863. *The Heath Anthology of American Literature*. Ed. Paul Lauter et al. 5th ed. Vol. B. Boston: Houghton, 2006. 2601-09. Print. 5 vols.

Wellek, René. *A History of Modern Criticism, 1750-1950*. Vol. 5. New Haven: Yale UP, 1986. Print. 8 vols. 1955-92.

If you are using only one volume of a multivolume work and the volume has an individual title, you may cite the book without reference to the other volumes in the work.

Caro, Robert A. *Master of the Senate*. New York: Knopf, 2002. Print.

Although not required, supplementary information about the complete multivolume work may follow the basic citation: the volume number, preceded by *Vol.* and followed by the word *of*; the title of the complete work (italicized); the total number of volumes; and, if the work appeared over a period of years, the inclusive publication dates.

Caro, Robert A. *Master of the Senate*. New York: Knopf, 2002. Print. Vol. 3

of *The Years of Lyndon Johnson*. 3 vols. to date. 1982- .

If the volume you are citing is part of a multivolume scholarly edition (see 5.5.10), you may similarly give supplementary information about the entire edition. Follow the publication information for the volume with the appropriate volume number, preceded by *Vol.* and followed by the word *of*; the title of the complete work (italicized); the name of the general editor of the multivolume edition, followed by a comma and *gen. ed.*; the total number of volumes; and the inclusive publication dates for the edition (see the entry for Howells). If the entire edition was edited by one person, state the editor's name after the title of the edition rather than after the title of the volume.

Howells, W. D. *Their Wedding Journey*. Ed. John K. Reeves. Bloomington:

Indiana UP, 1968. Print. Vol. 5 of *A Selected Edition of W. D. Howells*.

Edwin H. Cady, gen. ed. 32 vols. 1968-83.

5.5.15. A Book in a Series

If the title page or a preceding page indicates that the book you are citing is part of a series (see fig. 25), include the series name, neither italicized nor enclosed in quotation marks, and the series number (if any), followed by a period, at the end of the listing, after the medium of publication. Use common abbreviations for words in the series name (see 7.4), including *Ser.* if *Series* is part of the name.

Anderson, Danny, and Jill S. Kuhnheim, eds. *Cultural Studies in the*

Curriculum: Teaching Latin America. New York: MLA, 2003. Print.

Teaching Langs., Lits., and Cultures.

Murck, Alfreda. *Poetry and Painting in Song China: The Subtle Art of*

Dissent. Cambridge: Harvard UP, 2000. Print. Harvard-Yenching Inst.

Monograph Ser. 50.

Neruda, Pablo. *Canto General*. Trans. Jack Schmitt. Berkeley: U of

California P, 1991. Print. Latin Amer. Lit. and Culture 7.

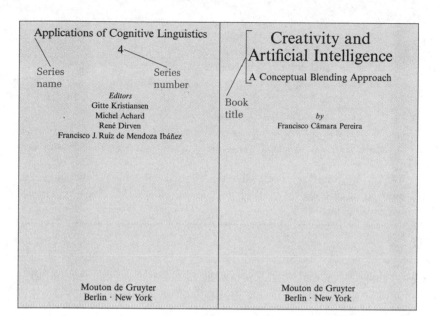

Fig. 25. A book in a series. The title page or a preceding page may indicate that the book is part of a series. This book would be listed as follows (see 7.5 on shortening publishers' names): "Câmara Pereira, Francisco. *Creativity and Artificial Intelligence: A Conceptual Blending Approach*. Berlin: Mouton, 2007. Print. Applications of Cognitive Linguistics 4."

5.5.16. A Republished Book or Journal Issue

To cite a republished book—for example, a paperback version of a book originally published in a clothbound version—give the original publication date, followed by a period, before the publication information for the book you are citing (see fig. 26).

Atwood, Margaret. *The Blind Assassin*. 2000. New York: Knopf-Random, 2001. Print.

Douglas, Mary. *Purity and Danger: An Analysis of the Concepts of Pollution and Taboo*. 1966. London: Routledge, 1993. Print.

García Márquez, Gabriel. *Love in the Time of Cholera*. Trans. Edith Grossman. 1988. New York: Vintage-Random, 2003. Print.

Holier, Denis, ed. *A New History of French Literature*. 1989. Cambridge: Harvard UP, 1994. Print.

BACK BAY BOOKS / LITTLE, BROWN AND COMPANY

HACHETTE BOOK GROUP USA

237 PARK AVENUE, NEW YORK, NY 10017

VISIT OUR WEB SITE AT WWW.HACHETTEBOOKGROUPUSA.COM

Original publication date

ORIGINALLY PUBLISHED IN HARDCOVER BY

LITTLE, BROWN AND COMPANY, JULY 1951

FIRST BACK BAY PAPERBACK EDITION, JANUARY 2001

Date of republication

Fig. 26. A republished book. Give the original publication date before the publication information for the book you are citing: "1951. New York: Back Bay–Little, 2001."

New material added to the republication, such as an introduction, should be cited after the original publication date.

> Dreiser, Theodore. *Sister Carrie*. 1900. Introd. Richard Lingeman. New
> York: New Amer. Lib.-Penguin, 2000. Print.

To cite a republished book that was originally issued under a different title, first state the new title and publication facts, followed by *Rpt. of* ("Reprint of"), the original title, and the original date.

> *The WPA Guide to 1930s Alabama*. Tuscaloosa: U of Alabama P, 2000.
> Print. Rpt. of *Alabama: A Guide to the Deep South*. 1941.

To cite a book that is a reprint of a special issue of a journal, begin the entry with the name of the person or persons who edited the book, followed by a comma and the abbreviation *ed.* (or *eds.* if there are multiple editors). Next give the title of the book (italicized), the publication information for the book, and the medium of publication consulted. Conclude the entry with *Rpt. of spec. issue of*, the name of the journal (italicized), the journal's volume and issue numbers (separated by a period: "9.1"), the year of publication (in parentheses), a colon, a space, and the complete pagination of the issue.

> Appiah, Kwame Anthony, and Henry Louis Gates, Jr., eds. *Identities*.
> Chicago: U of Chicago P, 1995. Print. Rpt. of spec. issue of *Critical
> Inquiry* 18.4 (1992): 625-884.

5.5.17. A Publisher's Imprint

Publishers often group some of their books under imprints, or special names (see fig. 27). Among Doubleday's many imprints, for example, have been Anchor Books, Crime Club, and Double D Western. If an imprint appears on a title page along with the publisher's name, state the imprint and follow it by a hyphen and the name of the publisher ("Anchor-Doubleday," "Collier-Macmillan," "Vintage-Random").

> Cassidy, Frederic, and Joan Houston Hall, eds. *Dictionary of American Regional English*. 4 vols. to date. Cambridge: Belknap-Harvard UP, 1985- . Print.
>
> Morrison, Toni. *Sula*. 1973. New York: Vintage-Random, 2004. Print.
>
> Rhodes, Dan. *Timoleon Vieta Come Home: A Sentimental Journey*. Orlando: Harvest-Harcourt, 2004. Print.

Fig. 27. A publisher's imprint. This information on the title page would appear in the works-cited list as "New York: Perennial-Harper."

5.5.18. A Book with Multiple Publishers

If the title page lists two or more publishers—not just two or more offices of the same publisher—include all of them, in the order given, as part of the publication information, putting a semicolon after the name of each but the last (see fig. 28).

> Duff, J. Wight. *A Literary History of Rome: From the Origins to the Close of the Golden Age*. Ed. A. M. Duff. 3rd ed. 1953. London: Benn; New York: Barnes, 1967. Print.

UNIVERSITY OF TORONTO PRESS

Toronto and Buffalo

ROUTLEDGE

London

Fig. 28. Multiple publishers. These copublishers would be listed as "Toronto: U of Toronto P; London: Routledge."

Tomlinson, Janis A., ed. *Goya: Images of Women*. Washington: Natl. Gallery
of Art; New Haven: Yale UP, 2002. Print.

Wells, H. G. *The Time Machine*. 1895. London: Dent; Rutland: Tuttle, 1992.
Print.

5.5.19. A Brochure, Pamphlet, or Press Release

Treat a brochure or pamphlet as you would a book.

Modern Language Association. *Language Study in the Age of
Globalization: The College-Level Experience*. New York: MLA, n.d.
Print.

Washington, DC. New York: Trip Builder, 2000. Print.

Document a press release the same way, but cite the day and month of
the release, if available, along with the year.

Modern Language Association. *Modern Language Association Announces
New and Improved MLA Language Map*. New York: MLA, 18 Apr.
2006. Print.

5.5.20. A Government Publication

Government publications emanate from many sources and so present special problems in bibliographic citation. In general, if you do not know the writer of the document, cite as author the government agency that issued it—that is, state the name of the government first, followed by the name of the agency, using an abbreviation if the context makes it clear. (But see below for citing a document whose author is known.)

> California. Dept. of Industrial Relations.
>
> United States. Cong. House.

If you are citing two or more works issued by the same government, substitute three hyphens for the name in each entry after the first. If you also cite more than one work by the same government agency, use an additional three hyphens in place of the agency in the second entry and each subsequent one.

> United States. Cong. House.
>
> ---. ---. Senate.
>
> ---. Dept. of Health and Human Services.

The title of the publication, italicized, should follow immediately

In citing the *Congressional Record* (abbreviated *Cong. Rec.*), give only the date, page numbers, and medium of publication consulted.

> *Cong. Rec.* 7 Feb. 1973: 3831-51. Print.

In citing other congressional documents, include such information as the number and session of Congress, the house (*S* stands for Senate, *HR* for House of Representatives), and the type and number of the publication. Types of congressional publications include bills (S 33, HR 77), resolutions (S. Res. 20, H. Res. 50), reports (S. Rept. 9, H. Rept. 142), and documents (S. Doc. 333, H. Doc. 222, Misc. Doc. 67).

The usual publication information comes next (i.e., place, publisher, date, and the medium of publication consulted). Most federal publications, regardless of the branch of government issuing them, are published by the Government Printing Office (GPO), in Washington, DC; its British counterpart is Her (or His) Majesty's Stationery Office (HMSO), in London. Documents issued by the United Nations and most local governments, however, do not all emanate from a central office; give the publication information that appears on the title page.

> Great Britain. Ministry of Agriculture, Fisheries, and Food. *Our*
>> *Countryside, the Future: A Fair Deal for Rural England.* London:
>> HMSO, 2000. Print.

New York State. Commission on the Adirondacks in the Twenty-First
    Century. *The Adirondack Park in the Twenty-First Century.* Albany:
    State of New York, 1990. Print.

---. Committee on State Prisons. *Investigation of the New York State
    Prisons.* 1883. New York: Arno, 1974. Print.

United Nations. *Consequences of Rapid Population Growth in Developing
    Countries.* New York: Taylor, 1991. Print.

---. Centre on Transnational Corporations. *Foreign Direct Investment, the
    Service Sector, and International Banking.* New York: United Nations,
    1987. Print.

---. Dept. of Economic and Social Affairs. *Industrial Development for the
    Twenty-First Century: Sustainable Development Perspectives.* New
    York: United Nations, 2007. Print.

United States. Cong. House. Permanent Select Committee on Intelligence.
    Al-Qaeda: The Many Faces of an Islamist Extremist Threat. 109th
    Cong., 2nd sess. H. Rept. 615. Washington: GPO, 2006. Print.

---.---. Joint Committee on the Investigation of the Pearl Harbor Attack.
    Hearings. 79th Cong., 1st and 2nd sess. 32 vols. Washington: GPO,
    1946. Print.

---. ---. Senate. Subcommittee on Constitutional Amendments of the
    Committee on the Judiciary. *Hearings on the "Equal Rights"
    Amendment.* 91st Cong., 2nd sess. S. Res. 61. Washington: GPO,
    1970. Print.

---. Dept. of Labor. *Child Care: A Workforce Issue.* Washington: GPO, 1988.
    Print.

---. Dept. of State. *U.S. Climate Action Report—2002: Third National
    Communication of the United States of America under the United
    Nations Framework Convention on Climate Change.* Washington:
    GPO, 2002. Print.

If known, the name of the document's author may either begin the
entry or, if the agency comes first, follow the title and the word *By* or
an abbreviation (such as *Ed.* or *Comp.*).

Poore, Benjamin Perley, comp. *A Descriptive Catalogue of the Government
    Publications of the United States, September 5, 1774-March 4, 1881.*

US 48th Cong., 2nd sess. Misc. Doc. 67. Washington: GPO, 1885.
Print.

or

United States. Cong. *A Descriptive Catalogue of the Government
Publications of the United States, September 5, 1774-March 4, 1881.*
Comp. Benjamin Perley Poore. 48th Cong., 2nd sess. Misc. Doc. 67.
Washington: GPO, 1885. Print.

To cite an online government document, see 5.6. To cite a legal
source, see 5.7.14.

5.5.21. The Published Proceedings of a Conference

Treat the published proceedings of a conference like a book, but add
pertinent information about the conference (unless the book title includes such information).

Brady, Brigid, and Patricia Verrone, eds. *Proceedings of the Northeast
Region Annual Meeting, Conference on Christianity and Literature:
Christ Plays in Ten-Thousand Places: The Christ-Figure in Text and
Interpretation.* 22 Oct. 2005, Caldwell Coll. N.p.: Northeast Regional
Conf. on Christianity and Lit., n.d. Print.

Chang, Steve S., Lily Liaw, and Josef Ruppenhofer, eds. *Proceedings of the
Twenty-Fifth Annual Meeting of the Berkeley Linguistics Society,
February 12-15, 1999: General Session and Parasession on Loan
Word Phenomena.* Berkeley: Berkeley Linguistics Soc., 2000. Print.

Cite a presentation in the proceedings like a work in a collection of
pieces by different authors (see 5.5.6).

Hualde, José Ignacio. "Patterns of Correspondence in the Adaptation
of Spanish Borrowings in Basque." *Proceedings of the Twenty-Fifth
Annual Meeting of the Berkeley Linguistics Society, February 12-15,
1999: General Session and Parasession on Loan Word Phenomena.* Ed.
Steve S. Chang, Lily Liaw, and Josef Ruppenhofer. Berkeley: Berkeley
Linguistics Soc., 2000. 348-58. Print.

5.5.22. A Book in a Language Other Than English

Cite a book published in a language other than English like any other
book. Give the author's name, title, and publication information as
they appear in the book and conclude with the medium of publication consulted. You may need to look in the colophon (a listing at the
back of the book) for some or all of the publication information found
on the title or copyright page of English-language books. If it seems
necessary to clarify the title, provide a translation, in square brackets: "*Gengangere [Ghosts]*." Similarly, you may use square brackets
to give the English name of a foreign city—"Wien [Vienna]"—or you
may substitute the English name, depending on your readers' knowledge of the language. Shorten the publisher's name appropriately (see
7.5). For capitalization in languages other than English, see 3.8.

> Bessière, Jean, ed. *Mythologies de l'écriture: Champs critiques*. Paris: PUF,
>   1990. Print.
>
> Esquivel, Laura. *Como agua para chocolate: Novelas de entregas*
>   *mensuales, con recetas, amores y remedios caseros*. Madrid:
>   Mondadori, 1990. Print.
>
> Maraini, Dacia. *Amata scrittura: Laboratorio di analisi, letture, proposte,*
>   *conversazioni*. Ed. Viviana Rosi and Maria Pia Simonetti. Milano:
>   Rizzoli, 2000. Print.
>
> Poche, Emanuel. *Prazské Palace*. Praha [Prague]: Odeon, 1977. Print.
>
> Šklovskij, Viktor. "Искусство, как прием" ["Art as Device"]. О теории
>   прозы [*On the Theory of Prose*]. 1929. Ann Arbor: Ardis, 1985. 7-23.
>   Print.

5.5.23. A Book Published before 1900

When citing a book published before 1900, you may omit the name
of the publisher and use a comma, instead of a colon, after the place
of publication.

> Brome, Richard. *The Dramatic Works of Richard Brome*. 3 vols. London,
>   1873. Print.
>
> Dewey, John. *The School and Society*. Chicago, 1899. Print.

Segni, Bernardo, trans. *Rettorica et poetica d'Aristotile*. By Aristotle.
    Firenze, 1549. Print.

5.5.24. A Book without Stated Publication Information or Pagination

When a book does not indicate the publisher, the place or date of publication, or pagination, supply as much of the missing information as you can, using square brackets to show that it did not come from the source.

New York: U of Gotham P, [2008].

If the date can only be approximated, put it after a *c.*, for *circa* 'around': "[c. 2008]." If you are uncertain about the accuracy of the information you supply, add a question mark: "[2008?]." Use the following abbreviations for information you cannot supply.

n.p.	No place of publication given
n.p.	No publisher given
n.d.	No date of publication given
n. pag.	No pagination given

Inserted before the colon, the abbreviation *n.p.* indicates *no place*; after the colon, it indicates *no publisher*. *N. pag.* explains the absence of page references in citations of the work.

NO PLACE

N.p.: U of Gotham P, 2008.

NO PUBLISHER

New York: n.p., 2008.

NO DATE

New York: U of Gotham P, n.d.

NO PAGINATION

New York: U of Gotham P, 2008. N. pag.

The following examples show uses of the notations described above.

Bauer, Johann. *Kafka und Prag*. [Stuttgart]: Belser, [1971?]. Print.

Malachi, Zvi, ed. *Proceedings of the International Conference on Literary and Linguistic Computing.* [Tel Aviv]: [Fac. of Humanities, Tel Aviv U], n.d. Print.

Michelangelo. *The Sistine Chapel.* New York: Wings, 1992. N. pag. Print.

Photographic View Album of Cambridge. [Eng.]: n.p., n.d. N. pag. Print.

Sendak, Maurice. *Where the Wild Things Are.* New York: Harper, 1963. N. pag. Print.

5.5.25. An Unpublished Dissertation

Enclose the title of an unpublished dissertation in quotation marks; do not italicize it. Then write the descriptive label *Diss.*, and add the name of the degree-granting university, followed by a comma and the year. Conclude with the work's medium.

Kane, Sonia. "Acts of Coercion: Father-Daughter Relationships and the Pressure to Confess in British Women's Fiction, 1778-1814." Diss. City U of New York, 2003. Print.

Kelly, Mary. "Factors Predicting Hospital Readmission of Normal Newborns." Diss. U of Michigan, 2001. Print.

To cite a master's thesis, substitute the appropriate label (e.g., *MA thesis, MS thesis*) for *Diss.* On documenting other unpublished writing, see 5.7.12.

5.5.26. A Published Dissertation

Cite a published dissertation as you would a book, but add pertinent dissertation information before the publication facts. If the dissertation was privately published, state *privately published* in place of the publisher's name.

Dietze, Rudolf F. *Ralph Ellison: The Genesis of an Artist.* Diss. U Erlangen-Nürnberg, 1982. Nürnberg: Carl, 1982. Print. Erlanger Beiträge zur Sprach- und Kunstwissenschaft 70.

Fullerton, Matilda. *Women's Leadership in the Public Schools: Towards a Feminist Educational Leadership Model.* Diss. Washington State U, 2001. Ann Arbor: UMI, 2001. Print.

Wendriner, Karl Georg. *Der Einfluss von Goethes* Wilhelm Meister *auf das Drama der Romantiker*. Diss. U Bonn, 1907. Leipzig: privately published, 1907. Print.

See 5.6.2 for dissertations on the Web, 5.4.8 for dissertation abstracts published in the print version of *Dissertation Abstracts* or *Dissertation Abstracts International*, and 5.6.4 for dissertation abstracts on the Web.

5.6. CITING WEB PUBLICATIONS

5.6.1. Introduction

In performing research on the World Wide Web, you may access bibliographic databases, academic journals, archives of print publications, critical editions, reference works, dissertations, and a wide variety of other documents and recordings. Citations of Web publications share some traits with those of print publications and other traits with those of reprinted works, broadcasts, and live performances. For example, most works on the Web have an author, a title, and publication information and are thus analogous to print publications. But while readers seeking a cited print publication can be reasonably assured that a copy in a local library will be identical to that consulted by the author, they can be less certain that a Web publication will be so. Electronic texts can be updated easily and at irregular intervals. They may also be distributed in multiple databases and accessed through a variety of interfaces displayed on different kinds of equipment. Multiple versions of any work may be available. In this sense, then, accessing a source on the Web is akin to commissioning a performance. Any version of a Web source is potentially different from any past or future version and must be considered unique. Scholars therefore need to record the date of access as well as the publication data when citing sources on the Web.

Publications on the Web present special challenges for documentation. Because of the fluidity of the network and the many hypertextual links between works accessed there, it is often difficult to determine where one work stops and another begins. How, for example, does one define a Web site? One definition would consider all pages affiliated with a particular domain name, like www.mla.org, to constitute a site.

Another view would consider all the pages organized by a particular editor or project team as a site, even if the project is housed under a larger body's domain name or distributed over several domains; the *Victorian Women Writers Project*, for example, appears under Indiana University's domain name (www.indiana.edu). Since both views have merit, the guidelines presented here do not take one side but instead offer a method to record the relation of works on the Web to the information hierarchies surrounding them.

In the past, this handbook recommended including URLs of Web sources in works-cited-list entries. Inclusion of URLs has proved to have limited value, however, for they often change, can be specific to a subscriber or a session of use, and can be so long and complex that typing them into a browser is cumbersome and prone to transcription errors. Readers are now more likely to find resources on the Web by searching for titles and authors' names than by typing URLs. You should include a URL as supplementary information only when the reader probably cannot locate the source without it or when your instructor requires it. If you present a URL, give it immediately following the date of access, a period, and a space. Enclose the URL in angle brackets, and conclude with a period. If a URL must be divided between two lines, break it only after the double slashes or a single slash; do not introduce a hyphen at the break or allow your word-processing program to do so. If possible, give the complete address, including *http*, for the specific work you are citing (see fig. 29).

Eaves, Morris, Robert Essick, and Joseph Viscomi, eds. *The William Blake Archive*. Lib. of Cong., 28 Sept. 2007. Web. 20 Nov. 2007. <http://www.blakearchive.org/blake/>.

The recommendations in this section mostly treat peer-reviewed, scholarly sources and primary sources for which a considerable amount of relevant publication information is available. In truth, though, many sources do not supply all desired information—for instance, many texts do not include reference markers, such as page or paragraph numbers, so it is difficult if not impossible to direct a reader to the exact location of the material you are citing. Thus, while aiming for comprehensiveness, writers must often settle for citing whatever information is available to them. Since the Web can deliver sound and images as well as written text, you may want to describe your source in your text or endnotes when there is a risk that readers will not appreciate important aspects of the work. MLA style is flexible,

Fig. 29. The URL of a Web publication. If you decide to present a URL in your works-cited-list entry, place the entire URL in angle brackets: "<http://www.blakearchive.org/blake/>."

and sometimes you must improvise to record features not anticipated by this handbook. In some cases, citation formats devised to handle complex print publications may serve as a basis for improvisation; see in particular the sections on an article in a reference book (5.5.7), scholarly editions (5.5.10), translations (5.5.11), and government publications (5.5.20). Remember to be consistent in your formatting throughout your work. Since sites and other resources on the Web sometimes disappear altogether, you should consider downloading or printing the material you use during your research, so that you can verify it if it is inaccessible later.

Section 5.6.2 explains how to cite the vast majority of works found on the Web: nonperiodical publications. Section 5.6.3 covers works in scholarly journals. Section 5.6.4 explains how to cite works from periodical publications that are collected in electronic databases. Publishers well known for their periodical publications in media not online, such as newspapers, magazines, and regular news broadcasts, also publish works at nonperiodical, or irregular, intervals on the Web. Thus, it is important to look carefully at the work you are consulting and establish the context for its publication. Note that 5.6 addresses only sources accessed on the Web. For electronic publications you consult apart from a network, such as digital files stored on your computer and on CD-ROMs, see 5.7.17–18.

5.6.2. A Nonperiodical Publication

a. Introduction

Most works on the Web are nonperiodical—not released on a regular schedule. This section begins by describing the basic entry for nonperiodical works on the Web. Web sites sponsored by newspapers and magazines are generally nonperiodical and documented as shown in 5.6.2b. Sometimes it is important to indicate that a work consulted on the Web also appeared in another medium. For example, you may want to give bibliographic data for a book that was scanned for viewing on the Web or the full description of a film that was digitized for viewing in your browser. This section concludes with guidelines for citing such works.

b. A Work Cited Only on the Web

An entry for a nonperiodical publication on the Web usually contains most of the following components, in sequence:

1. Name of the author, compiler, director, editor, narrator, performer, or translator of the work (for more than one author, see 5.5.4; for a corporate author, see 5.5.5; for an anonymous work, see 5.5.9)
2. Title of the work (italicized if the work is independent; in roman type and quotation marks if the work is part of a larger work [see 3.6.2–3])
3. Title of the overall Web site (italicized), if distinct from item 2
4. Version or edition used (see 5.5.13)
5. Publisher or sponsor of the site; if not available, use *N.p.*

6. Date of publication (day, month, and year, as available); if nothing is available, use *n.d.*
7. Medium of publication (*Web*)
8. Date of access (day, month, and year)

Each item is followed by a period except the publisher or sponsor, which is followed by a comma (see fig. 30). Untitled works may be identified by a genre label (e.g., *Home page, Introduction, Online posting*), neither italicized nor enclosed in quotation marks, in the place where the title goes (see 5.5.8 and 5.7.7–10 for additional guidance on the use of genre labels). If not otherwise recorded in the entry, the name of a creator of the overall Web site, such as its editor, may be listed following the title of the site (see the Yager example). If you cannot find some of this information, cite what is available.

Antin, David. Interview by Charles Bernstein. *Dalkey Archive Press*. Dalkey Archive P, n.d. Web. 21 Aug. 2007.

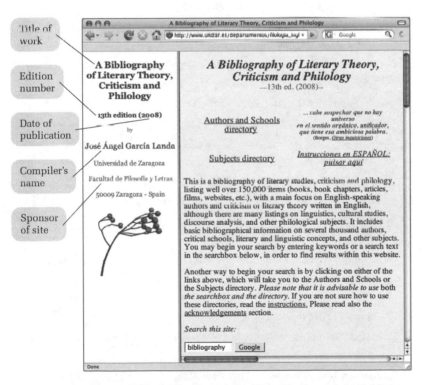

Fig. 30. A nonperiodical publication on the Web. Updates of this bibliography are issued in numbered editions.

185

Committee on Scholarly Editions. "Guidelines for Editors of Scholarly
    Editions." *Modern Language Association*. MLA, 25 Sept. 2007. Web.
    15 May 2008.

Concerto Palatino, perf. "Canzon à 6 per l'Epistola." By Giovanni Priuli.
    Boston Early Music Festival and Exhibition. Boston Early Music
    Festival, 2003. Web. 20 July 2007.

"de Kooning, Willem." *Encyclopaedia Britannica Online*. Encyclopaedia
    Britannica, 2008. Web. 15 May 2008.

Eaves, Morris, Robert Essick, and Joseph Viscomi, eds. *The William Blake
    Archive*. Lib. of Cong., 8 May 2008. Web. 15 May 2008.

García Landa, José Ángel, comp. *A Bibliography of Literary Theory,
    Criticism and Philology*. 13th ed. U de Zaragoza, 2008. Web. 15 May
    2008.

Green, Joshua. "The Rove Presidency." *The Atlantic.com*. Atlantic Monthly
    Group, Sept. 2007. Web. 15 May 2008.

"Hourly News Summary." *National Public Radio*. Natl. Public Radio, 20 July
    2007. Web. 20 July 2007.

Lessig, Lawrence. "Free Debates: More Republicans Call on RNC." *Lessig
    2.0*. N.p., 4 May 2007. Web. 15 May 2008.

Liu, Alan, ed. Home page. *Voice of the Shuttle*. Dept. of English, U of
    California, Santa Barbara, n.d. Web. 15 May 2008.

"Maplewood, New Jersey." Map. *Google Maps*. Google, 15 May 2008. Web.
    15 May 2008.

Quade, Alex. "Elite Team Rescues Troops behind Enemy Lines." *CNN.com*.
    Cable News Network, 19 Mar. 2007. Web. 15 May 2008.

Salda, Michael N., ed. *The Cinderella Project*. Vers. 1.2. U of Southern
    Mississippi, Oct. 2005. Web. 15 May 2008.

"The Scientists Speak." Editorial. *New York Times*. New York Times, 20 Nov.
    2007. Web. 15 May 2008.

"Six Charged in Alleged N.J. Terror Plot." *WNBC.com*. WNBC, 8 May 2007.
    Web. 9 May 2007.

Tyre, Peg. "Standardized Tests in College?" *Newsweek*. Newsweek, 16 Nov.
    2007. Web. 15 May 2008.

"Utah Mine Rescue Funeral." *CNN.com*. Cable News Network, 21 Aug.
    2007. Web. 21 Aug. 2007.

"Verb Tenses." Chart. *The OWL at Purdue.* Purdue U Online Writing Lab,
2001. Web. 15 May 2008.

Yager, Susan, narr. "The Former Age." By Geoffrey Chaucer. *Chaucer
Metapage.* Ed. Mark E. Allen et al. U of North Carolina, 13 Feb. 2007.
Web. 30 Nov. 2007.

If you need to include a URL, follow the guidelines in 5.6.1.

c. A Work on the Web Cited with Print Publication Data

If the nonperiodical work you are citing also appeared in print, you
may determine that it is important to include the bibliographic data
for the print publication as part of your entry. A book that was scanned
for access in a database, for example, is usually cited in this way (see
fig. 31). Begin the entry with the relevant facts about print publication
as described in 5.5. See in particular the guidelines for a work in an
anthology (5.5.6), a translation (5.5.11), a multivolume work (5.5.14),
a government publication (5.5.20), and an unpublished dissertation
(5.5.25). Instead of concluding with *Print* as the medium of publication, record the following information in sequence:

1. Title of the database or Web site (italicized)
2. Medium of publication consulted (*Web*)
3. Date of access (day, month, and year)

If the guidelines in 5.5 call for inclusive page numbers and they are
not present in the source, use *N. pag.* Supplementary bibliographic
information that in 5.5 follows the medium of publication should be
included immediately before item 1 above. Here are examples of entries for nonperiodical publications on the Web that have a previous
or concurrent publication in print.

Bierce, Ambrose. "Academy." *The Devil's Dictionary. The Collected Works of
Ambrose Bierce.* Vol. 7. New York: Neale, 1911. N. pag. *The Ambrose
Bierce Project.* Web. 15 May 2008.

Bown, Jennifer M. "Going Solo: The Experience of Learning Russian in a
Non-traditional Environment." Diss. Ohio State U, 2004. *OhioLINK.*
Web. 15 May 2008.

Cascardi, Anthony J. *Ideologies of History in the Spanish Golden Age.*
University Park: Pennsylvania State UP, 1997. *Penn State Romance
Studies.* Web. 12 Mar. 2007.

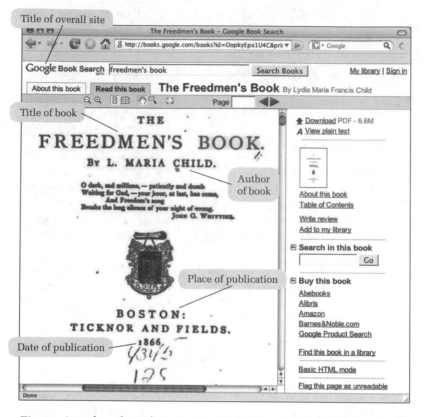

Fig. 31. A work on the Web cited with print publication data, This nineteenth-century book was scanned for access through *Google Book Search*. Since the book was published before 1900, you do not need to include the name of the publisher (see 5.5.23). Following the print publication data are the title of the overall Web site, the medium of publication consulted, and the date of access: "Child, L. Maria, ed. *The Freedmen's Book*. Boston, 1866. *Google Book Search*. Web. 15 May 2008."

Child, L. Maria, ed. *The Freedmen's Book*. Boston, 1866. *Google Book Search*. Web. 15 May 2008.

Heim, Michael Henry, and Andrzej W. Tymowski. *Guidelines for the Translation of Social Science Texts*. New York: ACLS, 2006. *American Council of Learned Societies*. Web. 15 May 2008.

United States. Dept. of Justice. Office of Juvenile Justice and Delinquency Prevention. *Law Enforcement and Juvenile Crime*. By Howard N.

Snyder. 2001. *National Criminal Justice Reference Service.* Web.
15 May 2008.

Whitman, Walt. *Leaves of Grass.* Brooklyn, 1855. *The Walt Whitman
Archive.* Web. 12 Mar. 2007.

Whittier, John G. "A Prayer." *The Freedmen's Book.* Ed. L. Maria Child.
Boston, 1866. 178. *Google Book Search.* Web. 15 May 2008.

You may add supplementary information about the database or Web
site (such as the name of its editor, sponsor, or publisher) following
its name.

Ovid. *Metamorphoses.* Trans. Arthur Golding. London, 1567. *The Perseus
Digital Library.* Ed. Gregory Crane. Tufts U. Web. 12 Mar. 2007.

If you need to include a URL, follow the guidelines in 5.6.1. See
5.6.4 for periodical print publications in online databases.

d. A Work on the Web Cited with Publication Data for Another Medium besides Print

The Web presents images (still and moving) and sound as well as
written text. It is sometimes important to indicate that a source online is available in another medium besides print. If you viewed a
digitized version of a film on the Web, for example, you may want to
include in your entry the details usually cited for a film. To document
sources such as these, begin the entry by following the recommendations in 5.7, but drop the medium of original publication (e.g., *Television, Photograph*). Conclude the entry with the following items:

1. Title of the database or Web site (italicized)
2. Medium of publication consulted (*Web*)
3. Date of access (day, month, and year)

Supplementary bibliographic information that in 5.7 follows the medium of publication should be included immediately before item 1
above. Be mindful of the distinction between sources accessed entirely
on the Web and digital files used apart from an electronic network; for
the latter, follow the directions in 5.7.18. Here are examples of entries
for works available on the Web and in another medium besides print.

Currin, John. *Blond Angel.* 2001. Indianapolis Museum of Art. *IMA: It's My
Art.* Web. 9 May 2007.

The Great Train Robbery. Dir. Edward Porter. Thomas Edison, 1903.
Internet Archive. Web. 5 June 2008.

Lange, Dorothea. *The Migrant Mother*. 1936. Prints and Photographs Div.,
Lib. of Cong. *Dorothea Lange: Photographer of the People*. Web.
9 May 2007.

"Protest on Behalf of Southern Women." 1932. Mary Cornelia Barker
Papers. Robert W. Woodruff Lib., Emory U. *Online Manuscript
Resources in Southern Women's History*. Web. 5 June 2008.

If you need to include a URL, follow the guidelines in 5.6.1.

5.6.3. A Scholarly Journal

Some scholarly journals exist only in electronic form on the Web,
while others appear both in print and on the Web. This section addresses journals published independently on the Web; periodicals collected in online databases are covered in 5.6.4. Following the legacy
of print periodicals, most scholarly journals on the Web are organized
by volume number (usually on an annual basis) and include issue
numbers and the dates of publication. To cite a work in a scholarly
journal on the Web, including an article, a review, an editorial, and a
letter to the editor, begin the entry by following the recommendations
in 5.4 for citing works in print periodicals, but do not give *Print* as
the medium of publication. A periodical publication on the Web may
not include page numbers, or it may include page numbers in a new
sequence for each item rather than continuously across the entire issue. In such cases, use *n. pag.* in place of inclusive page numbers (see
fig. 32). Conclude the entry with the following items:

1. Medium of publication consulted (*Web*)
2. Date of access (day, month, and year)

If the guidelines you are following in 5.4 call for supplementary bibliographic information after the medium of publication, this information should be included immediately before item 1 above. Here are
examples of entries for scholarly journals on the Web.

Armstrong, Grace. Rev. of *Fortune's Faces: The* Roman de la Rose *and the
Poetics of Contingency*, by Daniel Heller-Roazen. *Bryn Mawr Review of
Comparative Literature* 6.1 (2007): n. pag. Web. 5 June 2008.

Dionísio, João, and Antonio Cortijo Ocaña, eds. *Mais de pedras que de
livros / More Rocks Than Books*. Spec. issue of *eHumanista* 8 (2007):
1-263. Web. 5 June 2008.

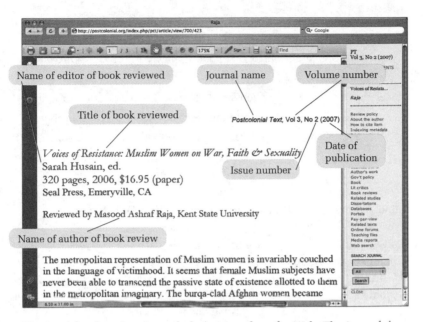

Fig. 32. A book review in a scholarly journal on the Web. The journal does not organize its contents with page numbering, so *n. pag.* is used in the place where inclusive page numbers are usually listed: "*Postcolonial Text* 3.2 (2007): n. pag."

Landauer, Michelle. "Images of Virtue: Reading, Reformation and the Visualization of Culture in Rousseau's *La nouvelle Héloïse*." *Romanticism on the Net* 46 (2007): n. pag. Web. 8 Nov. 2007.

Nater, Miguel. "El beso de la Esfinge: La poética de lo sublime en *La amada inmóvil* de Amado Nervo y en los *Nocturnos* de José Asunción Silva." *Romanitas* 1.1 (2006): n. pag. Web. 5 June 2008.

Ouellette, Marc. "Theories, Memories, Bodies, and Artists." Editorial. *Reconstruction* 7.4 (2007): n. pag. Web. 5 June 2008.

Raja, Masood Ashraf. Rev. of *Voices of Resistance: Muslim Women on War, Faith, and Sexuality*, ed. Sarah Husain. *Postcolonial Text* 3.2 (2007): n. pag. Web. 5 June 2008.

Schmidt-Nieto, Jorge R. "The Political Side of Bilingual Education: The Undesirable Becomes Useful." *Arachne@Rutgers* 2.2 (2002): n. pag. Web. 5 June 2008.

Shah, Parilah Mohd, and Fauziah Ahmad. "A Comparative Account of the
    Bilingual Education Programs in Malaysia and the United States."
    GEMA Online Journal of Language Studies 7.2 (2007): 63-77. Web.
    5 June 2008.
Shehan, Constance L., and Amanda B. Moras. "Deconstructing Laundry:
    Gendered Technologies and the Reluctant Redesign of Household
    Labor." *Michigan Family Review* 11 (2006): n. pag. Web. 8 Nov. 2007.

If you need to include a URL, follow the guidelines in 5.6.1.

5.6.4. A Periodical Publication in an Online Database

Many databases include digital scans of entire periodicals that were
previously published in print; often these scans present facsimiles of
the printed works. Other databases aggregate articles from disparate
periodicals, sometimes organizing the articles by subject. In some databases, typographic features and even the pagination found in print
versions may be altered or lost. Sometimes copyrighted third-party
materials (illustrations or text) in a print version may have been elim-
inated because permission for the electronic publication could not
be cleared. Web presentations of periodicals may include enhance-
ments, such as hypertextual links, sound recordings, and film clips,
that are not present in their print counterparts.

To cite a work from a periodical in an online database, such as
an article, a review, an editorial, or a letter to the editor, begin the
entry by following the recommendations in 5.4 for citing works in
print periodicals, but drop the medium of original publication (*Print*).
A periodical article on the Web may not include page numbers. If
possible, give the inclusive page numbers or, when pagination is not
continuous, the first page number and a plus sign; if pagination is not
available, use *n. pag.* Conclude the entry with the following items:

1. Title of the database (italicized)
2. Medium of publication consulted (*Web*)
3. Date of access (day, month, and year)

If the guidelines you are following in 5.4 call for supplementary bibliographic information after the medium of publication, this information should be included immediately before item 1 above (see the
Richardson entry). Here are examples of entries for periodical publications collected in online databases.

Chan, Evans. "Postmodernism and Hong Kong Cinema." *Postmodern Culture* 10.3 (2000): n. pag. *Project Muse.* Web. 5 June 2008.

Evangelista, Stefano. Rev. of *Victorian and Edwardian Responses to the Italian Renaissance*, ed. John E. Law and Lene Østermark-Johansen. *Victorian Studies* 48.4 (2006): 729-31. *Academic Search Premier.* Web. 12 Mar. 2007.

France, Anatole. "Pour la Paix, pour la Liberté." *New Age* 5 Sept. 1907: 297-98. *The Modernist Journals Project.* Web. 5 June 2008.

Lal, Ananda. Letter. *TDR* 51.3 (2007): 17-18. *Project Muse.* Web. 30 Nov. 2007.

Miller, Steven, and Sara Guyer, eds. *Literature and the Right to Marriage.* Spec. issue of *Diacritics* 35.4 (2005): 1-124. *Project Muse.* Web. 5 June 2008.

Richardson, Lynda. "Minority Students Languish in Special Education System." *New York Times* 6 Apr. 1994, late ed.: A1+. Pt. 1 of a series, A Class Apart: Special Education in New York City. *LexisNexis.* Web. 15 Aug. 2007.

Rosenberg, Mark. "Something Old, Something New. . . ." Editorial. *Canadian Journal on Aging / La revue canadienne du vieillissement* 26.2 (2007): 81. *Project Muse.* Web. 30 Nov. 2007.

Tolson, Nancy. "Making Books Available: The Role of Early Libraries, Librarians, and Booksellers in the Promotion of African American Children's Literature." *African American Review* 32.1 (1998): 9-16. *JSTOR.* Web. 5 June 2008.

If you need to include a URL, follow the guidelines in 5.6.1.

5.7. CITING ADDITIONAL COMMON SOURCES

5.7.1. A Television or Radio Broadcast

The information in an entry for a television or radio broadcast usually appears in the following order:

1. Title of the episode or segment, if appropriate (in quotation marks)

2. Title of the program or series (italicized)
3. Name of the network (if any)
4. Call letters and city of the local station (if any)
5. Broadcast date
6. Medium of reception (e.g., *Radio, Television*)
7. Supplementary information

For instance, among the examples below, "Frederick Douglass" is an episode of the program *Civil War Journal*. Use a comma between the call letters and the city and between the city and the broadcast date ("KETC, Saint Louis, 13 Jan. 2006"). A period follows each of the other items. For the inclusion of other information that may be pertinent (e.g., performers, director, narrator, number of episodes), see the sample entries. In general, information relating to a particular episode follows the title of the episode, while information pertinent to a series follows the title of the series.

"Death and Society." Narr. Joanne Silberner. *Weekend Edition Sunday*. Natl.
Public Radio. WUWM, Milwaukee, 25 Jan. 1998. Radio.

Don Giovanni. By Wolfgang Amadeus Mozart. Perf. James Morris, Bryn
Terfel, and Carol Vaness. Lyric Opera of Chicago. Cond. Yakov
Kreizberg. Nuveen-Lyric Opera of Chicago Radio Network. WFMT,
Chicago, 8 June 1996. Radio.

"Frederick Douglass." *Civil War Journal*. Narr. Danny Glover. Dir. Craig
Haffner. Arts and Entertainment Network. 6 Apr. 1993. Television.

"The Phantom of Corleone." Narr. Steve Kroft. *Sixty Minutes*. CBS. WCBS,
New York, 10 Dec. 2006. Television.

If your reference is primarily to the work of a particular individual, cite that person's name before the title.

Wadey, Maggie, adapt. "The Buccaneers." By Edith Wharton. Perf. Mira
Sorvino, Alison Elliott, and Carla Gugino. 3 episodes. *Masterpiece
Theatre*. Introd. Russell Baker. PBS. WGBH, Boston, 27 Apr.-11 May
1997. Television.

Welles, Orson, dir. "The War of the Worlds." By H. G. Wells. Adapt. Howard
Koch. *Mercury Theatre on the Air*. CBS Radio. WCBS, New York,
30 Oct. 1938. Radio.

If you are citing a transcript of a program, list its medium of publication and add the description *Transcript* at the end of the entry.

Fresh Air. Narr. Terry Gross. Natl. Public Radio. WHYY, n.p., 20 May 2008.
  Print. Transcript.

See 5.7.7 for interviews on television and radio broadcasts; see also 5.6.2d for television and radio broadcasts on the Web, 5.7.2–3 for sound, film, and video recordings, 5.7.4 for performances, and 5.7.17 for television and radio programs on CD-ROM.

5.7.2. A Sound Recording

In an entry for a commercially available recording, which person is cited first (e.g., the composer, conductor, ensemble, or performer) depends on the desired emphasis. List the title of the recording (or the titles of the works included), the artist or artists (when distinct from a first-listed person or group), the manufacturer (*Capitol*), and the year of issue (if the year is unknown, write *n.d.*). Indicate the medium, neither italicized nor enclosed in quotation marks, after the date of publication: *Audiocassette, Audiotape* (reel-to-reel tape), *CD* (compact disc), or *LP* (long-playing record). Place a comma between the manufacturer and the date; periods follow the other items.

In general, italicize titles of recordings (*Nuevo*). You may wish to indicate, in addition to the year of issue, the date of recording (see the entries for Beethoven and Ellington).

Beethoven, Ludwig van. *Symphony No. 9 in D Minor "Choral."* Perf.
  Elisabeth Schwarzkopf, Elisabeth Höngen, Hans Hopf, and Otto
  Edelmann. Chor und Orchester der Bayreuther Festspiele. Cond.
  Wilhelm Furtwängler. Rec. 29 July 1951. EMI, 1998. CD. Great
  Recordings of the Century.

Ellington, Duke, cond. *First Carnegie Hall Concert.* Duke Ellington Orch.
  Rec. 23 Jan. 1943. Prestige, 1977. LP.

Holiday, Billie. *The Essence of Billie Holiday.* Columbia, 1991. CD.

Joplin, Scott. *Treemonisha.* Perf. Carmen Balthrop, Betty Allen, and Curtis
  Rayam. Houston Grand Opera Orch. and Chorus. Cond. Gunther
  Schuller. Deutsche Grammophon, 1976. Audiocassette.

Kronos Quartet. *Nuevo.* Nonesuch, 2002. CD.

The Mamas and the Papas. *Gold.* Comp. Andy McKaie. Geffen, 2005. CD.

If you are citing a specific song, place its title in quotation marks.

Bartoli, Cecilia. "Quel chiaro rio." By Christoph W. Gluck. *Dreams and Fables*. London, 2001. CD.

Camper Van Beethoven. "Ambiguity Song." *Telephone Free Landslide Victory*. Rough Trade, n.d. LP.

Holiday, Billie. "God Bless the Child." Rec. 9 May 1941. *The Essence of Billie Holiday*. Columbia, 1991. CD.

Kronos Quartet and Tambuco. "Sensemaya." By Silvestre Revueltas. *Nuevo*. Nonesuch, 2002. CD.

Treat a spoken-word recording as you would a musical recording. Begin with the speaker, the writer, or the production director, depending on the desired emphasis. If relevant, you may add the date of the work's original publication immediately after the title.

Hermann, Edward, narr. *John Adams*. By David McCullough. Simon, 2001. Audiocassette.

Maloney, Michael, narr. *Selections from* The Diary of Samuel Pepys. Naxos, 2003. CD.

Neruda, Pablo. "Arte Poetica." *The Caedmon Poetry Collection: A Century of Poets Reading Their Work*. Harper, 2000. CD.

Shakespeare, William. *Othello*. Dir. John Dexter. Perf. Laurence Olivier, Maggie Smith, Frank Finley, and Derek Jacobi. RCA Victor, 1964. LP.

Welles, Orson, dir. *The War of the Worlds*. By H. G. Wells. Adapt. Howard Koch. Rec. 30 Oct. 1938. Evolution, 1969. LP.

Do not italicize or enclose in quotation marks the title of a private or archival recording or tape. Include the date recorded (if known) and the location and identifying number of the recording.

Wilgus, D. K. Southern Folk Tales. Rec. 23-25 Mar. 1965. Audiotape. Archives of Folklore, U of California, Los Angeles. B.76.82.

In citing the libretto, the booklet, the liner notes, or other material accompanying a recording, give the author's name, the title of the material (if any), and a description of the material (*Libretto*). Then provide the usual bibliographic information for a recording.

Boyd, Malcolm. Booklet. *The Bach Album*. Deutsche Grammophon, 1992. CD.

Colette. Libretto. *L'enfant et les sortilèges*. Music by Maurice Ravel. Orch.
　　National Bordeaux-Aquitaine. Cond. Alain Lombard. Valois, 1993. CD.

Lewiston, David. Liner notes. *The Balinese Gamelan: Music from the*
　　Morning of the World. Nonesuch, n.d. LP.

See 5.6.2d for sound recordings on the Web and 5.7.5 for a libretto
published independently.

5.7.3. A Film or a Video Recording

An entry for a film usually begins with the title, italicized, and includes the director, the distributor, the year of release, and the medium
consulted. You may include other data that seem pertinent—such as
the names of the screenwriter, performers, and producer—between
the title and the distributor. For films dubbed or subtitled in English,
you may give the English title and follow it with the original title,
italicized, in square brackets.

It's a Wonderful Life. Dir. Frank Capra. Perf. James Stewart, Donna Reed,
　　Lionel Barrymore, and Thomas Mitchell. RKO, 1946. Film.

Like Water for Chocolate [*Como agua para chocolate*]. Screenplay by Laura
　　Esquivel. Dir. Alfonso Arau. Perf. Lumi Cavazos, Marco Lombardi, and
　　Regina Torne. Miramax, 1993. Film.

If you are citing the contribution of a particular individual, begin
with that person's name.

Chaplin, Charles, dir. *Modern Times*. Perf. Chaplin and Paulette Goddard.
　　United Artists, 1936. Film.

Jhabvala, Ruth Prawer, adapt. *A Room with a View*. By E. M. Forster. Dir.
　　James Ivory. Prod. Ismail Merchant. Perf. Maggie Smith, Denholm
　　Eliot, Helena Bonham Carter, and Daniel Day-Lewis. Cinecom Intl.,
　　1985. Film.

Mifune, Toshiro, perf. *Rashomon*. Dir. Akira Kurosawa. Daiei, 1950. Film.

Rota, Nino, composer. *Juliet of the Spirits* [*Giulietta degli spiriti*]. Dir.
　　Federico Fellini. Perf. Giulietta Masina. Rizzoli, 1965. Film.

Cite a DVD (digital videodisc), videocassette, laser disc, slide program, or filmstrip as you would a film. Include the original release
date when it is relevant.

Alcohol Use and Its Medical Consequences: A Comprehensive Teaching Program for Biomedical Education. Prod. Project Cork, Dartmouth Medical School. Milner-Fenwick, 1982. Slide program.

Don Giovanni. By Wolfgang Amadeus Mozart. Dir. Joseph Losey. Perf. Ruggero Raimondi and Kiri Te Kanawa. Paris Opera Orch. and Chorus. Cond. Loren Maazel. 1979. Columbia, 2002. DVD.

It's a Wonderful Life. Dir. Frank Capra. Perf. James Stewart, Donna Reed, Lionel Barrymore, and Thomas Mitchell. 1946. Republic, 2001. DVD.

Looking at Our Earth: A Visual Dictionary. Natl. Geographic Educ. Services, 1992. Sound filmstrip.

Mifune, Toshiro, perf. *Rashomon.* Dir. Akira Kurosawa. 1950. Home Vision, 2001. Videocassette.

Noujaim, Jehane, dir. *Control Room.* Lions Gate, 2004. DVD.

Renoir, Jean, dir. *Grand Illusion* [*La grande illusion*]. Perf. Jean Gabin and Erich von Stroheim. 1938. Voyager, 1987. Laser disc.

For television broadcasts of films, adapt the guidelines in 5.7.1; for films or film clips on CD-ROM, see 5.7.17; for films or film clips on the Web, see 5.6.2d.

5.7.4. A Performance

An entry for a performance (play, opera, dance, concert) usually begins with the title, contains facts similar to those given for a film (see 5.7.3), and concludes with the site of the performance (usually the theater and city, separated by a comma and followed by a period), the date of the performance, and (in the place where the medium of publication is usually recorded) an indication that you are citing a performance.

Heartbreak House. By George Bernard Shaw. Dir. Robin Lefevre. Perf. Philip Bosco and Swoosie Kurtz. Roundabout Theatre Company. Amer. Airlines Theatre, New York. 1 Oct. 2006. Performance.

South African Suite. Chor. Arthur Mitchell, Augustus Van Heerder, and Laveen Naidu. Dance Theatre of Harlem. Cadillac Palace Theatre, Chicago. 1 June 2002. Performance.

> Les vêpres siciliennes. By Giuseppe Verdi. Libretto by Eugène Scribe and
> Charles Duveyrier. Dir. Federico Tiezzi. Cond. John Nelson. Perf.
> Daniela Dessì, David Kuebler, and Ferruccio Furlanetto. Teatro
> dell'Opera, Rome. 17 Jan. 1997. Performance.

If you are citing the contribution of a particular individual or group,
begin with the appropriate name.

> Culkin, Kieran, perf. *Suburbia*. By Eric Bogosian. Second Stage Theatre,
> New York. 16 Sept. 2006. Performance.
>
> Domingo, Plácido, perf. *Sly*. By Ermanno Wolf-Ferrari. With Cynthia
> Lawrence and Juan Pons. Metropolitan Opera. Cond. Marco Armiliato.
> Metropolitan Opera House, New York. 4 May 2002. Performance.
>
> Joplin, Scott. *Treemonisha*. Dir. Frank Corsaro. Perf. Carmen Balthrop,
> Betty Allen, and Curtis Rayam. Houston Grand Opera Orch. and
> Chorus. Cond. Gunther Schuller. Miller Theatre, Houston. 18 May
> 1975. Performance.

For television and radio broadcasts of performances, see 5.7.1; for
sound recordings of performances, see 5.7.2; for films and video recordings of performances, see 5.7.3.

5.7.5. A Musical Score or Libretto

Treat a published score or libretto like a book. For a score, begin with
the composer's name, and then give the title, italicized, as it appears
on the title page, capitalizing the abbreviations *no.* and *op.* Continue
with the date of composition (if the year is unknown, write *N.d.*), the
place of publication, the name of the publisher, the date of publication, and the medium of publication consulted. If the score is part of
a series, include the information about the series after the medium of
publication.

> Donizetti, Gaetano. *Don Pasquale: An Opera in Three Acts with Italian-
> English Text*. 1842. New York: Belwin, 1969. Print. Kalmus Vocal
> Scores.

An entry for a libretto follows the same sequence, but the librettist is
listed first and the composer after the title.

Oakes, Meredith. *The Tempest: An Opera in Three Acts.* Composed by

Thomas Adès. London: Faber Music, 2004. Print.

See 5.6.2 for scores on the Web, 5.7.1 for television and radio broadcasts of music, 5.7.2 for sound recordings of musical compositions and materials accompanying sound recordings, 5.7.3 for films and video recordings of musical performances, and 5.7.4 for musical performances.

5.7.6. A Work of Visual Art

To cite a painting, lithograph, sculpture, or similar work, state the artist's name first when available. In general, italicize the title and then list the date of composition (if the year is unknown, write *N.d.*). Indicate the medium of composition. Name the institution that houses the work (e.g., a museum), or, for a work in a private collection, give the name of the collection (*Collection of . . .*), and then provide the name of the city where the institution or collection is located. If the collector is unknown or wishes to be anonymous, use *Private collection* without a city name.

Bearden, Romare. *The Train.* 1974. Photogravure and aquatint. Museum of

Mod. Art, New York.

Heckman, Albert. *Windblown Trees.* N.d. Lithograph on paper. Private

collection.

Perutz, Dolly Hellman. *Bird Flying Machine.* 1973. Bronze. Central Park,

New York.

Rembrandt Harmensz van Rijn. *Aristotle with a Bust of Homer.* 1653. Oil

on canvas. Metropolitan Museum of Art, New York.

Seurat, Georges. *Man Leaning on a Fence.* 1880-81? Graphite on paper.

Collection of André Bromberg, n.p.

Cite a photograph in a museum or collection as you would a painting or sculpture.

Evans, Walker. *Penny Picture Display.* 1936. Photograph. Museum of Mod.

Art, New York.

If you use a reproduction of a painting, sculpture, or photograph, state not only the institution or private owner and the city (if available) but also the complete publication information for the source in which the reproduction appears, including the page, slide, figure, or plate number, whichever is relevant. Indicate the medium of reproduction.

> Eakins, Thomas. *Spinning.* 1881. Private collection. *Thomas Eakins.* Ed.
> Darrel Sewell. Philadelphia: Philadelphia Museum of Art in assn. with
> Yale UP, 2001. Plate 91. Print.
> Moholy-Nagy, Lászlò. *Photogram.* N.d. Museum of Mod. Art, New York.
> *The Contest of Meaning: Critical Histories of Photography.* Ed. Richard
> Bolton. Cambridge: MIT P, 1989. 94. Print.

See 5.6.2d for works of visual art on the Web and 5.7.17 for works of visual art on CD-ROM.

5.7.7. An Interview

For purposes of documentation, there are two kinds of interviews: those published or broadcast and those conducted by the researcher. Begin with the name of the person interviewed. If the interview is part of a publication, recording, or program, enclose the title of the interview, if any, in quotation marks; if the interview was published independently, italicize the title. If the interview is untitled, use the descriptive label *Interview*, neither italicized nor enclosed in quotation marks. The interviewer's name may be added if known and pertinent to your paper (see the sample entries for Breslin and Wiesel). Conclude with the appropriate bibliographic information and the medium of publication.

> Blanchett, Cate. "In Character with: Cate Blanchett." *Notes on a Scandal.*
> Dir. Richard Eyre. Fox Searchlight, 2006. DVD.
> Breslin, Jimmy. Interview by Neal Conan. *Talk of the Nation.* Natl. Public
> Radio. WBUR, Boston, 26 Mar. 2002. Radio.
> Gordimer, Nadine. Interview. *New York Times* 10 Oct. 1991, late ed.: C25.
> Print.
> Lansbury, Angela. Interview. *Off-Camera: Conversations with the Makers
> of Prime-Time Television.* By Richard Levinson and William Link. New
> York: Plume-NAL, 1986. 72-86. Print.
> Wiesel, Elie. Interview by Ted Koppel. *Nightline.* ABC. WABC, New York,
> 18 Apr. 2002. Television.

> Wolfe, Tom. Interview. *The Wrong Stuff: American Architecture.* Dir. Tom
>   Bettag. Carousel, 1983. Videocassette.

To cite an interview that you conducted, give the name of the person interviewed, the kind of interview (*Personal interview, Telephone interview*), and the date.

> Pei, I. M. Personal interview. 22 July 1993.
>
> Reed, Ishmael. Telephone interview. 10 Dec. 2007.

See 5.6.2b for interviews on the Web.

5.7.8. A Map or Chart

In general, treat a map or chart like an article or book, but add the appropriate descriptive label (*Map, Chart*).

> *Japanese Fundamentals.* Chart. Hauppauge: Barron, 1992. Print.
>
> *Michigan.* Map. Chicago: Rand, 2000. Print.
>
> "Western Boundaries of Brazil, 1600, 1780, and the Present." Map.
>   *Brazilian Narrative Traditions in a Comparative Context.* By Earl
>   E. Fitz. New York: MLA, 2005. 43. Print.

See 5.6.2b for maps and charts on the Web.

5.7.9. A Cartoon or Comic Strip

To cite a cartoon or comic strip, state the artist's name; the title of the cartoon or comic strip (if any), in quotation marks; and the descriptive label *Cartoon* or *Comic strip*, neither italicized nor enclosed in quotation marks. Conclude with the usual publication information and the medium of publication.

> Karasik, Paul. Cartoon. *New Yorker* 14 Apr. 2008: 49. Print.
>
> Trudeau, Garry. "Doonesbury." Comic strip. *Star-Ledger* [Newark] 4 May
>   2002: 26. Print.

See 5.5.12 for graphic narratives.

5.7.10. An Advertisement

To cite an advertisement, state the name of the product, company, or institution that is the subject of the advertisement, followed by the descriptive label *Advertisement*, neither italicized nor enclosed in quotation marks. Conclude with the usual publication information and the medium of publication consulted.

Air Canada. Advertisement. CNN. 15 May 1998. Television.

The Fitness Fragrance by Ralph Lauren. Advertisement. *GQ* Apr. 1997:
    111-12. Print.

Head and Shoulders. Advertisement. *Newsweek* 17 Mar. 2008: 2. Print.

5.7.11. A Lecture, a Speech, an Address, or a Reading

In a citation of an oral presentation, give the speaker's name; the title of the presentation (if known), in quotation marks; the meeting and the sponsoring organization (if applicable); the location; and the date. Use an appropriate descriptive label (*Address, Lecture, Keynote speech, Reading*), neither italicized nor enclosed in quotation marks, to indicate the form of delivery.

Alter, Robert, and Marilynne Robinson. "The Psalms: A Reading and
    Conversation." 92nd Street Y, New York. 17 Dec. 2007. Reading.

Matuozzi, Robert. "Archive Trauma." Archive Trouble. MLA Annual
    Convention. Hyatt Regency, Chicago. 29 Dec. 2007. Address.

5.7.12. A Manuscript or Typescript

To cite a manuscript or typescript, state the author, the title or a description of the material (e.g., *Notebook*), the date of composition (at least the year; if the year is unknown, write *N.d.*), and the form of the material—*MS* for a manuscript (i.e., a work written by hand), *TS* for a typescript (i.e., a work prepared by machine). Give the name and location of the library, research institution, or personal collection housing the material, if relevant.

Chaucer, Geoffrey. *The Canterbury Tales*. 1400-1410. MS Harley 7334.
    British Lib., London.

Dickinson, Emily. "Distance Is Not the Realm of Fox." 1870? MS. Pierpont
Morgan Lib., New York.

Henderson, George Wylie. *Baby Lou and the Angel Bud*. N.d. TS. Collection
of Roslyn Kirkland Allen, New York.

Jones, Celia. "Shakespeare's Dark Lady Illuminated." 1988. TS.

See 5.6.2d for manuscripts and typescripts on the Web.

5.7.13. A Letter, a Memo, or an E-Mail Message

As bibliographic entries, letters fall into three general categories:
* Published letters
* Unpublished letters in archives
* Letters received by the researcher

Treat a published letter like a work in a collection (see 5.5.6), adding
the date of the letter and the number (if the editor assigned one).

Woolf, Virginia. "To T. S. Eliot." 28 July 1920. Letter 1138 of *The Letters of
Virginia Woolf*. Ed. Nigel Nicolson and Joanne Trautmann. Vol. 2. New
York: Harcourt, 1976. 437-38. Print.

If you use more than one letter from a published collection, however,
provide a single entry for the entire work and cite the letters individu-
ally in the text, following the form recommended for cross-references
in works-cited lists (see 5.3.6).

In citing an unpublished letter, follow the guidelines for manuscripts and typescripts (see 5.7.12).

Benton, Thomas Hart. Letter to Charles Fremont. 22 June 1847. MS. John
Charles Fremont Papers. Southwest Museum Lib., Los Angeles.

Cite a letter that you received as follows:

Hatch, James C. Letter to the author. 5 Apr. 2008. TS.

Treat memos similarly: give the name of the writer of the memo,
a description of the memo that includes the recipient, the date of
the document, and the medium of delivery. Any title of the memo
should be enclosed in quotation marks and placed immediately after
the writer's name.

Cahill, Daniel J. Memo to English dept. fac., Brooklyn Technical High
School, New York. 1 June 2000. TS.

To cite e-mail, give the name of the writer; the title of the message
(if any), taken from the subject line and enclosed in quotation marks;
a description of the message that includes the recipient (e.g., *Message
to the author*); the date of the message; and the medium of delivery.

Boyle, Anthony T. "Re: Utopia." Message to Daniel J. Cahill. 21 June 1997.
E-mail.

Harner, James L. Message to the author. 20 Aug. 2002. E-mail.

5.7.14. A Legal Source

The citation of legal documents and law cases may be complicated.
If your paper requires many such references, consult the most recent
edition of *The Bluebook: A Uniform System of Citation* (Cambridge:
Harvard Law Rev. Assn.; print), an indispensable guide in this field.
The Bluebook uses footnotes instead of parenthetical references keyed
to a list of works cited, however, so its recommendations must be
adapted to MLA style.

In general, do not italicize or enclose in quotation marks the titles
of laws, acts, and similar documents in either the text or the list of
works cited (Declaration of Independence, Constitution of the United
States, Taft-Hartley Act). Such titles are usually abbreviated, and the
works are cited by sections. The years are added if relevant. Although
lawyers and legal scholars adopt many abbreviations in their citations, use only familiar abbreviations when writing for a more general
audience (see ch. 7). References to the United States Code, which is
often abbreviated *USC*, begin with the title number.

17 USC. Sec. 304. 2000. Print.

In the above entry, title 17 refers to laws concerned with copyrights.
Alphabetize a USC entry as if it began *United States Code*. When including more than one reference to the code, list the entries in numerical order by title and, within titles, by section.

If you are citing an act in the works-cited list, state the name of the
act, its Public Law number, its Statutes at Large volume number and
inclusive page numbers, the date it was enacted, and its medium of

publication. Use the abbreviations *Pub. L.* for Public Law and *Stat.* for Statutes at Large.

> Aviation and Transportation Security Act. Pub. L. 107-71. 115 Stat. 597-
>
> 647. 19 Nov. 2001. Print.

Names of law cases are similarly abbreviated ("Brown v. Board of Educ.," for the case of Oliver Brown versus the Board of Education of Topeka, Kansas), but the first important word of each party's name is always spelled out. Names of cases, unlike those of laws, are italicized in the text but not in bibliographic entries. When you cite a case, include, in addition to the names of the first plaintiff and the first defendant, the volume, name (not italicized), and inclusive page or reference numbers of the law report cited; the name of the court that decided the case; the year of the decision; and appropriate publication information for the medium consulted. Once again, considerable abbreviation is the norm.

> Brown v. Board of Educ. 347 US 483-96. Supreme Court of the US. 1954.
>
> *Supreme Court Collection.* Legal Information Inst., Cornell U Law
>
> School, n.d. Web. 3 Aug. 2007.

It is common in legal scholarship to refer to a case by the first nongovernmental party. Thus, for a case named *NLRB v. Yeshiva University*, scholars are likely to use *Yeshiva* as a short title. But in MLA style readers need the first part of the name (*NLRB*) to locate the full citation in the list of works cited. You should bear this in mind when formulating parenthetical references to legal sources.

To cite a government publication, see 5.5.20.

5.7.15. An Article in a Microform Collection of Articles

If you are citing an article that was provided by a reference source such as *NewsBank*, which formerly selected periodical articles and made them available on microfiche, begin the entry with the original publication information, followed by the medium of publication. Then add the relevant information concerning the microform from which you derived the article—title of source (italicized), volume number, year (in parentheses), and appropriate identifying numbers ("fiche 42, grids 5–6").

Chapman, Dan. "Panel Could Help Protect Children." *Winston-Salem*
Journal 14 Jan. 1990: 14. Microform. *NewsBank: Welfare and Social*
Problems 12 (1990): fiche 1, grids A8-11.

5.7.16. An Article Reprinted in a Loose-Leaf Collection of Articles

If you are citing a reprinted article that was provided by an information service such as the Social Issues Resources Series (SIRS), which
formerly selected articles from periodicals and published them in
loose-leaf volumes, each dedicated to a specific topic, begin the entry
with the original publication information, followed by the medium of
publication. Then add the relevant information for the loose-leaf volume in which the article is reprinted, treating the volume like a book
(see 5.5)—title (italicized), name of editor (if any), volume number (if
any), city of publication, publisher, year of publication, and article
number (preceded by the abbreviation *Art.*).

Edmondson, Brad. "AIDS and Aging." *American Demographics* Mar. 1990:
28+. Print. *The AIDS Crisis*. Ed. Eleanor Goldstein. Vol. 2. Boca Raton:
SIRS, 1991. Art. 24.

See 5.6.3–4 for articles on the Web.

5.7.17. A Publication on CD-ROM or DVD-ROM

Citations for publications on CD-ROM or DVD-ROM are similar to
those for print sources, with the following important differences.

Vendor's name. The persons or groups responsible for supplying the
information in publications on CD-ROM and DVD-ROM are sometimes also the publishers of the works. But many information pro-
viders choose instead to lease the data to vendors (e.g., ProQuest)
for distribution. It is important to state the vendor's name in your
works-cited list, if it is given in your source, because the information provider may have leased versions of the data to more than one
vendor and the versions may not be identical. Usually the vendor's
name is recorded in the part of the entry reserved for supplementary
information.

Publication dates. Some databases published on CD-ROM or DVD-ROM are updated regularly (e.g., annually, quarterly). Updates add information and may also correct or otherwise alter information that previously appeared in the database. Therefore, a works-cited-list entry for material derived from such a database commonly contains the publication date of the document, as indicated in the source, as well as the publication date of the database (or date of the most recent update) (see 5.7.17b).

The sections below contain recommendations for citing nonperiodical publications on CD-ROM or DVD-ROM (5.7.17a), materials from periodically published databases on CD-ROM or DVD-ROM (5.7.17b), and multidisc publications (5.7.17c).

a. A Nonperiodical Publication on CD-ROM or DVD-ROM

Many publications on CD-ROM or DVD-ROM are issued as books are—that is, without a plan to update or otherwise revise the work regularly. Cite a nonperiodical publication on CD-ROM or DVD-ROM as you would a book, but add a description of the medium of publication. When the information provider and the publisher are the same, no vendor's name appears, and only one publication date is given. The typical works-cited-list entry for the source consists of the following items:

1. Author's name (if given). If only an editor, a compiler, or a translator is identified, cite that person's name, followed by the appropriate abbreviation (*ed.*, *comp.*, *trans.*).
2. Title of the publication (italicized)
3. Name of the editor, compiler, or translator (if relevant)
4. Edition, release, or version (if relevant)
5. Place of publication
6. Name of the publisher
7. Date of publication
8. Medium of publication consulted
9. Supplementary information

If you cannot find some of this information, cite what is available.

Afro-Louisiana History and Genealogy, 1699-1860. Ed. Gwendolyn Midlo
   Hall. Baton Rouge: Louisiana State UP, 2000. CD-ROM.

English Poetry Full-Text Database. Rel. 2. Cambridge: Chadwyck-Healey,
   1993. CD-ROM.

Le Robert électronique. Paris: Robert, 1992. CD-ROM.

If publication information for a printed source or printed analogue is
indicated, begin the citation with that information. Give the publication data for the CD-ROM or DVD-ROM following the record of the
medium of publication.

Aristotle. *The Complete Works of Aristotle: The Revised Oxford*
   Translation. Ed. Jonathan Barnes. 2 vols. Princeton: Princeton UP,
   1984. CD-ROM. Clayton: InteLex, 1994.

If the work you are citing is part of another work, state which part.
If the work is of a type likely to be published on its own, such as a
book, italicize the title; if not, enclose the title in quotation marks. If
the source supplies page numbers, paragraph numbers, screen numbers, or some other kind of section numbers, state the range of the
numbers in the part if a single numbering encompasses all the parts.

"The Chemistry of Air Pollution." *Magill's Survey of Science.* 1998 ed.
   Pasadena: Salem, 1998. CD-ROM.

Coleridge, Samuel Taylor. "Dejection: An Ode." *The Complete Poetical*
   Works of Samuel Taylor Coleridge. Ed. Ernest Hartley Coleridge. Vol. 1.
   Oxford: Clarendon, 1912. 362-68. CD-ROM. *English Poetry Full-Text*
   Database. Rel. 2. Cambridge: Chadwyck-Healey, 1993.

"Parque." *Le Robert électronique.* Paris: Robert, 1992. CD-ROM.

b. Material from a Periodically Published Database on CD-ROM or DVD-ROM

Some periodicals (journals, magazines, newspapers) and periodically
published reference works, such as annual bibliographies and collections of abstracts, are published both in print and on CD-ROM or
DVD-ROM as databases or as parts of databases. To cite such a work,
begin with the publication data for the printed source or printed analogue, as identified in the disc publication. If the print version is a
book or a pamphlet, follow the guidelines in 5.5; if the print version
is an article in a periodical, follow 5.4. The typical works-cited-list
entry consists of the following items:

   1. Author's name (if given)

2. Publication information for the printed source or printed analogue (including title and date of print publication)
3. Medium of publication consulted
4. Title of the database (italicized)
5. Name of the vendor
6. Publication date of the database

If you cannot find some of this information, cite what is available.

Guidelines for Family Television Viewing. Urbana: ERIC Clearinghouse on
Elementary and Early Childhood Educ., 1990. CD-ROM. *ERIC.* Silver-
Platter. June 1993.

Krach, Peg. "Myth and Facts about Alcohol Abuse in the Elderly." *Nursing*
Feb. 1998: 25+. Abstract. CD-ROM. *Periodical Abstracts Ondisc.* UMI-
ProQuest. Feb. 1998.

Rodríguez, Miguel Angel. "Teatro de los Puppets: Diversión y educación."
Opinión 6 Sept. 1993: 1D. CD-ROM. *Ethnic Newswatch.* Dataware
Technologies. 1995.

United States. Cong. House. Committee on the Judiciary. *Report on the
Fair Use of Copyrighted Works.* 102nd Cong., 1st sess. CD-ROM.
Congressional Masterfile 2. Congressional Information Service. Dec.
1996.

c. A Multidisc Publication

If you are citing a CD-ROM or DVD-ROM publication of more than
one disc, complete the entry either with the total number of discs or
with a specific disc number if you use material from only one.

The Complete New Yorker. New York: New Yorker, 2005. DVD-ROM.
8 discs.

United States. Dept. of State. *Patterns of Global Terrorism.* 1994. CD-ROM.
National Trade Data Bank. US Dept. of Commerce. Dec. 1996. Disc 2.

5.7.18. A Digital File

Digital files can exist independently from the Web or a published disc.
Examples are a PDF file stored on your computer, a document created
by a peer using a word processor, a scanned image you received as an

e-mail attachment, and a sound recording formatted for playing on a digital audio player. In general, determine the kind of work you are citing (e.g., a book, a typescript, a photograph, a sound recording), and follow the relevant guidelines in this handbook for formatting the entry in the works-cited list. In the place reserved for the medium of publication, record the digital file format, followed by the word *file*—*PDF file*, Microsoft Word *file*, *JPEG file*, *MP3 file*, *XML file*, and so on—neither italicized (except for titles of software programs) nor enclosed in quotation marks. The file type is usually indicated by the extension at the end of the file name, after a period: OurCulturalCommonwealth.pdf. If you cannot identify the file type, use *Digital file*.

American Council of Learned Societies. Commission on
Cyberinfrastructure for the Humanities and Social Sciences. *Our Cultural Commonwealth*. New York: ACLS, 2006. PDF file.

Cortez, Juan. "Border Crossing in Chicano Narrative." 2007. *Microsoft Word* file.

Delano, Jack. *At the Vermont State Fair*. 1941. Lib. of Cong., Washington. JPEG file.

Hudson, Jennifer, perf. "And I Am Telling You I'm Not Going." *Dreamgirls: Music from the Motion Picture*. Sony BMG, 2006. MP3 file.

Your research may require that you cite more facts about the file, such as its date or name. For example, you may encounter multiple versions of a document with the same author and title, such as a sequence of drafts an author made in developing a work. Record such facts in the place reserved for the version or edition of a work.

Cortez, Juan. "Border Crossing in Chicano Narrative." File last modified on 4 Apr. 2007. *Microsoft Word* file.

5.8. A WORK IN MORE THAN ONE PUBLICATION MEDIUM

If a work you used is published in more than one medium (e.g., a book with a CD-ROM), follow the format for the medium of the component you primarily consulted. In the place for the medium of publication, specify alphabetically all the media you consulted.

Bauman, H-Dirksen L., Jennifer L. Nelson, and Heidi M. Rose, eds. *Signing the Body Poetic: Essays on American Sign Language Literature.* Berkeley: U of California P, 2006. DVD, print.

Burnard, Lou, Katherine O'Brien O'Keeffe, and John Unsworth, eds. *Electronic Textual Editing.* New York: MLA, 2006. CD-ROM, print.

Or, if you consulted only one part:

Rahtz, Sebastian. "Storage, Retrieval, and Rendering." *Electronic Textual Editing.* Ed. Lou Burnard, Katherine O'Brien O'Keeffe, and John Unsworth. New York: MLA, 2006. 310-33. Print.

⑥ Documentation: Citing Sources in the Text

6.1. PARENTHETICAL DOCUMENTATION AND THE LIST OF WORKS CITED

The list of works cited at the end of your research paper plays an important role in your acknowledgment of sources (see ch. 5), but the list does not in itself provide sufficiently detailed and precise documentation. You must indicate to your readers not only what works you used in writing the paper but also what you derived from each source and where in the work you found the material. The most practical way to supply this information is to insert a brief parenthetical acknowledgment in your paper wherever you incorporate another's words, facts, or ideas. Usually the author's last name and a page reference are enough to identify the source and the specific location from which you borrowed material.

> Medieval Europe was a place both of "raids, pillages, slavery, and extortion" and of "traveling merchants, monetary exchange, towns if not cities, and active markets in grain" (Townsend 10).

The parenthetical reference "(Townsend 10)" indicates that the quotations come from page 10 of a work by Townsend. Given the author's last name, your readers can find complete publication information for the source in the alphabetically arranged list of works cited that follows the text of your paper.

> Townsend, Robert M. *The Medieval Village Economy*. Princeton: Princeton UP, 1993. Print.

The sample references in 6.4 offer recommendations for documenting many other kinds of sources.

6.2. INFORMATION REQUIRED IN PARENTHETICAL DOCUMENTATION

In determining the information needed to document sources accurately, keep the following guidelines in mind.

References in the text must clearly point to specific sources in the list of works cited. The information in your parenthetical references in the text must match the corresponding information in the entries in your list of works cited. For a typical works-cited-list entry, which begins with the name of the author (or editor, translator, or narrator), the parenthetical reference begins with the same name. When the list contains only one work by the author cited, you need give only the author's last name to identify the work: "(Patterson 183–85)." If your list contains more than one author with the same last name, you must add the first initial—"(A. Patterson 183–85)" and "(L. Patterson 230)"—or, if the initial is shared too, the full first name. If two or three names begin the entry, give the last name of each person listed: "(Rabkin, Greenberg, and Olander vii)." If the work has more than three authors, follow the form in the bibliographic entry: either give the first author's last name followed by *et al.*, without any intervening punctuation—"(Lauter et al. 2601–09)"—or give all the last names. If there is a corporate author, use its name, shortened or in full (see 6.4.5). If the work is listed by title, use the title, shortened or in full; if two or more anonymous works have the same title, add a publication fact, such as a date, that distinguishes the works (see 6.4.4). If the list contains more than one work by the author, add the cited title, shortened or in full, after the author's last name (see 6.4.6).

Identify the location of the borrowed information as specifically as possible. Sources include a variety of reference markers to help users locate passages. For sources that use page numbering, give the relevant page number or numbers in the parenthetical reference (see esp. 6.4.2) or, if you cite from more than one volume of a multivolume work, the volume and page numbers (see 6.4.3). In a reference to a common work of literature, it is sometimes helpful to give information other than, or in addition to, the page number—for example, the chapter, book, or stanza number or the numbers of the act, scene, and line (see 6.4.8). You may omit page numbers when citing complete works (see 6.4.1). A page reference is similarly unnecessary if you use a passage from a one-page work. Electronic publications sometimes include paragraph numbers or other kinds of reference numbers (see 6.4.2). Of course, sources such as films, television broadcasts, performances, and electronic sources with no pagination or other type of reference markers cannot be cited by number. Such works are usually cited in their entirety (see 6.4.1) and often by title (see 6.4.4).

6.3. READABILITY

Keep parenthetical references as brief—and as few—as clarity and accuracy permit. Give only the information needed to identify a source, and do not add a parenthetical reference unnecessarily. Identify sources by author and, if necessary, title; do not use abbreviations such as *ed.*, *trans.*, and *comp.* after the name. If you are citing an entire work, for example, rather than a specific part of it, the author's name in the text may be the only documentation required. The statement "Booth has devoted an entire book to the subject" needs no parenthetical documentation if the list of works cited includes only one work by Booth. If, for the reader's convenience, you wish to name the book in your text, you can recast the sentence: "Booth has devoted an entire book, *The Rhetoric of Fiction*, to the subject."

Remember that there is a direct relation between what you integrate into your text and what you place in parentheses. If, for example, you include an author's name in a sentence, you need not repeat the name in the parenthetical page citation that follows, provided that the reference is clearly to the work of the author you mention. The paired sentences below illustrate alternative ways of identifying authors. Note that sometimes one version is more concise than the other.

AUTHOR'S NAME IN TEXT

Tannen has argued this point (178-85).

AUTHOR'S NAME IN REFERENCE

This point has already been argued (Tannen 178-85).

AUTHORS' NAMES IN TEXT

Others, like Jakobson and Waugh (210-15), hold the opposite point of view.

AUTHORS' NAMES IN REFERENCE

Others hold the opposite point of view (e.g., Jakobson and Waugh 210-15).

AUTHOR'S NAME IN TEXT

Only Daiches has seen this relation (2: 776-77).

AUTHOR'S NAME IN REFERENCE

Only one scholar has seen this relation (Daiches 2: 776-77).

AUTHOR'S NAME IN TEXT

It may be true, as Robertson maintains, that "in the appreciation of medieval art the attitude of the observer is of primary importance . . ." (136).

AUTHOR'S NAME IN REFERENCE

It may be true that "in the appreciation of medieval art the attitude of the observer is of primary importance . . ." (Robertson 136).

To avoid interrupting the flow of your writing, place the parenthetical reference where a pause would naturally occur (preferably at the end of a sentence), as near as possible to the material documented. The parenthetical reference precedes the punctuation mark that concludes the sentence, clause, or phrase containing the borrowed material.

In his *Autobiography*, Benjamin Franklin states that he prepared a list of thirteen virtues (135-37).

A reference directly after a quotation follows the closing quotation mark.

In the late Renaissance, Machiavelli contended that human beings were by nature "ungrateful" and "mutable" (1240), and Montaigne thought them "miserable and puny" (1343).

If the quotation, whether of poetry or prose, is set off from the text (sec 3.7.2–4), type a space after the concluding punctuation mark of the quotation and insert the parenthetical reference.

John K. Mahon adds a further insight to our understanding of the War of 1812:

> Financing the war was very difficult at the time. Baring Brothers, a banking firm of the enemy country, handled routine accounts for the United States overseas, but the firm would take on no loans. The loans were in the end absorbed by wealthy Americans at great hazard—also, as it turned out, at great profit to them. (385)

Elizabeth Bishop's "In the Waiting Room" is rich in evocative detail:

> It was winter. It got dark
> early. The waiting room
> was full of grown-up people,

> arctics and overcoats,
>
> lamps and magazines. (6-10)

For guidelines on citing common works of literature, see 6.4.8. If you need to document several sources for a statement, you may cite them in a note to avoid unduly disrupting the text (see 6.5.2).

When you borrow from a source several times in succession, you may be able to make your citations more concise by using one of the following techniques. However, always give your citations in full if these techniques would create ambiguity about your sources.

If you borrow more than once from the same source within a single paragraph and no borrowing from another source intervenes, you may give a single parenthetical reference after the last borrowing.

> *Romeo and Juliet* presents an opposition between two worlds: "the world
> of the everyday . . . and the world of romance." Although the two lovers
> are part of the world of romance, their language of love nevertheless
> becomes "fully responsive to the tang of actuality" (Zender 138, 141).

Here it is clear that the first page number in the parenthesis must apply to the first quotation and the second number to the second quotation.

But suppose you decide to break the first quotation into two parts. Then the parenthetical citation will be ambiguous, because three quotations will be followed by two numbers. It will not be clear how the page numbers should be matched to the borrowings. In that case, the citations should be separated. You can use another technique for making citations more economical—not repeating what is understood.

> *Romeo and Juliet* presents an opposition between two worlds: "the world
> of the everyday," associated with the adults in the play, and "the world of
> romance," associated with the two lovers (Zender 138). Romeo and Juliet's
> language of love nevertheless becomes "fully responsive to the tang of
> actuality" (141).

The second parenthetical citation, "(141)," omits the author's name. This omission is acceptable because the reader will conclude that the author must be Zender. No other understanding is possible. If you include material from a different source between the two borrowings, however, you must repeat this author's name in the second citation: "(Zender 141)."

A third technique is to define a source in the text at the start.

According to Karl F. Zender, *Romeo and Juliet* presents an opposition between two worlds: "the world of the everyday," associated with the adults in the play, and "the world of romance," associated with the two lovers (138). Romeo and Juliet's language of love nevertheless becomes "fully responsive to the tang of actuality" (141).

This technique can be useful when an entire paragraph is based on material from a single source. When a source is stated in this way and followed by a sequence of borrowings, it is important to signal at the end of the borrowings that you are switching to another source or to your own ideas. For example:

According to Karl F. Zender, *Romeo and Juliet* presents an opposition between two worlds: "the world of the everyday," associated with the adults in the play, and "the world of romance," associated with the two lovers (138). Romeo and Juliet's language of love nevertheless becomes "fully responsive to the tang of actuality" (141). I believe, in addition, that . . .

Work Cited

Zender, Karl F. "Loving Shakespeare's Lovers: Character Growth in *Romeo and Juliet.*" *Approaches to Teaching Shakespeare's* Romeo and Juliet. Ed. Maurice Hunt. New York: MLA, 2000. 137-43. Print.

6.4. SAMPLE REFERENCES

Each of the following sections concludes with a list of the works cited in the examples. Note that the lists for the first five sections (6.4.1–5) do not include more than one work by the same author. On citing two or more works by an author or authors, see 6.4.6.

6.4.1. Citing an Entire Work, Including a Work with No Page Numbers

If you wish to cite an entire work—whether a print source; a nonprint source such as a film, television broadcast, or performance; or a Web publication that has no pagination or other type of reference markers—it is often preferable to include in the text, rather than in a parenthetical reference, the name of the person (e.g., author, editor, director, performer) that begins the corresponding entry in the works-cited list. (See 6.4.4 for citing a work by title.)

> Fukuyama's *Our Posthuman Future* includes many examples of this trend.

> But Anthony Hunt has offered another view.

> Kurosawa's *Rashomon* was one of the first Japanese films to attract a Western audience.

> Chan considers the same topic in the context of Hong Kong cinema.

> The utilitarianism of the Victorians "attempted to reduce decision-making about human actions to a 'felicific calculus'" (Everett).

Works Cited

Chan, Evans. "Postmodernism and Hong Kong Cinema." *Postmodern Culture* 10.3 (2000): n. pag. *Project Muse.* Web. 20 May 2002.

Everett, Glenn. "Utilitarianism." *The Victorian Web*. Ed. George P. Landow. U Scholars Programme, Natl. U of Singapore, 11 Oct. 2002. Web. 18 May 2007.

Fukuyama, Francis. *Our Posthuman Future: Consequences of the Biotechnology Revolution*. New York: Farrar, 2002. Print.

Hunt, Anthony. "Singing the Dyads: The Chinese Landscape Scroll and Gary Snyder's *Mountains and Rivers without End*." *Journal of Modern Literature* 23.1 (1999): 7-34. Print.

Kurosawa, Akira, dir. *Rashomon*. Perf. Toshiro Mifune. Daiei, 1950. Film.

6.4.2. Citing Part of a Work

If you quote, paraphrase, or otherwise use a specific passage in a book, an article, or another work, give the relevant page or section (e.g., paragraph) number or numbers. When the author's name is in your text, give only the number reference in parentheses, but if the context does not clearly identify the author, add the author's last name before the reference. Leave a space between them, but do not insert punctuation or, for a page reference, the word *page* or *pages* or the abbreviation *p.* or *pp.* If you used only one volume of a multivolume work and included the volume number in the bibliographic entry, you need give only page numbers in the reference (see the Lauter et al. example), but if you used more than one volume of the work, you must cite both volume and page numbers (see 6.4.3).

If your source uses explicit paragraph numbers rather than page numbers—as, for example, some electronic publications do—give the relevant number or numbers preceded by the abbreviation *par.* or *pars.* (see the Chan example); if the author's name begins such a citation, place a comma after the name. If another kind of section is numbered in the source (e.g., sections; see the Committee on Scholarly Editions example), either write out the word for the section or use a standard abbreviation (see ch. 7); if the author's name begins such a citation, place a comma after the name. When a source has no page numbers or any other kind of reference numbers, no number can be given in the parenthetical reference. The work must be cited in its entirety (see 6.4.1), though you may indicate in your text an approximate location of the cited passage (e.g., "in the final third of his article, Jones argues for a revisionist interpretation"). Do not count unnumbered paragraphs.

Although writings describing utopia have always seemed to take place far from the everyday world, in fact "all utopian fiction whirls contemporary actors through a costume dance no place else but here" (Rabkin, Greenberg, and Olander vii).

Between 1968 and 1988, television coverage of presidential elections changed dramatically (Hallin 5).

The cluster on literacy in the anthology by Lauter and his coeditors is a resource for teaching the place of oral cultures in postbellum America (155-66).

Litvak calls Winters's mumbling a "labor of disarticulation" (167).

Chan claims that "Eagleton has belittled the gains of postmodernism" (par. 41).

The Committee on Scholarly Editions provides an annotated bibliography on the theory of textual editing (sec. 4).

Works Cited

Chan, Evans. "Postmodernism and Hong Kong Cinema." *Postmodern*
    Culture 10.3 (2000): n. pag. *Project Muse*. Web. 20 May 2002.

Committee on Scholarly Editions. "Guidelines for Editors of Scholarly
    Editions." *Modern Language Association*. MLA, 25 Sept. 2007. Web.
    22 Jan. 2008.

Hallin, Daniel C. "Sound Bite News: Television Coverage of Elections,
    1968-1988." *Journal of Communication* 42.2 (1992): 5-24. Print.

Lauter, Paul, et al., eds. *The Heath Anthology of American Literature*.
    5th ed. Vol. C. Boston: Houghton, 2006. Print.

Litvak, Joseph. "The Aesthetics of Jewishness: Shelley Winters." *Aesthetic*
    Subjects. Ed. Pamela R. Matthews and David McWhirter. Minneapolis:
    U of Minnesota P, 2003. 153-70. Print.

Rabkin, Eric S., Martin H. Greenberg, and Joseph D. Olander. Preface. *No*
    Place Else: Explorations in Utopian and Dystopian Fiction. Ed. Rabkin,
    Greenberg, and Olander. Carbondale: Southern Illinois UP, 1983. vii-ix.
    Print.

6.4.3. Citing Volume and Page Numbers of a Multivolume Work

When citing a volume number as well as a page reference for a multi-volume work, separate the two by a colon and a space: "(Wellek 2: 1–10)." Use neither the words *volume* and *page* nor their abbreviations. The functions of the numbers in such a citation are understood. If, however, you wish to refer parenthetically to an entire volume of a multivolume work, there is no need to cite pages. Place a comma after the author's name and include the abbreviation *vol.*: "(Wellek, vol. 2)." If you integrate such a reference into a sentence, spell out *volume*: "In volume 2, Wellek deals with. . . ."

> The anthology by Lauter and his coeditors contains both Stowe's "Sojourner Truth, the Libyan Sibyl" (B: 2601-09) and Gilman's "The Yellow Wall-Paper" (C: 578-90).

> Between 1945 and 1972, the political-party system in the United States underwent profound changes (Schlesinger, vol. 4).

Works Cited

Lauter, Paul, et al., eds. *The Heath Anthology of American Literature.*
    5th ed. 5 vols. Boston: Houghton, 2006. Print.
Schlesinger, Arthur M., Jr., gen. ed. *History of U.S. Political Parties.* 4 vols.
    New York: Chelsea, 1973. Print.

6.4.4. Citing a Work Listed by Title

In a parenthetical reference to a work alphabetized by title in the list
of works cited, the full title (if brief) or a shortened version precedes
the page, paragraph, section, or reference number or numbers (if any;
see 6.2), unless the title appears in your text. When abbreviating the
title, begin with the word by which it is alphabetized. Do not, for
example, shorten *Glossary of Terms Used in Heraldry* to *Heraldry*,
since this abbreviation would lead your reader to look for the bibliographic entry under *h* rather than *g.* If you are citing two or more
anonymous works that have the same title, find a publication fact that
distinguishes the works in their works-cited-list entries, and add it to
their parenthetical references (see the "Snowy Owl" example). This
fact could be the date of publication or the title of the work that encompasses the cited work. If you wish to cite a specific definition in
a dictionary entry, give the relevant designation (e.g., number, letter)
after the abbreviation *def.* (see the "Noon" example).

> The nine grades of mandarins were "distinguished by the color of the
> button on the hats of office" ("Mandarin").

> International espionage was as prevalent as ever in the 1990s ("Decade").

> Even *Sixty Minutes* launched an attack on modern art, in a segment
> entitled "Yes . . . but Is It Art?"

> In winter the snowy owl feeds primarily on small rodents ("Snowy Owl,"
> *Hinterland*), but in spring it also feeds on the eggs of much larger
> waterfowl, such as geese and swans ("Snowy Owl," *Arctic*).

> Milton's description of the moon at "her highest noon" signifies the "place
> of the moon at midnight" ("Noon," def. 4b).

> *Voice of the Shuttle* has links to many helpful resources.

Works Cited

"Decade of the Spy." *Newsweek* 7 Mar. 1994: 26-27. Print.

"Mandarin." *The Encyclopedia Americana.* 1994 ed. Print.

"Noon." *The Oxford English Dictionary.* 2nd ed. Oxford: Oxford UP, 1992.
    CD-ROM.

"Snowy Owl." *Arctic Studies Center.* Natl. Museum of Natural History of
    the Smithsonian Inst., 2004. Web. 8 Aug. 2007.

"Snowy Owl." *Hinterland Who's Who.* Canadian Wildlife Service, 2006. Web.
    8 Aug. 2007.

Voice of the Shuttle. Ed. Alan Liu. Dept. of Eng., U of California, Santa
    Barbara, n.d. Web. 8 Aug. 2007.

"Yes . . . but Is It Art?" Narr. Morley Safer. *Sixty Minutes.* CBS. WCBS, New
    York, 19 Sept. 1993. Television.

6.4.5. Citing a Work by a Corporate Author

To cite a work by a corporate author, you may use the author's name
followed by a page reference: "(United Nations, Economic Commission for Africa 79–86)." It is better, however, to include a long name
in the text, so that the reading is not interrupted with an extended
parenthetical reference. When giving the name of a corporate author
in parentheses, shorten terms that are commonly abbreviated (see
7.4): "(Natl. Research Council 15)."

In 1963 the United Nations Economic Commission for Africa predicted
that Africa would evolve into an advanced industrial economy within fifty
years (1-2, 4-6).

According to a study sponsored by the National Research Council, the
population of China around 1990 was increasing by more than fifteen
million annually (15).

Works Cited

National Research Council. *China and Global Change: Opportunities for
    Collaboration.* Washington: Natl. Acad., 1992. *National Academies
    Press.* Web. 15 Mar. 2007.

United Nations. Economic Commission for Africa. *Industrial Growth in
    Africa.* New York: United Nations, 1963. Print.

6.4.6. Citing Two or More Works by the Same Author or Authors

In a parenthetical reference to one of two or more works by the same author, put a comma after the author's last name and add the title of the work (if brief) or a shortened version and the relevant page reference: "(Frye, *Double Vision* 85)," "(Durant and Durant, *Age* 214–48)." If you state the author's name in the text, give only the title and page reference in parentheses: "(*Double Vision* 85)," "(*Age* 214–48)." If you include both the author's name and the title in the text, indicate only the pertinent page number or numbers in parentheses: "(85)," "(214–48)."

Shakespeare's *King Lear* has been called a "comedy of the grotesque" (Frye, *Anatomy* 237).

For Northrop Frye, one's death is not a unique experience, for "every moment we have lived through we have also died out of into another order" (*Double Vision* 85).

Moulthrop sees the act of reading hypertext as "struggle": "a chapter of chances, a chain of detours, a series of revealing figures in commitment out of which come the pleasures of the text" ("Traveling").

Hypertext, as one theorist puts it, is "all about connection, linkage, and affiliation" (Moulthrop, "You Say," par. 19).

Works Cited

Frye, Northrop. *Anatomy of Criticism: Four Essays.* Princeton: Princeton UP, 1957. Print.

---. *The Double Vision: Language and Meaning in Religion.* Toronto: U of Toronto P, 1991. Print.

Moulthrop, Stuart. "Traveling in the Breakdown Lane: A Principle of Resistance for Hypertext." *Mosaic* 28.4 (1995): 55-77. *University of Baltimore.* Web. 15 Mar. 2007.

---. "You Say You Want a Revolution? Hypertext and the Laws of Media." *Postmodern Culture* 1.3 (1991): n. pag. *Project Muse.* Web. 3 Apr. 1997.

6.4.7. Citing Indirect Sources

Whenever you can, take material from the original source, not a secondhand one. Sometimes, however, only an indirect source is available—for example, someone's published account of another's spoken remarks. If what you quote or paraphrase is itself a quotation, put the abbreviation *qtd. in* ("quoted in") before the indirect source you cite in your parenthetical reference. (You may document the original source in a note; see 6.5.1.)

> Samuel Johnson admitted that Edmund Burke was an "extraordinary man" (qtd. in Boswell 2: 450).

Work Cited

> Boswell, James. *The Life of Johnson*. Ed. George Birkbeck Hill and L. F. Powell. 6 vols. Oxford: Clarendon, 1934-50. Print.

6.4.8. Citing Common Literature

In a reference to a commonly studied prose work, such as a novel or play, that is available in several editions, it is helpful to provide more information than just a page number from the edition used; a chapter number, for example, would help readers to locate a quotation in any copy of a novel. In such a reference, give the page number first, add a semicolon, and then give other identifying information, using appropriate abbreviations: "(130; ch. 9)," "(271; bk. 4, ch. 2)."

> In *A Vindication of the Rights of Woman*, Mary Wollstonecraft recollects many "women who, not led by degrees to proper studies, and not permitted to choose for themselves, have indeed been overgrown children" (185; ch. 13, sec. 2).

When you cite an unpaginated source, the chapter number or similar designation may be the only identifying information you can give.

> Douglass notes that he had "no accurate knowledge" of his date of birth, "never having had any authentic record containing it" (ch. 1).

In citing commonly studied verse plays and poems, omit page numbers altogether and cite by division (act, scene, canto, book, part) and line, with periods separating the various numbers—for example, "*Iliad* 9.19" refers to book 9, line 19, of Homer's *Iliad*. If you are citing only line numbers, do not use the abbreviation *l.* or *ll.*, which can be confused with numerals. Instead, initially use the word *line* or *lines* and then, having established that the numbers designate lines, give the numbers alone (see fig. 33).

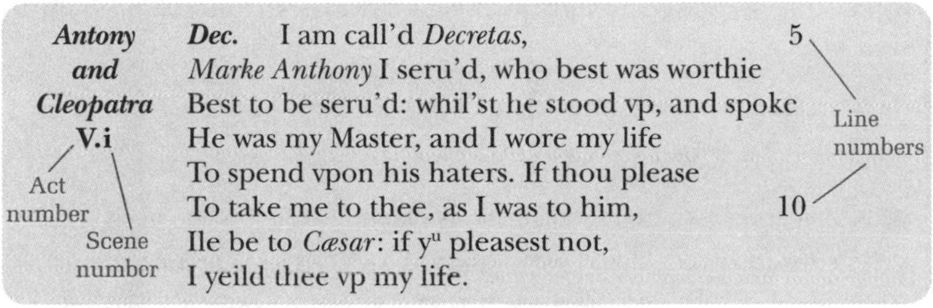

Fig. 33. A verse play with numbered divisions. Unless instructed otherwise, use arabic numerals for citations of acts, scenes, and other numbered divisions of works; titles of famous works are often abbreviated: "(*Ant.* 5.1.5–12)."

In general, use arabic numerals rather than roman numerals for division and page numbers. Although you must use roman numerals when citing pages of a preface or another section that are so numbered, designate volumes, parts, books, and chapters with arabic numerals even if your source does not. Some instructors prefer roman numerals, however, for citations of acts and scenes in plays (*King Lear* IV.i), but if your instructor does not require this practice, use arabic numerals (*King Lear* 4.1; see fig. 33). On numbers, see 3.5.

When citing scripture, provide an entry in the works-cited list for the edition you consulted. While general terms like Bible, Talmud, and Koran are not italicized, full and shortened titles of specific editions are italicized (see 3.6.5). The first time you borrow from a particular work of scripture in your manuscript, state in the text or in a parenthetical citation the element that begins the entry in the works-cited list (usually the title of the edition but sometimes an editor's or a translator's name). Identify the borrowing by divisions of the work—for the Bible, give the name of the book and chapter and verse numbers—rather than by a page number. Subsequent citations of the same edition may provide division numbers alone (see the *New Jerusalem Bible* example).

When included in parenthetical references, the titles of the books of the Bible and of famous literary works are often abbreviated (1 Chron. 21.8, Rev. 21.3, *Oth*. 4.2.7–13, *FQ* 3.3.53.3). The most widely used and accepted abbreviations for such titles are listed in 7.7. Follow prevailing practices for other abbreviations (*Troilus* for Chaucer's *Troilus and Criseyde*, "Nightingale" for Keats's "Ode to a Nightingale," etc.).

> In "Marching Song," Nesbit declares, "Our arms and hearts are strong for all who suffer wrong . . ." (line 11).

> One Shakespearean protagonist seems resolute at first when he asserts, "Haste me to know't, that I, with wings as swift / As meditation . . . / May sweep to my revenge" (*Ham*. 1.5.35-37), but he soon has second thoughts; another tragic figure, initially described as "too full o' th' milk of human kindness" (*Mac*. 1.5.17), quickly descends into horrific slaughter.

> In one of the most vivid prophetic visions in the Bible, Ezekiel saw "what seemed to be four living creatures," each with the faces of a man, a lion, an ox, and an eagle (*New Jerusalem Bible*, Ezek. 1.5-10). John of Patmos echoes this passage when describing his vision (Rev. 4.6-8).

Works Cited

Douglass, Frederick. *Narrative of the Life of Frederick Douglass*. Boston, 1845. *Department of History, University of Rochester*. Web. 15 Mar. 2007.

Nesbit, E[dith]. "Marching Song." 1887. *Ballads and Lyrics of Socialism: 1883-1908*. London: Fabian Soc.; Fifield, 1908. 9. *Victorian Women Writers Project*. Web. 15 Mar. 2007.

The New Jerusalem Bible. Henry Wansbrough, gen. ed. New York: Doubleday, 1985. Print.

Shakespeare, William. *Hamlet*. Ed. Barbara A. Mowat and Paul Werstine. New York: Washington Square-Pocket, 1992. Print.

---. *Macbeth*. Ed. Barbara A. Mowat and Paul Werstine. New York: Washington Square-Pocket, 1992. Print.

Wollstonecraft, Mary. *A Vindication of the Rights of Woman*. Ed. Carol H. Poston. New York: Norton, 1975. Print.

6.4.9. Citing More Than One Work in a Single Parenthetical Reference

If you wish to include two or more works in a single parenthetical reference, cite each work as you normally would in a reference, and use semicolons to separate the citations.

(Fukuyama 42; McRae 101-33)

(Natl. Research Council 25-35; "U.S.'s Paulson")

(Craner 308-11; Moulthrop, pars. 39-53)

(*Guidelines*; Hallin 18-24)

Keep in mind, however, that a long parenthetical reference such as the following example may prove intrusive and disconcerting to your reader:

(Taylor A1; Moulthrop, pars. 39-53; Armstrong, Yang, and Cuneo 80-82; Craner 308-11; Fukuyama 42)

To avoid an excessive disruption, cite multiple sources in a note rather than in parentheses in the text (see 6.5.2).

Works Cited

Armstrong, Larry, Dori Jones Yang, and Alice Cuneo. "The Learning Revolution: Technology Is Reshaping Education—at Home and at School." *Business Week* 28 Feb. 1994: 80-88. Print.

Craner, Paul M. "New Tool for an Ancient Art: The Computer and Music." *Computers and the Humanities* 25.5 (1991): 303-13. Print.

Fukuyama, Francis. *Our Posthuman Future: Consequences of the Biotechnology Revolution*. New York: Farrar, 2002. Print.

Guidelines for Family Television Viewing. Urbana: ERIC Clearinghouse on Elementary and Early Childhood Educ., 1990. CD-ROM. *ERIC*. SilverPlatter. Oct. 1993.

Hallin, Daniel C. "Sound Bite News: Television Coverage of Elections, 1968-1988." *Journal of Communication* 42.2 (1992): 5-24. Print.

McRae, Murdo William, ed. *The Literature of Science: Perspectives on Popular Science Writing*. Athens: U of Georgia P, 1993. Print.

Moulthrop, Stuart. "You Say You Want a Revolution? Hypertext and the Laws of Media." *Postmodern Culture* 1.3 (1991): n. pag. *Project Muse*. Web. 8 Aug. 2007.

National Research Council. *China and Global Change: Opportunities for Collaboration*. Washington: Natl. Acad., 1992. *National Academies Press*. Web. 15 Mar. 2007.

Taylor, Paul. "Keyboard Grief: Coping with Computer-Caused Injuries." *Globe and Mail* [Toronto] 27 Dec. 1993: A1+. Print.

"U.S.'s Paulson Urges China to Open Financial Markets." *CNN.com*. Cable News Network, 7 Mar. 2007. Web. 15 Mar. 2007.

6.5. USING NOTES WITH PARENTHETICAL DOCUMENTATION

Two kinds of notes may be used with parenthetical documentation:

- Content notes offering the reader comment, explanation, or information that the text cannot accommodate
- Bibliographic notes containing either several sources or evaluative comments on sources

In providing this sort of supplementary information, place a superscript arabic numeral at the appropriate place in the text and write the note after a matching numeral either at the end of the text (as an endnote) or at the bottom of the page (as a footnote). See the examples in 6.5.1–2.

6.5.1. Content Notes

In your notes, avoid lengthy discussions that divert the reader's attention from the primary text. In general, comments that you cannot fit into the text should be omitted unless they provide essential justification or clarification of what you have written. You may use a note, for example, to give full publication facts for an original source for which you cite an indirect source and perhaps to explain why you worked from secondary material.

Brooks's "The Ballad of Chocolate Mabbie" is a poem about a series of proposed metonymic relations (Mabbie next to the grammar school gate, Mabbie next to Willie Boone) that concludes with the speaker's hopeful recognition that if Mabbie aligns herself with like figures (her "chocolate companions") she will achieve a positive sense of self-reliance ("Mabbie on Mabbie to be").[1]

Note

1. In this paper, I follow the definition of *metonymy* as a figure of contiguity. For a good definition of the term, see Martin.

Works Cited

Brooks, Gwendolyn. "The Ballad of Chocolate Mabbie." *Selected Poems.* New York: Perennial-Harper, 2006. 7. Print.

Martin, Wallace. "Metonymy." *The New Princeton Encyclopedia of Poetry and Poetics.* Ed. Alex Preminger and T. V. F. Brogan. Princeton: Princeton UP, 1993. *Literature Online.* Web. 26 Mar. 2008.

6.5.2. Bibliographic Notes

Use notes for evaluative comments on sources and for references containing numerous citations.

Many observers conclude that health care in the United States is inadequate.[1]

Technological advancements have brought advantages as well as unexpected problems.[2]

Notes

1. For strong points of view on different aspects of the issue, see Public Agenda Foundation 1-10 and Sakala 151-88.

2. For a sampling of materials that reflect the range of experiences related to recent technological changes, see Taylor A1; Moulthrop, pars. 39-53; Armstrong, Yang, and Cuneo 80-82; Craner 308-11; and Fukuyama 42.

Works Cited

Armstrong, Larry, Dori Jones Yang, and Alice Cuneo. "The Learning
    Revolution: Technology Is Reshaping Education—at Home and at
    School." *Business Week* 28 Feb. 1994: 80-88. Print.

Craner, Paul M. "New Tool for an Ancient Art: The Computer and Music."
    Computers and the Humanities 25.5 (1991): 303-13. Print.

Fukuyama, Francis. *Our Posthuman Future: Consequences of the
    Biotechnology Revolution.* New York: Farrar, 2002. Print.

Moulthrop, Stuart. "You Say You Want a Revolution? Hypertext and the
    Laws of Media." *Postmodern Culture* 1.3 (1991): n. pag. *Project Muse.*
    Web. 8 Aug. 2007.

Public Agenda Foundation. *The Health Care Crisis: Containing Costs,
    Expanding Coverage.* New York: McGraw, 1992. Print.

Sakala, Carol. "Maternity Care Policy in the United States: Toward a More
    Rational and Effective System." Diss. Boston U, 1993. Print.

Taylor, Paul. "Keyboard Grief: Coping with Computer-Caused Injuries."
    Globe and Mail [Toronto] 27 Dec. 1993: A1+. Print.

Abbreviations

7.1. INTRODUCTION

Abbreviations are used regularly in the list of works cited and in tables but rarely in the text of a research paper (except within parentheses). In choosing abbreviations, keep your audience in mind. While economy of space is important, clarity is more so. Spell out a term if the abbreviation may puzzle your readers.

When abbreviating, always use accepted forms. In appropriate contexts, you may abbreviate the names of days, months, and other measurements of time (see 7.2); the names of states, provinces, countries, and continents (see 7.3); terms and reference words common in scholarship (see 7.4); publishers' names (see 7.5); and the titles of well-known and commonly studied works (see 7.7).

The trend in abbreviation is to use neither periods after letters nor spaces between letters, especially for abbreviations made up of all capital letters.

BC	MA	S
NJ	CD-ROM	US

The chief exception to this trend continues to be the initials used for personal names: a period and a space ordinarily follow each initial.

J. R. R. Tolkien

Most abbreviations that end in lowercase letters are followed by periods.

assn.	fig.	Mex.
Eng.	introd.	prod.

In most abbreviations made up of lowercase letters that each represent a word, a period follows each letter, but no space intervenes between letters.

a.m.	i.e.
e.g.	n.p.

But there are numerous exceptions.

mph	os
ns	rpm

7.2. TIME DESIGNATIONS

Spell out the names of months in the text but abbreviate them in the list of works cited, except for May, June, and July. Whereas words denoting units of time are also spelled out in the text (*second, minute, week, month, year, century*), some time designations are used only in abbreviated form (*a.m., p.m., AD, BC, BCE, CE*).

AD	after the birth of Christ (from the Latin *anno Domini* 'in the year of the Lord'; used before numerals ["AD 14"] and after references to centuries ["twelfth century AD"])
a.m.	before noon (from the Latin *ante meridiem*)
Apr.	April
Aug.	August
BC	before Christ (used after numerals ["19 BC"] and references to centuries ["fifth century BC"])
BCE	before the common era (used after numerals and references to centuries)
CE	common era (used after numerals and references to centuries)
cent.	century
Dec.	December
Feb.	February
Fri.	Friday
hr.	hour
Jan.	January
Mar.	March
min.	minute
mo.	month
Mon.	Monday
Nov.	November
Oct.	October
p.m.	after noon (from the Latin *post meridiem*)
Sat.	Saturday
sec.	second
Sept.	September
Sun.	Sunday
Thurs.	Thursday
Tues.	Tuesday
Wed.	Wednesday
wk.	week
yr.	year

7.3. GEOGRAPHIC NAMES

In the text, spell out the names of states, provinces, territories, and the like (other than federal districts stated after cities—e.g., Washington, DC), except usually in addresses and sometimes in parentheses. Likewise, spell out in the text the names of countries, with a few exceptions (e.g., USSR). In documentation, however, abbreviate the names of states, provinces, countries, and continents.

AB	Alberta
Afgh.	Afghanistan
Afr.	Africa
AK	Alaska
AL	Alabama
Alb.	Albania
Alg.	Algeria
Ant.	Antarctica
AR	Arkansas
Arg.	Argentina
Arm.	Armenia
AS	American Samoa
ASSR	Autonomous Soviet Socialist Republic
Aus.	Austria
Austral.	Australia
AZ	Arizona
Azer.	Azerbaijan
Bang.	Bangladesh
BC	British Columbia
Belg.	Belgium
Bol.	Bolivia
Bos.-Herz.	Bosnia-Herzegovina
Braz.	Brazil
Bulg.	Bulgaria
BWI	British West Indies
CA	California
Can.	Canada
CAR	Central African Republic
CO	Colorado
Col.	Colombia
CT	Connecticut
Czech Rep.	Czech Republic

DC	District of Columbia
DE	Delaware
Dem. Rep. Congo	Democratic Republic of Congo
Den.	Denmark
Dom. Rep.	Dominican Republic
Ecua.	Ecuador
Eng.	England
Equat. Guinea	Equatorial Guinea
Eth.	Ethiopia
Eur.	Europe
Fin.	Finland
FL	Florida
FM	Federated States of Micronesia
Fr.	France
Ga.	Georgia (republic)
GA	Georgia (US state)
Ger.	Germany
Gr.	Greece
Gt. Brit.	Great Britain
GU	Guam
Guat.	Guatemala
HI	Hawaii
Hond.	Honduras
Hung.	Hungary
IA	Iowa
ID	Idaho
IL	Illinois
IN	Indiana
Indon.	Indonesia
Ire.	Ireland
Isr.	Israel
It.	Italy
Jpn.	Japan
Kazakh.	Kazakhstan
KS	Kansas
KY	Kentucky
Kyrg.	Kyrgyzstan
LA	Louisiana
Lat. Amer.	Latin America
Leb.	Lebanon
Lith.	Lithuania

Lux.	Luxembourg
MA	Massachusetts
Madag.	Madagascar
MB	Manitoba
MD	Maryland
ME	Maine
Mex.	Mexico
MH	Marshall Islands
MI	Michigan
MN	Minnesota
MO	Missouri
Moz.	Mozambique
MP	Northern Mariana Islands
MS	Mississippi
MT	Montana
NB	New Brunswick
NC	North Carolina
ND	North Dakota
NE	Nebraska
Neth.	Netherlands
NH	New Hampshire
Nic.	Nicaragua
NJ	New Jersey
NL	Newfoundland and Labrador
NM	New Mexico
No. Amer.	North America
Norw.	Norway
NS	Nova Scotia
NT	Northwest Territories
NU	Nunavut
NV	Nevada
NY	New York
NZ	New Zealand
OH	Ohio
OK	Oklahoma
ON	Ontario
OR	Oregon
PA	Pennsylvania
Pak.	Pakistan
Pan.	Panama
Para.	Paraguay

PE	Prince Edward Island
Phil.	Philippines
PNG	Papua New Guinea
Pol.	Poland
Port.	Portugal
PR	Puerto Rico
PRC	People's Republic of China
PW	Palau
QC	Quebec, Québec
RI	Rhode Island
RSFSR	Russian Soviet Federalist Socialist Republic
Russ.	Russia
Russ. Fed.	Russian Federation
SC	South Carolina
Scot.	Scotland
SD	South Dakota
Serb. and Mont.	Serbia and Montenegro
Sing.	Singapore
SK	Saskatchewan
So. Afr.	South Africa
So. Amer.	South America
Sp.	Spain
Swed.	Sweden
Switz.	Switzerland
Tajik.	Tajikistan
Tanz.	Tanzania
Tas.	Tasmania
Thai.	Thailand
TN	Tennessee
Trin. and Tob.	Trinidad and Tobago
Turk.	Turkey
Turkm.	Turkmenistan
TX	Texas
UAE	United Arab Emirates
UK	United Kingdom
Ukr.	Ukraine
Uru.	Uruguay
US, USA	United States, United States of America
USSR	Union of Soviet Socialist Republics
UT	Utah
Uzbek.	Uzbekistan

VA	Virginia
Venez.	Venezuela
VI	Virgin Islands
VT	Vermont
WA	Washington
WI	Wisconsin
WV	West Virginia
WY	Wyoming
YT	Yukon Territory

7.4. COMMON SCHOLARLY ABBREVIATIONS AND REFERENCE WORDS

The following list includes abbreviations and reference words commonly used in humanities research studies in English. Abbreviations within parentheses are alternative but not recommended forms. The list provides some plurals of abbreviations (e.g., *nn*, *MSS*). Plurals of most other noun abbreviations not ending in *s* and longer than one letter can be formed through the addition of *s* (e.g., *adjs.*, *bks.*, *DVDs*, *figs.*, *insts.*, *pts.*). Most of the abbreviations listed would replace the spelled forms only in parentheses, tables, and documentation.

abbr.	abbreviation, abbreviated
abr.	abridgment, abridged, abridged by
acad.	academy
adapt.	adapter, adaptation, adapted by
adj.	adjective
adv.	adverb
Amer.	America, American
anon.	anonymous
app.	appendix
arch.	archaic
art.	article
assn.	association
assoc.	associate, associated
attrib.	attributed to
aux.	auxiliary verb
b.	born
BA	bachelor of arts

bib.	biblical
bibliog.	bibliographer, bibliography, bibliographic
biog.	biographer, biography, biographical
bk.	book
BL	British Library, London
BM	British Museum, London (library transferred to British Library in 1973)
BS	bachelor of science
bull.	bulletin
©, copr.	copyright ("© 2009")
c. (ca.)	circa, *or* around (used with approximate dates: "c. 1796")
cap.	capital, capitalize
CD	compact disc
CD-ROM	compact disc read-only memory
cf.	compare (not "see"; from the Latin *confer*)
ch. (chap.)	chapter
chor.	choreographer, choreographed by
col.	column
coll.	college
colloq.	colloquial
com	commercial (used as a suffix in Internet domain names: "www.nytimes.com")
comp.	compiler, compiled by
compar.	comparative
cond.	conductor, conducted by
conf.	conference
Cong.	Congress
Cong. Rec.	*Congressional Record*
conj.	conjunction
Const.	Constitution
cont.	contents; continued
(contd.)	continued
copr., ©	copyright
d.	died
DA	doctor of arts
DA, DAI	*Dissertation Abstracts, Dissertation Abstracts International*
DAB	*Dictionary of American Biography*
def.	definition; definite
dept.	department

dev.	development, developed by
dict.	dictionary
dir.	director, directed by
diss.	dissertation
dist.	district
distr.	distributor, distributed by
div.	division
DNB	*Dictionary of National Biography*
doc.	document
DVD	originally *digital videodisc* but now used to describe discs containing a wide range of data
DVD-ROM	digital videodisc read-only memory
ed.	editor, edition, edited by
EdD	doctor of education
edu	educational (used as a suffix in Internet domain names: "www.indiana.edu")
educ.	education, educational
e.g.	for example (from the Latin *exempli gratia*; rarely capitalized; set off by commas, unless preceded by a different punctuation mark)
e-mail	electronic mail
encyc.	encyclopedia
enl.	enlarged (as in "rev. and enl. ed.")
esp.	especially
et al.	and others (from the Latin *et alii, et aliae, et alia*)
etc.	and so forth (from the Latin *et cetera*; like most abbreviations, not appropriate in text)
ex.	example
fac.	faculty
facsim.	facsimile
fig.	figure
fl.	flourished, *or* reached greatest development or influence (from the Latin *floruit*; used before dates of historical figures when birth and death dates are not known: "fl. 1200")
fr.	from
front.	frontispiece
fut.	future
fwd.	foreword, foreword by
gen.	general (as in "gen. ed.")

gov	government (used as a suffix in Internet domain names: "www.census.gov")
govt.	government
GPO	Government Printing Office, Washington, DC
H. Doc.	House of Representatives Document
hist.	historian, history, historical
HMSO	Her (His) Majesty's Stationery Office, London
HR	House of Representatives
H. Rept.	House of Representatives Report
H. Res.	House of Representatives Resolution
HTML	hypertext markup language
http	hypertext transfer protocol (used at the beginning of an Internet address)
i.e.	that is (from the Latin *id est*; rarely capitalized; set off by commas, unless preceded by a different punctuation mark)
illus.	illustrator, illustration, illustrated by
inc.	including; incorporated
infin.	infinitive
inst.	institute, institution
intl.	international
introd.	introduction, introduced by
ips	inches per second (used in reference to tape recordings)
irreg.	irregular
ISP	Internet service provider
JD	doctor of law (from the Latin *juris doctor*)
jour.	journal
Jr.	Junior
KB	kilobyte
(l., ll.)	line, lines (avoided in favor of *line* and *lines* or, if clear, numbers only)
lang.	language
LC	Library of Congress
leg.	legal
legis.	legislator, legislation, legislature, legislative
lib.	library
lit.	literally; literature, literary
LLB	bachelor of laws (from the Latin *legum baccalaureus*)

LLD	doctor of laws (from the Latin *legum doctor*)
LLM	master of laws (from the Latin *legum magister*)
LP	long-playing phonograph record
ltd.	limited
MA	master of arts
mag.	magazine
MB	megabyte
MD	doctor of medicine (from the Latin *medicinae doctor*)
misc.	miscellaneous
mod.	modern
MS	master of science
MS, MSS	manuscript, manuscripts (as in "Bodleian MS Tanner 43"; cf. *TS, TSS*)
n, nn	note, notes (used immediately after the number of the page containing the text of the note or notes: "56n," "56n3," "56nn3–5")
n.	noun
narr.	narrator, narrated by
natl.	national
NB	take notice (from the Latin *nota bene*; always capitalized)
n.d.	no date of publication
NED	*A New English Dictionary* (cf. *OED*)
no.	number (cf. *numb.*)
nonstand.	nonstandard
n.p.	no place of publication; no publisher
n. pag.	no pagination
ns	new series
NS	New Style (calendar designation)
numb.	numbered (cf. *no.*)
obj.	object, objective
obs.	obsolete
OCLC	Online Computer Library Center
OED	*The Oxford English Dictionary* (formerly *A New English Dictionary* [*NED*])
op.	opus (work)
orch.	orchestra (also Italian *orchestra*, French *orchestre*, etc.), orchestrated by
org	organization (used as a suffix in Internet domain names: "www.mla.org")

orig.	original, originally
os	old series; original series
OS	Old Style (calendar designation)
P	Press (used in documentation; cf. *UP*)
p., pp.	page, pages (omitted before page numbers unless necessary for clarity)
par.	paragraph
part.	participle
PDF	portable document format
perf.	performer, performed by
PhD	doctor of philosophy (from the Latin *philosophiae doctor*)
philol.	philology, philological
philos.	philosophy, philosophical
pl.	plate; plural
poss.	possessive
pref.	preface, preface by
prep.	preposition
pres.	present
proc.	proceedings
prod.	producer, produced by
pron.	pronoun
pronunc.	pronunciation
PS	postscript
pseud.	pseudonym
pt.	part
pub. (publ.)	publisher, publication, published by
Pub. L.	Public Law
qtd.	quoted
r.	reigned
rec.	record, recorded
Ref.	Reference (used to indicate the reference section in a library)
reg.	registered; regular
rel.	relative; release
rept.	report, reported by
res.	resolution
resp.	respectively
rev.	review, reviewed by; revision, revised, revised by (spell out *review* where *rev.* might be ambiguous)

RLIN	Research Libraries Information Network
rpm	revolutions per minute (used in reference to phonograph recordings)
rpt.	reprint, reprinted, reprinted by
S	Senate
sc.	scene (omitted when act and scene numbers are used together for verse plays: "*King Lear* 4.1")
S. Doc.	Senate Document
sec. (sect.)	section
ser.	series
sess.	session
sic	thus in the source (in square brackets as an editorial interpolation, otherwise in parentheses; not followed by an exclamation point)
sing.	singular
soc.	society
spec.	special
Sr.	Senior
S. Rept.	Senate Report
S. Res.	Senate Resolution
st.	stanza
St., Sts. (S, SS)	Saint, Saints
Stat.	Statutes at Large
subj.	subject, subjective; subjunctive
substand.	substandard
supp.	supplement
syn.	synonym
trans. (tr.)	transitive; translator, translation, translated by
TS, TSS	typescript, typescripts (cf. *MS, MSS*)
U	University (also French *Université*, German *Universität*, Italian *Università*, Spanish *Universidad*, etc.; used in documentation; cf. *UP*)
univ.	university (used outside documentation—e.g., in parentheses and tables: "Montclair State Univ.")
UP	University Press (used in documentation: "Columbia UP")
URL	uniform resource locator
USC	United States Code

usu.	usually
var.	variant
vb.	verb
vers.	version
VHS	video home system (the recording and playing standard for videocassette recorders)
vol.	volume
vs. (v.)	versus (*v.* preferred in titles of legal cases)
writ.	writer, written by
www	World Wide Web (used in the names of servers, or computers, on the Web)

7.5. PUBLISHERS' NAMES

In the list of works cited, shortened forms of publishers' names immediately follow the cities of publication, enabling the reader to locate books or to acquire more information about them. Since publications like *Books in Print*, *Literary Market Place*, and *International Literary Market Place* list publishers' addresses, you need give only enough information so that your reader can look up the publishers in one of these sources. It is usually sufficient, for example, to give "Harcourt" as the publisher's name even if the title page shows "Harcourt Brace" or one of the other earlier names of that firm (Harcourt, Brace; Harcourt, Brace, and World; Harcourt Brace Jovanovich). If you are preparing a bibliographic study, however, or if publication history is important to your paper, give the publisher's name in full.

In shortening publishers' names, keep in mind the following points:

- Omit articles (*A*, *An*, *The*), business abbreviations (*Co.*, *Corp.*, *Inc.*, *Ltd.*), and descriptive words (*Books*, *House*, *Press*, *Publishers*). When citing a university press, however, always add the abbreviation *P* (Ohio State UP) because the university itself may publish independently of its press (Ohio State U).
- If the publisher's name includes the name of one person (Harry N. Abrams, W. W. Norton, John Wiley), cite the surname alone (Abrams, Norton, Wiley). If the publisher's name includes the names of more than one person, cite only the first of the surnames (Bobbs, Dodd, Faber, Farrar, Funk, Grosset, Harcourt, Harper, Houghton, McGraw, Prentice, Simon).

- Use standard abbreviations whenever possible (*Acad.*, *Assn.*, *Soc.*, *UP*; see 7.4).
- If the publisher's name is commonly abbreviated with capital initial letters and if the abbreviation is likely to be familiar to your audience, use the abbreviation as the publisher's name (GPO, MLA, UMI). If your readers are not likely to know the abbreviation, shorten the name according to the general guidelines given above (Mod. Lang. Assn.).

Following are examples of how various types of publishers' names are shortened:

Acad. for Educ. Dev.	Academy for Educational Development, Inc.
ACLS	American Council of Learned Societies
ALA	American Library Association
Basic	Basic Books
CAL	Center for Applied Linguistics
Cambridge UP	Cambridge University Press
Eastgate	Eastgate Systems
Einaudi	Giulio Einaudi Editore
ERIC	Educational Resources Information Center
Farrar	Farrar, Straus and Giroux, Inc.
Feminist	The Feminist Press at the City University of New York
Gale	Gale Research, Inc.
Gerig	Gerig Verlag
GPO	Government Printing Office
Harper	Harper and Row, Publishers, Inc.; HarperCollins Publishers, Inc.
Harvard Law Rev. Assn.	Harvard Law Review Association
HMSO	Her (His) Majesty's Stationery Office
Houghton	Houghton Mifflin Co.
Knopf	Alfred A. Knopf, Inc.
Larousse	Librairie Larousse
Little	Little, Brown and Company, Inc.
Macmillan	Macmillan Publishing Co., Inc.
McGraw	McGraw-Hill, Inc.
MIT P	The MIT Press
MLA	The Modern Language Association of America

NCTE	The National Council of Teachers of English
NEA	The National Education Association
Norton	W. W. Norton and Co., Inc.
Planeta	Editorial Planeta Mexicana
PUF	Presses Universitaires de France
Random	Random House, Inc.
Scribner's	Charles Scribner's Sons
Simon	Simon and Schuster, Inc.
SIRS	Social Issues Resources Series
State U of New York P	State University of New York Press
St. Martin's	St. Martin's Press, Inc.
UMI	University Microfilms International
U of Chicago P	University of Chicago Press
UP of Mississippi	University Press of Mississippi

7.6. SYMBOLS AND ABBREVIATIONS USED IN PROOFREADING AND CORRECTION

7.6.1. Selected Proofreading Symbols

Proofreaders use the symbols below when correcting typeset material. Many instructors also use them in marking student papers.

⌄	add an apostrophe or a single quotation mark
⌒	close up (basket⌒ball)
⋀	add a comma
ℛ	delete
⋀	insert
¶	begin a new paragraph
No ¶	do not begin a new paragraph
⊙	add a period
⌄⌄	add double quotation marks
#	add space
∽	transpose elements (usually with *tr* in margin) (th⁀er)

7.6.2. Common Correction Symbols and Abbreviations

		lack of parallelism
ab	faulty abbreviation
adj	improper use of adjective
adv	improper use of adverb
agr	faulty agreement
amb	ambiguous expression or construction
awk	awkward expression or construction
cap	faulty capitalization
d	faulty diction
dgl	dangling construction
frag	fragment
lc	use lowercase
num	error in use of numbers
p	faulty punctuation
ref	unclear pronoun reference
rep	unnecessary repetition
r-o	run-on sentence
sp	error in spelling
ss	faulty sentence structure
t	wrong tense of verb
tr	transpose elements
vb	wrong verb form
wdy	wordy writing

7.7. TITLES OF WORKS

In documentation, you may abbreviate the titles of works and parts of works. It is usually best to introduce an abbreviation in parentheses immediately after the first use of the full title in the text: "In *All's Well That Ends Well* (*AWW*), Shakespeare. . . ." Abbreviating titles is appropriate, for example, if you repeatedly cite a variety of works by the same author. In such a discussion, abbreviations make for more concise parenthetical documentation—"(*AWW* 3.2.100–29)," "(*MM* 4.3.93–101)"—than the usual shortened titles would: "(*All's Well* 3.2.100–29)," "(*Measure* 4.3.93–101)." For works not on the following lists, you may use the abbreviations you find in your sources, or you may devise simple, unambiguous abbreviations of your own.

7.7.1. Bible

The following abbreviations and spelled forms are commonly used for parts of the Bible (Bib.). While the Hebrew Bible and the Protestant Old Testament include the same parts in slightly different arrangements, Roman Catholic versions of the Old Testament also include works listed here as apocrypha.

HEBREW BIBLE OR OLD TESTAMENT (OT)

Amos	Amos
Cant. of Cant.	Canticle of Canticles (also called Song of Solomon and Song of Songs)
1 Chron.	1 Chronicles
2 Chron.	2 Chronicles
Dan.	Daniel
Deut.	Deuteronomy
Eccles.	Ecclesiastes (also called Qoheleth)
Esth.	Esther
Exod.	Exodus
Ezek.	Ezekiel
Ezra	Ezra
Gen.	Genesis
Hab.	Habakkuk
Hag.	Haggai
Hos.	Hosea
Isa.	Isaiah
Jer.	Jeremiah
Job	Job
Joel	Joel
Jon.	Jonah
Josh.	Joshua
Judg.	Judges
1 Kings	1 Kings
2 Kings	2 Kings
Lam.	Lamentations
Lev.	Leviticus
Mal.	Malachi
Mic.	Micah
Nah.	Nahum
Neh.	Nehemiah
Num.	Numbers

Obad.	Obadiah
Prov.	Proverbs
Ps.	Psalms
Qoh.	Qoheleth (also called Ecclesiastes)
Ruth	Ruth
1 Sam.	1 Samuel
2 Sam.	2 Samuel
Song of Sg.	Song of Songs (also called Canticle of Canticles and Song of Solomon)
Song of Sol.	Song of Solomon (also called Canticle of Canticles and Song of Songs)
Zech.	Zechariah
Zeph.	Zephaniah

NEW TESTAMENT (NT)

Acts	Acts
Apoc.	Apocalypse (also called Revelation)
Col.	Colossians
1 Cor.	1 Corinthians
2 Cor.	2 Corinthians
Eph.	Ephesians
Gal.	Galatians
Heb.	Hebrews
Jas.	James
John	John
1 John	1 John
2 John	2 John
3 John	3 John
Jude	Jude
Luke	Luke
Mark	Mark
Matt.	Matthew
1 Pet.	1 Peter
2 Pet.	2 Peter
Phil.	Philippians
Philem.	Philemon
Rev.	Revelation (also called Apocalypse)
Rom.	Romans
1 Thess.	1 Thessalonians
2 Thess.	2 Thessalonians
1 Tim.	1 Timothy

2 Tim.	2 Timothy
Tit.	Titus

SELECTED APOCRYPHA

Bar.	Baruch
Bel and Dr.	Bel and the Dragon
Ecclus.	Ecclesiasticus (also called Sirach)
1 Esd.	1 Esdras
2 Esd.	2 Esdras
Esth. (Apocr.)	Esther (Apocrypha)
Jth.	Judith
1 Macc.	1 Maccabees
2 Macc.	2 Maccabees
Pr. of Man.	Prayer of Manasseh
Sg. of 3 Childr.	Song of Three Children
Sir.	Sirach (also called Ecclesiasticus)
Sus.	Susanna
Tob.	Tobit
Wisd.	Wisdom (also called Wisdom of Solomon)
Wisd. of Sol.	Wisdom of Solomon (also called Wisdom)

7.7.2. Works by Shakespeare

Ado	*Much Ado about Nothing*
Ant.	*Antony and Cleopatra*
AWW	*All's Well That Ends Well*
AYL	*As You Like It*
Cor.	*Coriolanus*
Cym.	*Cymbeline*
Err.	*The Comedy of Errors*
F1	First Folio edition (1623)
F2	Second Folio edition (1632)
Ham.	*Hamlet*
1H4	*Henry IV, Part 1*
2H4	*Henry IV, Part 2*
H5	*Henry V*
1H6	*Henry VI, Part 1*
2H6	*Henry VI, Part 2*

3H6	*Henry VI, Part 3*
H8	*Henry VIII*
JC	*Julius Caesar*
Jn.	*King John*
LC	*A Lover's Complaint*
LLL	*Love's Labour's Lost*
Lr.	*King Lear*
Luc.	*The Rape of Lucrece*
Mac.	*Macbeth*
MM	*Measure for Measure*
MND	*A Midsummer Night's Dream*
MV	*The Merchant of Venice*
Oth.	*Othello*
Per.	*Pericles*
PhT	*The Phoenix and the Turtle*
PP	*The Passionate Pilgrim*
Q	Quarto edition
R2	*Richard II*
R3	*Richard III*
Rom.	*Romeo and Juliet*
Shr.	*The Taming of the Shrew*
Son.	*Sonnets*
TGV	*The Two Gentlemen of Verona*
Tim.	*Timon of Athens*
Tit.	*Titus Andronicus*
Tmp.	*The Tempest*
TN	*Twelfth Night*
TNK	*The Two Noble Kinsmen*
Tro.	*Troilus and Cressida*
Ven.	*Venus and Adonis*
Wiv.	*The Merry Wives of Windsor*
WT	*The Winter's Tale*

7.7.3. Works by Chaucer

BD	*The Book of the Duchess*
CkT	The Cook's Tale
ClT	The Clerk's Tale
CT	*The Canterbury Tales*
CYT	The Canon's Yeoman's Tale

FranT	The Franklin's Tale
FrT	The Friar's Tale
GP	The General Prologue
HF	*The House of Fame*
KnT	The Knight's Tale
LGW	*The Legend of Good Women*
ManT	The Manciple's Tale
Mel	The Tale of Melibee
MerT	The Merchant's Tale
MilT	The Miller's Tale
MkT	The Monk's Tale
MLT	The Man of Law's Tale
NPT	The Nun's Priest's Tale
PardT	The Pardoner's Tale
ParsT	The Parson's Tale
PF	*The Parliament of Fowls*
PhyT	The Physician's Tale
PrT	The Prioress's Tale
Ret	Chaucer's Retraction
RvT	The Reeve's Tale
ShT	The Shipman's Tale
SNT	The Second Nun's Tale
SqT	The Squire's Tale
SumT	The Summoner's Tale
TC	*Troilus and Criseyde*
Th	The Tale of Sir Thopas
WBT	The Wife of Bath's Tale

7.7.4. Other Works

Aen.	Vergil, *Aeneid*
Ag.	Aeschylus, *Agamemnon*
Ant.	Sophocles, *Antigone*
Bac.	Euripides, *Bacchae*
Beo.	*Beowulf*
Can.	Voltaire, *Candide*
Dec.	Boccaccio, *Decameron*
DJ	Byron, *Don Juan*
DQ	Cervantes, *Don Quixote*
Eum.	Aeschylus, *Eumenides*

FQ	Spenser, *The Faerie Queene*
Gil.	*Epic of Gilgamesh*
GT	Swift, *Gulliver's Travels*
Hept.	Marguerite de Navarre, *Heptameron*
Hip.	Euripides, *Hippolytus*
Il.	Homer, *Iliad*
Inf.	Dante, *Inferno*
LB	Wordsworth, *Lyrical Ballads*
Lys.	Aristophanes, *Lysistrata*
MD	Melville, *Moby-Dick*
Med.	Euripides, *Medea*
Mis.	Molière, *Le misanthrope*
Nib.	*Nibelungenlied*
Od.	Homer, *Odyssey*
OR	Sophocles, *Oedipus Rex* (also called *Oedipus Tyrannus* [*OT*])
Or.	Aeschylus, *Oresteia*
OT	Sophocles, *Oedipus Tyrannus* (also called *Oedipus Rex* [*OR*])
Par.	Dante, *Paradiso*
PL	Milton, *Paradise Lost*
Prel.	Wordsworth, *The Prelude*
Purg.	Dante, *Purgatorio*
Rep.	Plato, *Republic*
SA	Milton, *Samson Agonistes*
SGGK	*Sir Gawain and the Green Knight*
Sym.	Plato, *Symposium*
Tar.	Molière, *Tartuffe*

Appendix A:
Guides to Writing

A.1. INTRODUCTION

A good dictionary is an essential tool for all writers. Your instructor will probably recommend a standard American dictionary such as *The American Heritage College Dictionary*, *Merriam-Webster's Collegiate Dictionary*, or *The New Oxford American Dictionary*. Because dictionaries vary in matters like word division and spelling preference, you should, to maintain consistency, use the same one throughout your paper.

You should also keep on hand at least one reliable guide to writing. A selected list of writing guides appears below, classified under three headings: dictionaries of usage, guides to nondiscriminatory language, and books on style. Your instructor can help you choose among these titles.

A.2. DICTIONARIES OF USAGE

Bernstein, Theodore M. *The Careful Writer: A Modern Guide to English Usage*. 1965. New York: Free, 1998. Print.

Copperud, Roy H. *American Usage and Style: The Consensus*. New York: Van Nostrand, 1980. Print.

Follett, Wilson. *Modern American Usage: A Guide*. Rev. Erik Wensberg. Rev. ed. New York: Hill-Farrar, 1998. Print.

Fowler, H[enry] W. *Fowler's Modern English Usage*. Ed. R. W. Burchfield. Rev. 3rd ed. 1998. New York: Oxford UP, 2004. Print.

Garner, Bryan A. *Garner's Modern American Usage*. New York: Oxford UP, 2003. Print.

———. *The Oxford Dictionary of American Usage and Style*. New York: Oxford UP, 2000. Print.

Lovinger, Paul W. *The Penguin Dictionary of American English Usage and Style*. New York: Penguin, 2002. Print.

Mager, Nathan H., and Sylvia K. Mager. *Prentice Hall Encyclopedic Dictionary of English Usage*. 2nd ed. Englewood Cliffs: Prentice, 1992. Print.

Morris, William, and Mary Morris. *Harper Dictionary of Contemporary Usage*. 2nd ed. 1985. New York: Harper, 1992. Print.

Nicholson, Margaret. *A Dictionary of American-English Usage Based on Fowler's* Modern English Usage. New York: Oxford UP, 1957. Print.

Waite, Maurice, E. S. C. Weiner, and Andrew Delahunty, eds. *The Oxford Dictionary and Usage Guide to the English Language*. New York: Oxford UP, 1995. Print.

Weiner, E. S. C., and Andrew Delahunty, comps. *The Oxford Guide to English Usage*. 2nd ed. Oxford: Oxford UP, 1993. Print.

Wilson, Kenneth G. *The Columbia Guide to Standard American English*. New York: Columbia UP, 1993. Print.

A.3. GUIDES TO NONDISCRIMINATORY LANGUAGE

American Psychological Association. "Guidelines to Reduce Bias in Language." *Publication Manual of the American Psychological Association*. 5th ed. Washington: Amer. Psychological Assn., 2001. 61–76. Print.

Frank, Francine Wattman, and Paula A. Treichler. *Language, Gender, and Professional Writing: Theoretical Approaches and Guidelines for Nonsexist Usage*. New York: MLA, 1989. Print.

International Association of Business Communication. *Without Bias: A Guidebook for Nondiscriminatory Communication*. Ed. Judy E. Pickens, Patricia W. Rao, and Linda C. Roberts. 2nd ed. New York: Wiley, 1982. Print.

Maggio, Rosalie. *The Bias-Free Word Finder: A Dictionary of Nondiscriminatory Language*. Boston: Beacon, 1992. Print.

———. *The Dictionary of Bias-Free Usage: A Guide to Nondiscriminatory Language*. Phoenix: Oryx, 1991. Print.

———. *The Nonsexist Word Finder: A Dictionary of Gender-Free Usage*. 1987. Boston: Beacon, 1989. Print.

———. *Talking about People: A Guide to Fair and Accurate Language*. Phoenix: Oryx, 1997. Print.

Miller, Casey, and Kate Swift. *The Handbook of Nonsexist Writing*. 2nd ed. New York: Harper, 1988. Print.

———. *Words and Women*. Rev. ed. New York: Harper, 1991. Print.

Schwartz, Marilyn, and the Task Force of the Association of American University Presses. *Guidelines for Bias-Free Writing*. Bloomington: Indiana UP, 1995. Print.

Sorrels, Bobbye D. *The Nonsexist Communicator: Solving the Problems of Gender and Awkwardness in Modern English*. Englewood Cliffs: Prentice, 1983. Print.

Warren, Virginia L. "Guidelines for the Nonsexist Use of Language." *Proceedings and Addresses of the American Philosophical Association* 59.3 (1986): 471–84. Print.

A.4. BOOKS ON STYLE

Barzun, Jacques. *Simple and Direct: A Rhetoric for Writers.* 4th ed. New York: Harper, 2001. Print.

Beardsley, Monroe C. *Thinking Straight: Principles of Reasoning for Readers and Writers.* 4th ed. Englewood Cliffs: Prentice, 1975. Print.

Cook, Claire Kehrwald. *Line by Line: How to Edit Your Own Writing.* Boston: Houghton, 1985. Print.

Eastman, Richard M. *Style: Writing and Reading as the Discovery of Outlook.* 3rd ed. New York: Oxford UP, 1984. Print.

Elbow, Peter. *Writing without Teachers.* 2nd ed. New York: Oxford UP, 1998. Print.

———. *Writing with Power: Techniques for Mastering the Writing Process.* 2nd ed. New York: Oxford UP, 1998. Print.

Gibson, Walker. *Tough, Sweet, and Stuffy: An Essay on Modern American Prose Styles.* Westport: Greenwood, 1984. Print.

Gowers, Ernest. *The Complete Plain Words.* Ed. Sidney Greenbaum and Janet Whitcut. Rev. ed. 1990. Boston: Godine, 2002. Print.

Lanham, Richard A. *Style: An Anti-textbook.* Rev. 2nd ed. Philadelphia: Dry, 2007. Print.

Smith, Charles K. *Styles and Structures: Alternative Approaches to College Writing.* New York: Norton, 1974. Print.

Strunk, William, Jr., and E. B. White. *The Elements of Style.* 4th ed. New York: Longman-Allyn, 2000. Print.

Williams, Joseph M. *Style: Lessons in Clarity and Grace.* 9th ed. New York: Longman-Allyn, 2007. Print.

———. *Style: Toward Clarity and Grace.* 1990. Chicago: U of Chicago P, 1995. Print.

Appendix B: Specialized Style Manuals

Every scholarly field has its preferred style, or set of guidelines for writing. MLA style, as presented in this handbook, is widely accepted in humanities disciplines. The following manuals describe the styles of other disciplines.

Biblical Literature

Alexander, Patrick H., et al., eds. *The SBL Handbook of Style: For Ancient Near Eastern, Biblical, and Early Christian Studies*. Peabody: Hendrickson, 1999. Print.

Chemistry

Coghill, Anne M., and Lorrin R. Garson, eds. *The ACS Style Guide: Effective Communication of Scientific Information*. 3rd ed. Washington: Amer. Chemical Soc., 2006. Print.

Geology

United States. Geological Survey. *Suggestions to Authors of the Reports of the United States Geological Survey*. 7th ed. Washington: GPO, 1991. Print, Web.

Law

Association of Legal Writing Directors and Darby Dickerson. *ALWD Citation Manual: A Professional System of Citation*. 3rd ed. New York: Aspen, 2006. Print.

Harvard Law Review Association. *The Bluebook: A Uniform System of Citation*. 18th ed. Cambridge: Harvard Law Rev. Assn., 2005. Print.

Linguistics

"*Language* Style Sheet." *Linguistic Society of America*. Linguistic Soc. of Amer., n.d. Web. 20 May 2008.

Medicine

Iverson, Cheryl, et al. *AMA Manual of Style: A Guide for Authors and Editors*. 10th ed. New York: Oxford UP, 2007. Print.

Physics

American Institute of Physics. *AIP Style Manual*. 4th ed. New York: Amer. Inst. of Physics, 1990. Print, Web.

Political Science

American Political Science Association. Committee on Publications. *Style Manual for Political Science.* 2nd rev. ed. Washington: Amer. Political Science Assn., 2006. Print.

Psychology

American Psychological Association. *Publication Manual of the American Psychological Association.* 5th ed. Washington: Amer. Psychological Assn., 2001. Print.

Science

Council of Science Editors. Style Manual Committee. *Scientific Style and Format: The CSE Manual for Authors, Editors, and Publishers.* 7th ed. Reston: Council of Science Eds., 2006. Print.

Sociology

American Sociological Association. *ASA Style Guide.* 3rd ed. Washington: Amer. Sociological Assn., 2007. Print.

The *MLA Style Manual*, published by the MLA, addresses graduate students, scholars, and professional writers. While the information on documentation style it contains is essentially the same as that presented in the *MLA Handbook*, the *MLA Style Manual* gives more detail on working with sources in languages other than English. It includes extensive advice on preparing manuscripts for publication.

MLA Style Manual and Guide to Scholarly Publishing. 3rd ed. New York: MLA, 2008. Print.

There are also style manuals that address primarily editors and concern procedures for preparing a manuscript for publication.

The Chicago Manual of Style. 15th ed. Chicago: U of Chicago P, 2003. Print, Web.
Skillin, Marjorie E., et al. *Words into Type.* 3rd ed. Englewood Cliffs: Prentice, 1974. Print.
United States. Government Printing Office. *Style Manual.* 29th ed. Washington: GPO, 2000. CD-ROM, print, Web.

Index